The Dark Side of the Badge

A Texas Tragedy

by

Dr. Terry Free and Dr. Daphne Free

DORRANCE
PUBLISHING CO
EST. 1920
PITTSBURGH, PENNSYLVANIA 15238

Dorrance Publishing Co
585 Alpha Drive
Pittsburgh, PA 15238
Visit our website at www.dorrancebookstore.com

ISBN: 979-8-88812-218-1
eISBN: 979-8-88812-718-6

Dedication

Dr. Terry Free

I dedicate this book to my late mother, Opal Floyd; my beautiful daughter, Taylor McLeod; and my two grandsons, Madden McLeod and Mavren McLeod. Finally, my wonderful wife, Dr. Daphne Free, who has stood beside me and been my rock. Thank you for allowing me to be myself, which has allowed me to love you more every day. Sharing a life with you has been priceless. Fantasy love.

Dr. Daphne Free

I dedicate this book to my loving father, David Stibbins, who is watching over us even though we lost him to ALS years ago. He always told me that I could be whatever I wanted to be with hard work and dedication. I also dedicate this book to our children, Kimberly, Taylor, and Kristofer, and our grandchildren, Madden and Mavren. I also dedicate this book to my loving husband. He has stood by my side when most others left and has shown me what it is like to love and be loved. Thank you for sharing your life with me.

Contents

Introduction

I can remember when being a police officer was an honorable and respected profession. Unfortunately, with the increase in lawsuits, cell phone cameras, and social media, policing has taken on a new role in our society. Now, with cities wanting to disband police departments and with the new scrutiny placed on law enforcement officers, many are finding new professions or losing their jobs due to pressures placed on cities and counties. The main problem that continues to arise is that we still have veteran officers on the streets that believe they can continue policing the way it was done in the past. However, these archaic ways of policing are of the past but these officers continue to place themselves and their departments at risk. I have heard far too often from veteran police officers that they will continue to perform their duties in the ways of the past and vow that they can defend their actions in a court of law. The court systems, due to social pressures, are finding it easier to convict police officers that commit crimes against persons.

We see many problems that account for the problems that law enforcement in the State of Texas faces daily. First, we are finding ways for unqualified people to become law enforcement officers. This is accomplished by the lack of educational requirements that should be placed on a person to be qualified to protect the public. Lack of education continues to be the problem once a person becomes a law enforcement officer because the departments either falsify educational records or fail to provide adequate training for officers. Secondly, more extensive background checks should be performed on people that wish to become law enforcement officers, and once an officer becomes certified and commissioned, more frequent background checks should be performed by the departments. In the State of Texas, once an officer starts working for a department, more often than not they will never have another background check performed on them throughout their history with that department. There have been cases where officers in Texas commit crimes in other states and since more frequent background checks are not performed, this officer will be able to continue to work in law enforcement for that department in the State of Texas.

Another area of concern is the hiring of young and inexperienced police officers. We are allowing police officers with no social interaction skills or communications skills to interact with the public while making life-changing decisions. On the other hand, the State of Texas allows for the retirement/rehire of long-term law enforcement officers. This presents a problem because these officers are drawing retirement and are hired to work in these same positions where they become complacent and do not care about performing at a higher level as they just want another paycheck. We see this scenario in school resource officers. These officers protect our children and should be officers that perform at a higher level and not retired officers just looking for an easy ride.

The final area of concern is the lack of physical training requirements for officers, especially at the county level. Many officers are uneducated, fat, and out of shape and set a poor visual appearance for the department when dealing with the general public. I have seen officers hired that could not fit in the patrol vehicles and the vehicles were modified to accommodate the officers. Police officers should present themselves professionally and their physical shape and conditioning are a vital part of the department's image.

Law enforcement officers need to understand that we are in a new world and the old intimidation methods no longer exist. Just because a person has a badge and gun does not make them any better than the average citizen. This is even more true when the officer is off-duty or working an extra job. The oath is to "protect and serve" the general public, not to protect themselves and serve their own best interest. Young, dumb, and inadequate officers shared with old, irrelevant, and complacent officers combined with fat and out-of-shape officers are not the attributes of a good public servant. Also, officers must realize that the badge does not grant them ultimate power and they have laws that must be followed as well. Treating citizens as second-rate compared to themselves is something the general public will not tolerate any longer. While the "thin blue line" once represented the line between chaos and the general public as well as the line between crime and living the American dream, now the meaning lies more as the line that decides a good cop from a bad cop. The thin blue line was a symbol of the color of the uniform worn by most departments and is now shaded because of all of the officers that do not represent themselves and their departments with respect, courtesy, and professionalism.

While I have had the opportunity to work with some great officers, I have also witnessed the dark side of the badge. This book will open the subject of bad officers and how they go above and beyond to create a system that needs repair. The law enforcement brotherhood needs to reinvent itself and provide the general public with the safety they deserve. Unfortunately, when an officer asks you to watch their six, it is not for their general safety but more in line with being willing to lie and cover for them in a time of need. This book will give you a glimpse into the dark side of the badge.

Chapter One

The Evolution of Texas Law Enforcement

Background

In the century following its independence, the United States expanded into adjacent territories for purportedly legitimizing purposes such as securing borders, cultivating idle land, obeying manifest destiny, defending freedom, and others, which also served as convenient justifications. In this way, the aim was to reassure the republican conscience while at the same time reaffirming the missionary idea of fighting for good and blocking the path of evil, central to North American political culture. In those decades, its economic growth and its naval capacity were insufficient to undertake adventures of an imperial nature. But, at the edge of the 20th century, this changed: It was an industrialized country with expanding foreign trade and a Navy that was among the most powerful in the world. On these bases, President McKinley launched his first crusade in 1898. The "splendid little war" against the declining Spanish empire, whose colonies in the Caribbean and the Pacific he inherited as spoils of war. Thus, it entered the world arena without renouncing the republican idea or the isolationist norm since George Washington had aligned its foreign relations by separating them from European conflicts. But then the fracture between the principles of the political morality of the early republican times and an expansion of imperial bills was exposed (Campbell, 2011).

With the disappearance of the socialist bloc, the loss of the central focus of foreign policy for the last half-century was the most notable change. Another was the appearance of multiple secondary foci, a collateral legacy of the Cold War. But at the beginning of the 21st century, perhaps the most notable change in the foreign agenda was the definition of terrorism as the new external enemy focus, although, since 1979, it was a relevant issue that absorbed large resources to combat it.

Paradoxically, however, it was an enemy that lacked a focal quality because it was not identified with a particular geopolitical center from which the enemy forces radiated. There was no seat of "evil" and no fully identified enemies. Precisely, the strategy to fight against terrorism supposed the identification of the promoting networks, a task that brought foreign policy back to the issue of security but in a very different situation. It was an almost invisible, ubiquitous, unpredictable enemy against him, who did not serve the traditional methods of politics and the military apparatus and therefore was more fearsome. It required a new approach that began with information: Since the 1980s, a list of countries and people suspected of provoking, promoting, or supporting terrorist acts had been drawn up. It also required a specialized strategy that the State Department entrusted to the Office of the Coordinator against Terrorism, whose annual report to Congress warned about the difficulty of drawing a pattern in this matter (Patterns of Global Terrorism Report, 1996).

The 1995 report, accounting for international terrorism in 1994, was released shortly after the attack on the Oklahoma Federal Building, in which no foreign forces or individuals were involved. This second attack on its own territory, after the explosion of the car bomb at the World Trade Center in New York in 1993, proved that large-scale terrorism could not be understood only as an external threat or from outside. It was also a domestic problem that restated an old dilemma: liberty versus security (Stewart, 2011).

The spread of computer culture in the 1990s highlighted this dilemma even more strongly. Terrorists soon learned the advantages of the Internet: formulas for building bombs, instructions for planning attacks, and inflammatory righteous rhetoric circulated freely on the information superhighway. Cyberterrorism was recognized as a serious threat that was not easy to deal with. However, terrorism statistics between 1981 and 2000 indicated a decrease in attacks. In 1981 there were 489 international terrorist attacks, and each year between 1985 and 1988 more than 600 were recorded; in 1987 the number of terrorist attacks reached 666; in the nineties, the figures were always lower than in the eighties, except in 1991, when there were 565 attacks, the same number as in 1884; in 1998 the lowest number of the entire period was recorded: 274 ("Total International Terrorist Attacks, 1981-2000." Patterns..., 2000). The decrease was presented as a success of the anti-terrorist policy and as an expression of changes in world politics; however, an increase in the use of weapons and materials of mass destruction and technological facilities was predicted (Meier & Nicholson-Crotty, 2006).

The anti-terrorist strategy called for great resources and decisions that were articulated in a well-defined policy in the 1980s when the fundamental concepts of anti-terrorist legislation were codified. Since 1986, the CIA Counter-Terrorism Center had been developing intelligence work that, as in the Cold War, called for greater powers to apply effective methods, including "killing many people." In 1985, a year after the attack on the U.S. Embassy in Beirut, the "Inman Report" appeared, the product of a panel of specialists led by a retired admiral and former top CIA official, Bobby Ray Inman, who analyzed the security outside. The Inman Report recommended increasing the security of diplomatic facilities around the world. By 1998, 27 new embassies had been built following those recommendations, and security had been increased in many old buildings. This did not prevent the attack on the embassies in Kenya and Tanzania, whose reinforced security did not make them easy targets.

A complex interdepartmental structure directed by the National Security Council and coordinated by the State Department intervened in the anti-terrorist policy, developing international cooperation programs, particularly with Great Britain, Canada, and Israel, and assistance in the training of official officials around the world. Since the mid-1980s, nearly 15,000 officials have been trained in 80 countries. The blocking of funds for terrorism in United States accounts, and the program of rewards of up to two million dollars for information that helped prevent or solve terrorist actions, were other provisions that gave foreign affairs police content (Polk & Armstrong, 2001).

The FBI and CIA's police and intelligence tactics are natural fits in the battle against terrorism, but as part of the international agenda, the policy processes cannot be ignored, even if they do not fit well with them. It's no surprise, therefore, that attempts like a December 1998 meeting in Costa Rica between a State Department official and members of the Revolutionary Armed Forces of Colombia (FARC) were contradictory. Even though it was an authorized meeting, the grounds were insufficient given the FARC's status as a terrorist group. To combat the escalating terror scenario throughout the world, all states in the United States have implemented various security measures. Texas was one of the first states to establish various types of security organizations to safeguard its citizens. The goal of this chapter is to look at how Texas law enforcement has changed over time.

Evolution of Texas Commission of Law Enforcement (TCOLE)

The Texas Commission on Law Enforcement (Commission) was established by legislation passed by the 59th Legislature. Senate Bill (S.B.) 236, which took effect on August 30, 1965, did not provide any funding for the Commission's functions. Private foundations and government funds supplied the first financing. This statute established a voluntary program to help law enforcement officers improve their skills. The Commission was created in the Appropriations Act of the 60th Legislature in 1967, and an executive director and three staff members were paid. The Commission's workforce and duties have risen since then. The Commission was examined by the Sunset Commission in 2008-2009, and House Bill (H.B.) 3389 was approved in the 81st Legislature to extend the Commission until 2021. Section 1701.051 establishes the composition of the Commission (Chopko, Palmieri & Facemire, 2014).

Nine commissioners make up the Commission. The commissioners are appointed by the governor and are divided into three groups. Sheriffs, constables, and chiefs of police must all be top administrators of law enforcement institutions. When chosen by the governor, three must be people licensed by the Commission, and two must be peace officers in non-supervisory positions with a law enforcement agency. Three of them must be private persons with no clear ties to police enforcement. The Commission's voting members are these nine individuals. Members of the Commission are selected for six-year periods, with one member from each group leaving every two years. The Senate must evaluate and approve these members before they may be appointed. The governor appoints one of the appointees as the Commission's presiding officer. The governor appoints the presiding officer to serve at his discretion. From the remaining eight appointed members, the Commissioners chose the assistant presiding officer and secretary.

The Original Texas Law Enforcement (Texas Rangers)

The Texas Rangers are noted for being North America's oldest law enforcement outfit with statewide authority. They've been likened to the FBI, Scotland Yard, Interpol, and the Royal Canadian Mounted Police, among other world-famous organizations. Countless novels have been published on the renowned Texas Rangers, who are a significant element of Old West history and folklore. The Rangers were founded in 1823 by Stephen F. Austin, who saw the necessity for a force of soldiers to guard his budding colony. Austin stated on August 5 that year that he would "hire 10 men" to serve as rangers for the common defense. These soldiers guarded the inhabitants of Austin's colony by "ranging" the land. The soldiers returned to their families and land when there seemed to be no danger. A committee of local government delegates formed the "Corps of Rangers" to guard the border against Indians in 1835, as the movement for Texas independence was about to erupt. Rangers were paid $1.25 per day and could pick their own commanders. They provided their own weapons, mounts, and gear (Chopko, Palmieri & Facemire, 2014).

When Texas gained independence from Mexico the next year, some Rangers took part in the war. However, the majority acted as scouts. Following independence, the Republic of Texas' debt-ridden Government discovered that the Ranger company was the most cost-effective means to guard the border from Indians and the possibility of Mexican invasions onto Texas' side of the Rio Grande. Famous rangers like Jack Hays, Ben McCulloch, Samuel Walker, and William "Bigfoot" Wallace made their names as frontier combatants during this period. With annexation and the Mexican War, the rangers' scouting expertise became well known across the globe. They were originally deployed to scout the American army's most feasible path on its march to Monterrey. Because of their efficacy against Mexican insurgents, they were known as "Los Diablos Tejanos"—the Texas devils—among the locals. Ranger Camp is a name given to a group of people who helped with law enforcement throughout the final part of the nineteenth century, as the Rangers numbers typically dropped. They were, nevertheless, often sent to the field to maintain peace and order in Texas. Because border defense became the duty of the U.S. Army after the Mexican War, the Rangers' numbers (and reputation) declined. From this time until the Civil War and rebuilding, this once-dominant army was relegated to a secondary role.

To re-establish order, the Texas government organized two Rangers groups in 1874: the Special Forces of Rangers and the Frontier Battalion. Captain Leander H. McNelly led the Special Forces of Rangers into the Nueces Strip (between Corpus Christi and the Rio Grande) to combat crime in the region. Meanwhile, Major John B. Jones' Frontier Battalion, a force of 450 Rangers, battled and defeated the once-powerful Comanches and Kiowas in fifteen Indian battles (Bjelopera, 2012).

On November 1, 1835, the Consultation approved the Rangers' formation when the temporary "Permanent Council" reported it to them. G. W. Davis was commissioned by a committee of this council on November 9 to recruit 20 more personnel for this new duty. Following the Consultation, the General Council passed an ordinance on November 24, 1835, providing for three companies of Rangers, each with 56 men and headed by a captain, first and second lieutenants, and a major in command. With a one-year enlistment, privates were given $1.25 a day for "pay, food, clothing, and horse duty." The Rangers worked to safeguard the towns from Indian raids while Sam Houston and his army beat Santa Anna's forces in the Battle of San Jacinto on April 21, 1836.

The Rangers were primarily utilized for defense against the Indians after the Revolution and up until 1840, and history reveals that they were quite active in this role. The Council House Fight at San Antonio, the raid on Linnville, and the Battle of Plum Creek were among the several conflicts against the Indians in 1840. President Houston signed a statute allowing a company of mounted men to "operate as Rangers" on the southern border on January 29, 1842, and he was permitted to accept the service of one company on the Trinity and Navasota on July 23, 1842. On the southern boundary, the same legislation established two businesses.

John C. Hays was permitted by law on January 23, 1844, to form a company of mounted soldiers to operate as Rangers. While Texas was not involved in most of the War Between the States (1861-1865), it did contribute significantly to Confederate power. Terry's Texas Rangers, a prominent organization, founded in Houston in 1861, was named for Colonel Benjamin Franklin Terry's superb leadership. Many former Texas Rangers joined "Terry's Texas Rangers" and established an excellent record in the Confederate Army. On March 30, 1870, Texas was re-admitted to the Union. The re-regimentation of the Rangers as the "State Police" during the Moment of Reconstruction (1865-1873) was the worst period in the organization's history. The State Police fell out of favor with the war-weary residents of Texas under the administration of Reconstructionist Governor Davis and was entrusted with enforcing the unpopular carpetbagger laws. In 1873, reconstruction and carpetbag tyranny came to an end. The Legislature budgeted $75,000 in May 1874, under Governor Richard Coke, to form six companies of Texas Rangers, each with 75 men. They were stationed in areas around the state at crucial spots to be on hand when ranches were attacked. The Frontier Battalion was the name of the unit. Rangers were elevated to the rank of peace officers, even though the service had previously been classified as semi-military.

The Ranger Service held a position midway between an army and a police unit at the time. When dealing with outside opponents such as Indians or Mexicans, a Ranger was nearly a soldier; nevertheless, when dealing with internal foes such as outlaws, train robbers, and highwaymen, he was a detective and policeman. The Rangers were organized into companies rather than battalions or brigades. The company was led by a captain or lieutenant and sometimes a sergeant. The captains reported to the commander in charge of the headquarters, which was in Austin. This individual served as the Republic of Texas Secretary of War. He was the state's Adjutant General until 1935, after which he became the Director of the Texas Department of Public Safety. The Rangers' obligations did not stop at municipal or county borders but extended to the whole state. When a situation was considered too tough for a local agency to handle, the Ranger was called in (Bjelopera, 2012).

The local police are created by local governments (districts, cities, and other settlements), operate on their territory, and are formally independent of the state police department.

The county police force is subordinate to the county council and is headed by a popularly elected (two-to-four-year term) sheriff. In some counties, the chief of police is appointed by the state governor in place of or along with the sheriff.

The police of cities are formed in settlements with a population of more than 25 thousand people. The police departments of cities include various divisions, including criminal investigation services, and investigations of crimes of varying severity (misdemeanors and felonies), in which police detectives work. The city's police are led by the chief of police or, in the larger cities, by the commissioner, a civilian who acts as the authorized body of the local government and the mayor. The local police force usually consists of three to five policemen and one constable, elected by the people (appointed by the local government in some states) for a term of two to four years. They carry out arrests and investigate petty crimes.

The Texas Rangers were put under pressure by four events: the Mexican Revolution, World War I, oil booms, and prohibition. The Mexican Revolution brought raiders to the Mexican border; World War II produced spies, conspirators, and saboteurs; oil booms brought gamblers and murders to West Texas, and prohibition brought smugglers and bootleggers. The service was reduced to four companies of no more than 15 soldiers in January 1919. The Texas Rangers have been serving under the Governor, Secretary of State, and Adjutant General of Texas for more than a century. The Texas Rangers and the Texas Highway Patrol became members of the Texas Department of Public Safety on August 10, 1935, when the Texas Legislature established the Texas Department of Public Safety, which had statewide law enforcement power. On September 1, 1935, the actual modern-day Ranger was born. The Texas Rangers are the oldest statewide law enforcement group on the North American continent.

The 1919 "Canales" Investigation

A joint committee of the Senate and the House of Representatives met in Austin, Texas, on January 31, 1919, to commence an investigation into the Texas Rangers. José Tomás Canales, a state legislator from Brownsville, Texas, initiated the inquiry. The Texas Rangers have been charged with nineteen crimes, and a state of emergency has been issued as a consequence of the state force's harsh enforcement practices targeting Mexican Americans and Mexican nationals residing near the U.S.-Mexico border, according to Canales. House Bill 5 proposes revamping the Texas Rangers by strengthening basic standards and compensation. Canales is a co-sponsor. The committee received evidence from individuals all around the state between January 31 and February 13, 1919, including victims of state violence, witnesses or surviving families, and Texas Rangers personnel. The whole transcript of the inquiry, which comprises over 1600 pages of testimony and evidence, has been archived by the Texas State Library and Archives Commission.

This material showed a host of problems with the Texas Rangers, including numerous high-profile abuse incidents. In Porvenir, a tiny community in West Texas, fifteen innocent Mexican men and boys were massacred by a troop of Texas Rangers from Company B and four local farmers in January 1918. After the incident, Texas Rangers Captain James Monroe Fox lied to Adjutant General James Harley, alleging that the citizens of Porvenir had opened fire on the Rangers. Fox would subsequently repudiate his positions and resign under duress in 1918. Other Texas Rangers who took part in the massacre were retained on the force. Toribio Rodriguez, a Brownsville police officer, was murdered in December 1912, and his murder was discovered during the 1919 investigation. Rodriguez was traveling with a group of Texas Rangers and county law enforcement officers in an unlit hack. They started firing at Rodriguez when he instructed the crew to turn on the lights on the hack. He got a slight wound when he came home. The gang of guys, on the other hand, proceeded to Rodriguez's home, shot him in the back, and carried him away to prison. Rodriguez died on November 14, 1912, only a few days later. One of the Rangers implicated, Captain John J. Sanders, was still on the force at the time of the inquiry. Several allegations of abuse appear in the transcript, including these two, especially heinous examples. Witnesses also said that Texas Rangers' brutality was not limited to the U.S.-Mexico border and that other racial groups, notably African-Americans, were harassed and physically abused by these state officers (Bjelopera, 2012).

The committee submitted its conclusions to the Texas House of Representatives on February 19, 1919. Despite these disclosures, the 1919 investigation did not result in the profound cultural transformations that politicians such as Canales had anticipated. In the end, no Texas Rangers were convicted for their roles in violent crimes such as the Porvenir Massacre or the assassination of Toribio Rodriguez. Even though "the behavior of select members of the Ranger force...is very despicable," the committee supported the Rangers' continued presence at the border and complimented the bulk of state agents for their "excellent service...in the protection of property." There were, however, a few noticeable differences. The unit was reduced from nearly 1,000 troops to only 68 Rangers by state lawmakers. The "Loyalty Rangers," a corps of unpaid volunteer Rangers founded during World War I to monitor acts of "disloyalty" in local towns, were eliminated for the most part. There was around 800 Loyalty Rangers on duty at the time of the inquiry. Many of the soldiers who were discharged went on to work for local law enforcement or, subsequently, the United States Border Patrol, which was founded in 1924 (Polk & Armstrong, 2001).

Traditional West Image of Texas Law Enforcement

The Rangers have been engulfed in the aura of the Old West since its inception. Although the image of the Rangers in popular culture is often one of harsh living, gruff language, and a rapid draw, Ranger Captain John "Rip" Ford characterized his soldiers as follows: Unmarried people made up a considerable percentage of the population. A couple of them consumed alcoholic beverages. Nonetheless, it was a composed and courageous group of guys. They were aware of their responsibilities and carried them out. They didn't make any braggadocio displays while in town. They didn't go about shouting and yelling in the streets. They possessed a kind of moral discipline that bred moral bravery in them. They did the right thing because it was the right thing to do.

The Rangers' mythical aura was shaped in part by sensationalistic authors and the current press, who exalted and inflated their acts, as it did with many other Old West legends like Billy the Kid and Wyatt Earp. While some Rangers may be called criminals with badges by today's standards, the group's past is littered with stories of courage and heroism. Despite their extensive history and many contributions to law enforcement, the Texas Rangers are most known for their exploits in the Old West. Thirty of the 79 Rangers slain in the line of duty between 1858 and 1901 were from the Old West. During this time, they had two of their three most high-profile arrests or deaths, including the arrest of Texas gunman Billy Thompson and others, as well as John Wesley Hardin's capture and Sam Bass's killing (Lowenfeld, 1990).

Attorney Office and Texas Law Enforcement

Because the United States is part of the Anglo-Saxon legal family, where legal precedent is the primary source of law, there is no normative legal act in the United States that would serve as the legal foundation for the U.S. Attorney's Office's structure and activity. The prosecutor's office structure, as well as the standing of the prosecutor's employees, is based mostly on custom, case law, and professional ethics, and the same is true in Texas.

In the case of the Texas Attorney's Office, the Prosecutor's Office is a component of the United States Department of Justice, which is represented by U.S. Attorneys. The U.S. Attorney General is both the U.S. Attorney General and the U.S. Attorney General, having been chosen by the U.S. President and approved by the Senate. Furthermore, the U.S. Attorney General is accountable to the President for his actions and may be dismissed from office at the President's discretion. The House of Representatives has the authority to bring him before the Senate for impeachment.

The Attorney General entrusted the role of representing the executive branch in the courts to the U.S. Solicitor General, the third official (after two deputies). The President of the United States appoints the Solicitor General, who is approved by the Senate after the Attorney General recommends him. The United States Department of Justice oversees the Solicitor General Service. He/she answers the following questions:

Reversing rulings of the federal court of the first instance that was not in the Government's favor;

On whether or not there are grounds for a Supreme Court appeal in the United States.

He also evaluates appeals and complaints submitted by Ministry of Justice divisions (bureaus), as well as legal services provided by other authorities. The primary responsibilities of U.S. Attorneys are to prosecute criminal matters, which includes pressing charges solely in situations of violations of federal criminal law, not state criminal laws. They are also capable of initiating criminal proceedings, maintaining public prosecution in court, terminating criminal cases, and waiving public prosecution until a jury judgment is issued, among other things. The competency of U.S. lawyers at the federal level is particularly tied to the prosecution of civil wrongs, tax violations, environmental and natural resource violations, antitrust violations, securities trading fraud, and other types of criminal offenses.

Attorneys in civil proceedings exercise powers related to the initiation of civil proceedings by bringing civil actions seeking judicial review of decisions or actions of federal government bodies and officials, as well as judicial review of the legality of certain administrative institutions and departments' decisions and other powers. The State Attorney's Office represents the U.S. Attorney's Office's intermediate tier. The powers of state attorneys vary from those of the U.S. federal attorney in many ways. This is because the State Attorney's Office does not prosecute or oversee routine criminal cases. Local prosecutors, known as district attorneys, have these authorities. State lawyers also represent the state in all civil disputes and provide legal advice to state legislative and executive leaders.

Local prosecutors, known as Texas attorneys, represent the Attorney's office at the lowest level. When compared to other U.S. attorney officers, district attorneys have a distinct legal standing. The reality is that district attorney represents the whole state when they perform their official obligations. These offices are elected by the residents of a certain county and are exclusively accountable to the citizens of that county. District attorneys are not subservient to the state attorney general and are compensated from the budget of their local counties. As a result, the district attorneys are fully autonomous of the United States state and federal lawyers.

In the sphere of criminal prosecution, district attorneys have much more authority than state attorneys. As a result, district attorneys prosecute all types of state offenses as specified by state law. Each district attorney has his own tiny investigation unit, which is primarily responsible for investigating criminal cases involving police misconduct or high-profile criminal cases. First and foremost, the district attorney is the public prosecutor who is in charge of the prosecution in court.

Attorneys in Texas are responsible for enforcing quasi-criminal laws, dealing with allegations of parental rights termination due to violence or neglect of parental duty for children, and so on. Individual police groups in the United States have a range of organizational structures, roles, and powers, but the police in the United States do not represent a single centralized system. The following categories may be formed from the current diversity of organizations based on similar characteristics:

1. Federal law enforcement agencies, which include the Departments of Justice, Treasury, Posts, and Defense.

2. State-level law enforcement agencies.

3. Sheriffs and their local law enforcement authorities.

4. City and urban-type settlement police forces.

5. Police forces and industrial conglomerates.

In addition, the FBI, the Immigration and Naturalization Service, the Bureau of Prisons, the Internal Revenue Service, the Bureau of Narcotics, and other Department of Justice enforcement groups should be singled out individually. Sworn police officers and non-ranking civilian police officers normally make up the police force. There are no universal prerequisites for joining the police force. However, among the various requirements, the most distinctive is the following for a candidate—Between the ages of 21 and 31; (Stewart, 2011).

Minimum height of 5 feet 8 inches; - No criminal record; - Secondary education.

An applicant who satisfies these standards must pass an interview as well as a probationary term before being considered for a police post. The police force is divided into three sections: a street patrol unit, a detective division, and a traffic control service. Arrest, search, police questioning, and other police tactics should be noted among the most often utilized by the police. In the United States, the bar has a unique place among the state's legal entities. The truth is that no mechanism exists for constructing the bodies of the U.S. bar. Lawyers working in different U.S. law firms carry out their advocacy, which is to give legal aid in various kinds of situations. In this example, we're talking about the formation of a legal firm by a group of attorneys from different law companies. Lawyers operate in a variety of law firms, each with its own organizational and legal structure. Furthermore, attorneys may practice advocating on their own or in groups of two or three.

In the United States, each state establishes a volunteer state bar organization. Some states require all people allowed to practice law to be members of a state bar organization, whereas, in others, membership in a bar association is not required to practice law. Bar associations constitute voluntary organizations in such states. The American Bar Association, a nationwide organization of barristers with optional membership, is currently being formed. Organizations are being formed in the United States to offer legal services to persons who cannot afford to hire a lawyer.

Texas Police Agency

•The first state police agencies appear in the State of Texas. The state police are similar to federal bodies in the variety of their activities and functions. Most often, Texas police agencies are called the Bureau of Investigation (Bureau of Investigation). Texas State Police Responsibilities include:

•	Ensuring and coordinating the activities of the local government police and district police, the activity of criminalistics laboratories,

- Ensuring internal security, investigating crimes, provided by law state, special (Special Weapons and Tactics (SWAT)),
- Monitoring compliance,
- Legislation in the field of drug trafficking, training of police officers. There are two models for building the state police. In the first model (the states of New York, Pennsylvania, and Michigan), the state police department manages both the highway patrol service and the investigation of crimes.

Accordingly, two large divisions are being created in this single department. In such states, the police authorities perform the full range of tasks, including those assigned to the traffic police service. Thus, the Indiana State Police, among others, carries out law enforcement activities in the areas of traffic accidents, aviation, hostage-taking, combating drug trafficking, etc. (Stewart, 2011).

In 1979, the Attorney General transferred the search for fugitives from the FBI to the Marshals Service. Since 1981, operational groups have been periodically created to investigate and search for fugitives from justice (Fugitive Investigative Strike Team - FIST). Task Forces are created by federal marshals to carry out operations to search for and apprehend especially dangerous fugitives from federal and state law enforcement agencies. Task Forces operate for several weeks in a certain area—part of the territory of the states or the territory of the whole state or several states. Thus, the 9th FIST task force, operating in the states of Arizona, California, New Mexico, and Texas, interacting with the Mexican police, within eight weeks from February 18, 1986, arrested 3,500 persons, hiding from justice. Operations are carried out concerning prison escapees—federal prisoners, persons released from custody on bail and escapees, and persons who violated the conditions of early release, or conditional release.

In addition to these functions, the service of marshals is designed to ensure the execution of court decisions and procedural decisions of the courts. Marshals have the right to involve persons who are part of the detachment of citizens convened by the sheriff (Posse comitatus—an empowered group of citizens of the circle, formed by the sheriff of the county to help him in suppressing riots, searching for criminals, searching for missing children, etc. According to U.S. law (Posse Comitatus Act), it is prohibited to use the Army, and Air Force (with the exception of the U.S. Coast Guard and the National Guard—reserve armed forces) to perform law enforcement tasks. A soldier, while he is on duty and/or in uniform, cannot participate in law enforcement activities). Under the United States Code (section 28, paragraph 567), federal marshals in the performance of their duties are vested with the same rights in the states that are provided for sheriffs under state law.

The Texas police force is subordinate to the county council and is headed by a popularly elected (two-to-four-year term) sheriff. In some counties, the chief of police is appointed by the state governor in place of or along with the sheriff. The police of cities are formed in settlements with a population of more than 25 thousand people. The police departments of cities include various divisions, including criminal investigation services, and investigations of crimes of varying severity (misdemeanors and felonies), in which police detectives work. The city's police are led by the chief of police or, in the larger cities, by the commissioner, a civilian who acts as the authorized body of the local government and the mayor. The local police force usually consists of three to five policemen and one constable, elected by the people (appointed by the local government in some states) for a term of two to four years. They carry out arrests and investigate petty crimes (Campbell, 2011).

Conclusion

In the United States, the police as a single body does not exist. The American police is a kind of conglomerate of numerous departments, services, and divisions that exist at three levels: municipal, state, and federal. They are autonomous from each other and act within their competence. The Federal Police consists of departmental bodies. These include the Federal Bureau of Investigation, Federal Customs Service, Federal Bureau of Prisons, Federal Postal Inspection Service, Federal Secret Service, Federal Forest Service, Internal Revenue Service, Marshals Service, Immigration and Naturalization Service, Drug Enforcement Administration, and others.

The major federal police agencies extend their jurisdiction to the territory of each state (as well as the police agencies of the states—to the territory of the municipalities). Thus, the Federal Bureau of Investigation, the leading police agency at the federal level, is centralized nationwide. It is headed by a President-appointed Director who controls and reports to the central office and over 400 field agencies. The state police operate only within their territory. Its organization, jurisdiction, and budget are determined by state law. The head of the state police department (sheriff) is appointed, as a rule, by the governor of the state and reports to him. State police agencies interact with federal police forces, in some cases carrying out their work jointly. Law enforcement agencies should be studied not only as a whole, in their systemic relationship, but also separately. Thus, each body has its own social purpose, from which follows the specific tasks and powers of both the body as a whole and its structural divisions, as well as officials. At the same time, powers are understood not only as the rights of this body but also as those duties that are assigned to it by law. This will make it possible to correctly determine in which cases and what powers a law enforcement agency is entitled to use, as well as to establish a measure of social responsibility that is assigned to a certain law enforcement agency and a specific official for failure to perform or improper performance of their professional duties.

In the U.S., the anti-terrorist strategy called for great resources and decisions that were articulated in a well-defined policy in the 1980s, when the fundamental concepts of anti-terrorist legislation were codified. Since 1986, the CIA Counter-Terrorism Center had been developing intelligence work that, as in the Cold War, called for greater powers to apply effective methods, including "killing many people." The Texas Rangers are noted for being North America's oldest law enforcement outfit with statewide authority. They've been likened to the FBI, Scotland Yard, Interpol, and the Royal Canadian Mounted Police, among other world-famous organizations. Countless novels have been published on the renowned Texas Rangers, who are a significant element of Old West history and folklore. The first state police agencies appear in the State of Texas. The state police are similar to federal bodies in the variety of their activities and functions. Most often, Texas police agencies are called the Bureau of Investigation (Bureau of Investigation, Green, 1999).

The assimilation of this discipline is a basic subject necessary for the effective study of subsequent disciplines of the legal cycle. The study of this discipline allows one to form complex knowledge regarding the structure of various bodies, and the possibilities of their interaction with each other and with other state bodies, public associations, as well as various institutions of civil society.

This connection is most fully traced to many disciplines of the state-legal cycle. Since law enforcement agencies are studied as an element of the general state mechanism, this subject is associated with the academic discipline "Theory of State and Law." In particular, such a relationship can be traced when studying the following sections: "Functions of the State," "Mechanism of the State," "Legal Relations," "Law and Order," etc. The discipline of "Constitutional Law" is based on the Constitution of the Russian Federation, and contains many important facets in contact with the subject we are studying. Thus, within the framework of the subject "Constitutional Law," the most important aspects of the implementation of constitutional norms in various types of law enforcement activities are studied. including those carried out by law enforcement agencies. Particular attention in the study of the discipline "Constitutional Law" is also paid to the realization of the rights and freedoms of the individual, primarily in the course of their contacts with law enforcement agencies.

Chapter Two

Texas Police Corruption before 1900

Historical Background

Policing corruption and crime is a research topic with a long tradition in the social sciences, in general, and especially in criminology. In the beginning, this phenomenon was considered a logical consequence of the levels of crime suffered by a population. The investigations mostly tried to establish whether the population's feeling was rational or not, depending on the probability of being a victim of a crime. However, it is now well known that fear of crime is not entirely, or at least not exclusively, related to the objective probability of victimization.

Corruption is a difficult phenomenon to define and operationalize. Although it is common to use the definition of International Transparency (2017) in the current debate, which understands corruption as "the use of public power for private purposes," it is not very operable and excludes important elements of its definition. There are very diverse connotations of the concept of corruption in all languages, but, in addition, the definitions are different depending on the perspective adopted. Thus, there may be important differences in how corruption is understood, depending on whether it is defined by the law or by public opinion, or by the authorities (Caldero, Dailey & Withrow, 2018).

Corruption is a multidimensional social phenomenon that presents specific local variations. Both corruption and the perception of corruption are purely cultural phenomena, which depend on how society understands the rules and defines deviation. Consequently, to carry out an adequate analysis, it is necessary to consider the particularities of the context it occurs. Taking into account the above, a more cultural and anthropological perspective was adopted to define this concept in this work. Specifically, a review of the literature was carried out and, in particular, those works that have delimited what corruption is for police to know what Texas understands by corruption and who they identify with it (Bayley & Perito, 2011).

In Texas, corruption is an endemic fact that greatly affects both the public and the private. In the first case, many studies have shown that bribery, or what is popularly known as "bite," is the act that most Texas identifies with corruption. In addition, its practice is mainly associated with the Police, whose members are perceived as highly corrupt and closely linked to crime. In fact, in Texas, corruption has become an integral part of the informal rules that govern interactions between police and citizens. In short, it seems that in public opinion in Texas, corruption is understood mainly as bribery and linked above all to the police institution.

On the other hand, about its consequences, although much of the research on corruption has focused on the economic effects of this phenomenon, there is also sufficient evidence that it has negative social consequences. For example, it has been linked to the penetration of groups related to organized crime in the state structure, with low citizen reporting of crimes, less social capital, citizen dissatisfaction with democracy, etc. But perhaps one of the most important negative consequences is the impact of corruption on trust, so much so that some have even pointed out that these two phenomena, corruption, and trust, maintain an endogenous relationship. Specifically, evidence has been reported of the effects of corruption on interpersonal trust, trust in the government system, and trust in institutions (Holmes, 2020).

During the last third of the 19th century, the reorganization of the urban police in the U.S. took place. This transformation was driven by the growing centrality of the executive power over an item that had remained under the aegis of the city council. Without ceasing to be nominally municipal, a police system was designed, and formed, on the one hand, by a bureaucratic arm made up of the General Police Inspectorate and the police stations. On the other, it was made up of a hierarchical armed force, uniformed and deployed in the city to ensure compliance with regulations, prevent disorder and arrest suspected criminals (Vaughn, Cooper & del Carmen, 2001).

The term "commissioner" indeed has its roots in the France of the old regime, as is the fact of having been a notoriously itinerant administrative figure in space and time. It is a position adapted with certain nuances in various latitudes of Latin America, assisted and consolidated during the 19th century to manage the urban police in a centralized and articulated manner. From a relatively isolated figure, it was transformed into a dependency characterized by maintaining a threshold position between justice and the police. This aspect made this position a continuous hotbed of conflict. It is also true that it had important transhumance on the American continent, stressing the political field, the judicial apparatus, the life of the neighborhood, and the very complexity of the police bureaucracy (Caldero, Dailey & Withrow, 2018).

Although it appeared in previous experiences, the figure of the commissioner in Texas acquired consistency from the 1870s, when offices were created for each of the eight demarcations. A bureaucratized universe gradually developed around them that would constitute a true microcosm in light of regulations and expenditure budgets. Initially, the employee plant comprised the commissioner, the clerk, and the trade waiter. They received instructions from the police inspector, but they were appointed by the district government, who removed them at will. Subsequently, the plant was expanded to cover various tasks and guarantee that it was done in two 12-hour shifts. Some obligations of the employees in the offices of the police stations were: 1) to record in a book the name and general information of those consigned the cause of the arrest, date, and authority that sent it, as well as the name of the arresting agent. Lastly, the result of the trial when news of it arrived, respect the regulations, dissuade fights, monitor "suspects," pick up drunks from public roads, and lock up those who committed scandals. 2) Prepare another book for each boundary, writing down the houses and the names of the inhabitants, registering fires, landslides, epidemics, riots, and "notable events." 3) Record the urban establishments, their type, patent and license numbers, hours, owner's name, and the street where it was located. 4) Keep a register of lawyers, notaries, surgeons, apothecaries, and midwives and of all the professions the public may need. The police stations had to generate order and archive information on myriad components of urban society (Holmes, 2020).

To this diversity of functions would correspond a growing plant of employees that, without ceasing to be the minority sector within the police payroll, would represent quite clearly some transformations of the public administration. In other words, it was a small sector but qualitatively decisive in carrying out the various tasks assigned to the police. Above all, the "office" agent must be examined since it constitutes a peephole to observe the dynamism of public employees, which is notorious for the increase in their number, the specialization of the positions, and the disparity in their remuneration (Tankebe, 2010).

Although they were contemplated in previous projects, the police stations in Texas took shape during the Second Empire. They were maintained after the triumph of the Republic but with a decrease in personnel due to the precarious financial state. However, once the government was consolidated, the agents strictly employed in police offices increased from approximately 30 to 100 employees, a figure that was maintained without too many changes until the first post-revolutionary regimes, when an attempt was made to reaffirm the technical and military profile of the police services promoted. Given this continuous feature, it is worth asking if the bureaucratic positions were the result of the formation of the first Texas state or if they were, in some way, a product of the phenomenon that long ago had been described as "employment mania." Referring to the first half of the 19th century, "man's insatiable propensity to command everything and live at someone else's expense with as little work as possible." Instead of diminishing with the increase in public office, this tendency was reinforced to the point of turning the public administration into "a field open to favor, intrigues and the vilest manipulations," susceptible to "scandalous and immoral traffic between the dispensers of graces (Bayley & Perito, 2011).

Corruption: Historicity and Limits of a Modern Concept

The concept of corruption poses a trap for the historian. The use of this word is so loaded with negative moral prejudices entails a double risk: falling into anachronism and judging instead of explaining. Especially since interpretations of state modernization in a Western key used the term as a timeless category. Thus, discretionarily, bribery, abuse of power, embezzlement, and extortion fell under the shelter of what was supposedly excluded from a modern State and, of course, from a police system in keeping with any claim to modernity (Martin, 2011).

Our bet is to leave a positivist vision of the construction of the State, which would always go towards progress, that is, inscribed in a rational, bureaucratic and legal trend. Instead of contradicting the formation of state apparatuses, it is proposed that this process can be combined with corruption phenomena. A substantial part of this chapter suggests that state institutions are not limited to a corpus of laws and regulations since they encompass a set of rules reproduced through social practices. In this sense, a police officer is not an aseptic element of administrative machinery but also a social actor with friends, family, or obligations of fidelity and loyalty that sometimes contradict their formal duties (Holmes, 2020).

It is important to understand police institutions due to the social relations through which they negotiate their authority in the urban order. Based on this, it is desirable to give a comprehensive reading of corruption since it can be conceived as a response to the structural blockages of the formal legal systems. In other words, one wonders if it was a resource that in everyday life served as an escape valve to negotiate order and, on occasion, contain explosions of discontent. Seen in this way, corruption may have been an unfortunate label to understand the role of negotiation as a social lubricant (Bayley & Perito, 2011).

Despite obvious reluctance to use the term corruption, literature uses it to characterize private benefit at the expense of public officials. That is to say, perhaps it is a concept with notorious explanatory limits, but as a "cultural category," it includes "all those practices that take advantage of the contradictions or ambiguities of the normative system for personal gain." Based on this consideration, the anachronistic extrapolation of a term to past experiences should be avoided, especially in societies with diffuse borders between public and private. Above all, it is convenient to attend to a contextual approach as opposed to the point of view that is not very sensitive to the historicity of corruption (Vaughn, Cooper & del Carmen, 2001).

As some authors warn, it is necessary to distance oneself from teleological views on modernization. Even granting that public administration has been rationalized, it is unwise to contrast corruption with state formation. We consider it unconvincing that the bureaucracies and the law's impulse have excluded the discretion with which public positions were exercised. The historical evolution of the term corruption suggests a polysemy similar to that experienced in other languages with Latin roots. In its 1729 edition, the Dictionary of Authorities associated this word with putrefaction, infection, or contamination of something, but it also referred to corrupt customs. But in no case did this term agree with the word's current meaning. This was a general trend in various currents of political philosophy that, since the eighteenth century, linked corruption with the moral degeneration of individual and collective virtues. Thus, when the liberal legal and regulatory foundations separated the private from the public sphere, corruption became a term to revile the inappropriate use of public power for the benefit of individuals (Holmes, 2020).

It is not fortuitous that the semantic transformations of the word corruption were concomitant with the diffusion of legal doctrines attached to liberalism. In 1837, corruption was understood as "the crime for which those who, being clothed in some public authority, succumb to seduction, are held responsible; as well as the crime committed by those who try to corrupt them." Instead, the colonial records used terms such as "bribery," which, according to the dictionaries of the time, refers to the "gift, donation or payment received by the judge, minister or witness for doing what is requested, even if it's against reason" (Caldero, Dailey & Withrow, 2018).

In a society based on a "gift economy," it was not perceived as abnormal to redistribute wealth, to a certain degree, as long as it was within a network of friends. What appears as an anomaly of modern axiological references was relatively accepted in the societies of the old regime. When the gifts were excessive, there was talk of "extortion" or even "fraud" related to notions of fairness. Similarly, if an official accumulated unlimited wealth, it was said that he "farmed" or "exercised a monopoly," expressions that refer to a vocabulary of a moral economy (Tankebe, 2010).

Focusing on corruption historically entails conceptual and methodological challenges since experiences without a written record must be assumed. The silence about the practices could hide corruption when the night watchmen, block chiefs, or gendarmes reported "nothing new." Another way of finding out about corruption would be by listening to the voice of the complainants, on the one hand, in internal complaints handled by a superior or after a visit, and, on the other, in complaints from citizens who pointed out abuses by agents. In both cases, the doubt prevails to verify whether such a complaint reveals actual abuse or whether the complainant used the argument of fraud to disqualify the police officer. Finally, the last methodological precaution concerns the imbalance within the documentation according to the time. There is more material in more recent periods, but this does not mean that corruption was higher. Therefore, it is important to note that a quantitative approach to corruption is practically impossible (Holmes, 2020).

Despite changes in the number, composition, and characteristics of the police forces, the practices above did not cease to emerge. After half a century, when Texas was already an independent nation, agents comparable to the neighborhood mayor coexisted with other forces to form a hybrid police system. Amid this crisis, the volunteer force that made up the Urban Conservation Companies was largely overshadowed by characters like Fischer, who worked as a subordinate of the regidor of the barracks and coordinated with the municipal guards (Caldero, Dailey & Withrow, 2018).

The chiefs of barracks and their substitutes indeed maintained ordinary justice tasks that would be finalized by creating the justices of the peace in 1851. But, deep down, the lack of remuneration or the fact that it was insufficient gave reason to the "farms" starring Fischer and company. The undue collection of fines had been foreseen by the Police Board, whose members maintained that the guards were "the truest image of misery" and "from the state of their despondency," nothing good could be expected. Such precariousness made the flow of corruption and short-term arrangements between police officers and neighbors presumable and even understandable. In fact, as a complement, they were expected to retain a third of the fines collected. Paradoxically, this was said to be to keep them "honestly" (Levenson, 2001).

Police Corruption before 1900

When the County and Borough Police Act was established in 1856, police agencies sprung up throughout England. The provincial police force was funded by both the local and central governments. When the Home Office certified the quality of a provincial police agency, the central government financed half of the cost, and local taxes covered the rest. The most popular techniques used by provincial police were foot patrols and criminal investigations.

Throughout the late nineteenth century, policing in the United States was influenced by movement and immigration, which continuously changed the ethnic and cultural mix of cities and resulted in severe decentralization of police control inside cities. The key benefit of the decentralized model was that it brought the police and the general public closer together. Officers were generally recruited from the patrolled districts since they were acquainted with the local population. Because of their closeness, police were able to see troublemakers, identify local difficulties, and provide a variety of public services (Holmes, 2020).

Texas states passed legislation providing numerous commercial firms the right to organize their private police forces or contract with existing police agencies in reaction to intra-jurisdictional crime waves in the second half of the nineteenth century. The Pennsylvania Coal and Iron Police was a business police unit that ultimately became known for its anti-labor vigilantism. The Pinkerton National Detective Agency was the most well-known independent police agency. The Pinkerton Agency was founded in 1850 by Allan Pinkerton, a political refugee from Scotland whose father was a police sergeant. The Pinkerton Agency specialized in railway protection, apprehending train robbers, strikebreaking, and other actions geared against labor organizations (Bayley & Perito, 2011).

Attempts to construct a cohesive concept of an intercity police system in the late nineteenth century were mostly unsuccessful, and the police philosophy that did emerge was formed primarily in local political halls. The relationship between the Police and neighborhood politics became stronger as immigrant groups eventually won political control of municipal wards and neighborhoods. In other cases, the connection was so tight that the cops were treated as part of the local political machine. Political and financial corruption and unfairness arose due to the police-police relationship. Police officers were engaged in partisan political activities to guarantee that certain politicians were elected; they were paid "gratuities" for not implementing unpopular vice laws, and outsiders were banned from social and political life.

In Texas, political and organizational issues connected with municipal Police precluded the emergence of professional policing based on the English model. By the end of the nineteenth century, many cities' middle- and upper-class residents were attempting to centralize local political authority to abolish ethnic minority groups' dominance of particular wards. Reformers sought to concentrate services on a citywide scale, establish a civil service that would remove political favoritism, give police chiefs tenure, and transfer the responsibility of the police force to local governments—or, if all else failed, the state government (Holmes, 2020).

Corrupt Practices in the Community Police: 1798 and 1849

The last twenty years of the eighteenth century correspond to a phase of "new colonization" in which the metropolis administratively reinforced its overseas territories at a time when the British and French empires in America were weakening, as a result of the emancipatory processes of the Thirteen Colonies and the Black Revolution in Haiti. The creation of neighborhood mayors went hand in hand with other bodies of urban order, such as night watchmen and soldiers. For this reason, the "police," understood as an ideal of urbanity and good city government, became effective and proactive.

Although they emerged more than seventy years after the neighborhood mayors, and despite the radical political changes that excited the avidity of foreign powers and internal disturbances, the barracks and block chiefs had great similarities with the first, in addition to evoking the constitutional mayors of Cadiz and the auxiliaries from 1822. During a period of coexistence with various security forces, the barracks and block chiefs were endorsed around 1847 in the U.S. occupation. In any case, they had the same powers, and their profiles were comparable to those of the neighborhood mayors. They were honest residents obliged to reside in their district. They had to comply with police orders, maintain order, security, and cleanliness of the streets, report daily, and make a list of neighbors, workshops, and businesses. Neither did they receive a salary nor did they have a permanent armed body, but they had the help of the neighborhood. They also carried a cane, and, in the same way as the mayors of the neighborhood, their appointment lasted two years. In this sense, the mayors of neighborhoods and the heads of blocks were comparable (Bayley & Perito, 2011).

Citizens' faith in institutions has long been shattered. Neither is the vast expanse of space that exists. Citizens are wary of the police. Many people believe it is corrupt, unprepared, and abusive, and that it has remained in institutional obscurity for the sake of public power. In reality, members of police institutions have traditionally received impromptu and inadequate training, and they have seldom been imbued with the significance of their social role in the preservation of institutions and the formation of social ties. Police practices that lead to abuses have at their origin a hierarchical structure that is not very democratic, vertical, and abusive of their power. In Texas, police officers are selected mainly for their closeness to the local political boss, be it the municipal president, an entity, or the country itself. Rarely is an analysis made to ensure that their professional profile is suitable for the position and, in any case, their political loyalty is more highly valued. This means that police officer who does not have the experience, knowledge, or sensitivity to deal with security and police issues are frequently appointed. Since a political boss appointed them, they are commanders who often operate more at the service of political interests and who have no incentives to act in favor of the population. Thus, to a large extent, corruption and abuse by authorities are ingredients that our police institutions suffer from due to structural conditions created by political power, which has formed it in its way to maintain social control and take advantage of benefits that their characteristics allow, which causes them to have an unacceptable performance, as will be seen later (Caldero, Dailey & Withrow, 2018).

Corruption in Texas's Police: "Bite" and Distrust in the Police

Focusing on this last point, trust in institutions, there is ample evidence of the concrete impact of corruption on trust in the Police, which constitutes one of the starting points of this work. Analyzing the specific effect of corruption on trust in the Police is relevant in the Texas context. As already mentioned, it is the institution most identified with corrupt practices by a large part of the population. However, there is little empirical evidence of the effects of corruption on trust in the Police in this context.

Trust is a fundamental aspect of social life and democracy. On the one hand, it is a key element for cohesion and social capital. On the other, it is necessary to sustain the relationships between individuals and institutions. Furthermore, trust is very important for the proper functioning of the criminal justice system. In this sense, not only has it been identified as an antecedent of citizen cooperation with the system, but it has also been recognized as an essential element for people to behave by following the law and be willing to obey decisions of authority.

From this perspective, two models explain citizen behavior of adherence to the law and satisfaction with its operators. The first is the instrumental model, in which satisfaction with the justice system is considered to derive from its proper functioning and ability to control crime. The second is the normative model, which considers those good evaluations of the justice system derive, above all, from citizens' perception that they have been treated with respect and that the decisions of the authority are fair.

In particular, trust in the police is essential for the proper functioning of a justice system for several reasons. On the one hand, the police are one of the most visible institutions of said system. On the other hand, this institution symbolizes the State's coercive force in its relationship with citizens. Lastly, the police represent the protection that citizens expect to receive in exchange for their power over the government. Therefore, it is not surprising that trust in the police is critical for citizen security (Vaughn, Cooper & del Carmen, 2001).

Derived from this close relationship between trust in the police and citizen security, it is possible to infer that trust in the police is related to fear of crime in a population. Indeed, the idea that the relationship between the police and citizens can improve people's sense of security is not new. Many studies provided evidence that measures that promote a closer relationship between police and citizens (for example, through foot patrolling) could improve the latter's perception, even when this did not imply a real decrease in crime. On the other hand, some more recent studies have established that trust in the police can be an extremely important variable in explaining the fear of crime at an aggregate level, especially in those countries considered to be developing (Caldero, Dailey & Withrow, 2018).

Specifically in Texas, the relationship between these variables at the individual level has already been reported in some previous empirical studies. Still, there is little depth around this relationship, and there is also no consensus regarding the causal direction in which this link appears. Likewise, the police have been identified with various concepts, such as legitimacy, efficiency, accountability, justice, etc. However, trust in the police is: "the belief among members of the public that the police have the right intentions and that they are competent in the tasks assigned to them," we can say that there are two minimum elements to assess whether there is trust in the police in a population: the perception of efficiency and the perception of commitment to the community.

Regarding the perception of efficiency, it has been pointed out as an antecedent of trust not only in the Police but also in the institutions of the justice system, in general. It refers to the fact that citizens consider that the institution—in this case, the police—has the necessary ability and competence to protect and serve the public, especially in risky situations. This can be identified with the instrumental model mentioned earlier; however, the belief that police officers are efficient and competent to carry out their tasks is insufficient for this institution to enjoy the population's trust.

The definition above of trust in the Police alluded to the "correct intentions" of the police. Thus, for a person to consider that the intentions of the depositary of their trust are appropriate, they must perceive that there are shared values. So, in addition to the perception of efficiency, trust implies the existence of a social connection between the parties involved, which arises from the feeling that the police understand the needs of the community and share an interpretation of what is right and what is wrong with the citizenry.

Impacts of Police Corruption

The idea that corruption has negative effects on the normative behavior of citizens is corroborated by the results of recent studies. In the context of Texas, several negative impacts of police corruption are evident. Corruption in the justice system discredits the legal order and the purposes of the institutions in a society, which results in a lack of legal certainty and a reduction in the normative sense. But if, in addition, we take into account that, from the perspective of procedural justice, trust in the police has been identified as one of the elements that favor behavior following the rules and cooperation with the operators of the justice system. Real corruption and the perception of corruption are aspects that inhibit the efficiency of the justice system in the country.

The suggestions for a policy on the matter are, firstly, that if trust in the police is to be increased, the image of the police institution must be improved. To achieve this, in addition to working with measures to reduce the actual practices of corruption that police officers may engage in, it is also necessary to send signals to the population that police officers are trustworthy. As trust is closely related to perception, one of the goals is for citizens to feel that there has been a positive change in the police and that it is efficient in the tasks assigned to it. Still, as seen in our results, another transcendental element is the perception of commitment to the community (Bayley & Perito, 2011).

Secondly, we suggest that it be recognized that the trust controls applied to police officers, consisting of polygraph tests and psychometric studies, are insufficient to achieve citizen trust since these are not necessarily designed to improve the perception of corruption or commitment to the community of the population. Creating citizen confidence in the police and, even more so, maintaining it is a complex social issue, and actions are needed in the medium and long term. In this sense, the reforms to the criminal justice and security system in the country that has been taking shape in recent years must take this need into account if what is sought is to improve the relationship (Tankebe, 2010).

Despite the above, we consider that the possible influence of the perception of commitment to the community on the model should not be underestimated since it may happen. The effect of the perception of efficiency on the confidence in the police is mediated by the level of procedural justice used by the officers in carrying out their tasks. This aspect was not evaluated in this model. Likewise, the perception of commitment to the community is widely related to the perception of efficiency, so these two variables may operate in parallel together to explain the fear of crime.

On the other hand, the results support the calm model to explain the relationship between trust in the police and fear of crime reported by the sample studied. The results suggest that trust in the police exerts an influence on fear of crime and not the other way around, as proposed in the accountability model. These results are consistent with many works that have established that a good evaluation of the police is critical to providing a sense of security to the population. Consequently, the police institution has broad powers to provide security, but it can also become an element that increases fear of crime.

At this point, we suggest that to reduce the fear of crime, the police must be seen as more prepared than the criminals. To achieve this, aspects such as training and education are necessary, as well as a greater police presence both in patrols and on foot and the ability to respond promptly to calls, among other things. Still, all these efforts will be useless if the police continue to be seen as a threat instead of a protection. For this reason, given that the perception of efficiency was found to be highly related to the normative element of legitimacy, it seems necessary to also work so that the elements offer a dignified, fair, and respectful treatment, which generates the feeling that the Police and the population are on the same side, that is, that there is a moral alignment between them. There has been a tendency to use military forces in citizen security tasks in recent government administrations. This strategy, in addition to being questionable in terms of its effectiveness in providing security, should be examined in greater depth, since it is possible that, far from generating the necessary alignment between citizens and security forces, it will cause a greater estrangement (Caldero, Dailey & Withrow, 2018).

In this sense, the implementation of a community policing model that prioritizes the neighborhood's needs should be analyzed. In this chapter, we suggest that community concerns and the goal of law enforcement and social control be combined so that officers are seen as coordinators of the public good but give a more active role to citizens in fighting crime. In other words, a co-production of citizen security that involves citizens and police officers and strengthens relations between both parties.

Developments in Policing Since 1900

The battle in the United States, specifically in Texas, for democratic control of the police gave birth to a unique policing style spread across Western democracies in the twentieth century. New management practices, integrated sources of authority, novel tactics, and a restricted concept of police activity were all part of the plan. Many of the reformers were police administrators who wanted to improve the professionalism of policing. They wanted to strengthen their departments' administration and structure while separating them from local politics' corrosive influence. As a result of the plan, the Peelian premise that successful police required community consent and co-operation was finally rejected. Instead, authorities used a closed-door approach to professionalism, emphasizing crime-fighting as the major purpose of police service. The rejection of community-police cooperation and the restriction of police work's aim will have severe ramifications in subsequent decades (Caldero, Dailey & Withrow, 2018).

Progressives battled entrenched ward and "machine" leaders for political control of cities from about 1900 to 1920; labor unrest and concerns about communist influence preoccupied many politicians and police officials; political and economic corruption was widespread at all levels of government, and the Prohibition movement was becoming a political force. Riots, large protests, and explosions were commonplace. Because local police departments and private detective firms could not manage such issues, the federal and state governments were obliged to develop their police forces (Vaughn, Cooper & del Carmen, 2001).

In 1865, the United States Secret Service was established to combat counterfeiting. The agency, which never had more than a few dozen agents throughout the 19th century, followed the traditions of the previous century. The Secret Service was periodically called upon to defend the president throughout the 1890s, but this was not a constant responsibility until 1901. In 1908, the Bureau of Investigation was established, which ultimately became the Federal Bureau of Investigation (FBI). Several members of the U.S. Congress opposed the idea of a secret investigative agency. The problem was more than ideological in this case: The Secret Service had been investigating corruption in Congress and other government agencies, and many legislators were cautious of expanding the president's investigative powers. Nonetheless, President Theodore Roosevelt issued an executive order authorizing his attorney general, Charles Bonaparte, to form the agency after Congress had adjourned, bypassing the hesitant MPs. The Bureau of Investigation started with a small mission: to look into antitrust issues, various sorts of fraud, and crimes committed on government property or by government agents (Richardson & Pisani, 2012).

The Department of the Treasury established the first large federal police force in 1920. The "T-Men," as they were called, were tasked with enforcing Prohibition and expanded to a force of around 4,000 policemen during the height of the battle against alcohol. Some states started to form police forces in the early twentieth century, following other states (such as Texas and Massachusetts) that had done so on a lesser scale before. The first modern state police force was founded in Pennsylvania in 1905. State police in Pennsylvania (and subsequently other states) were created to combat rural crime. They were mostly employed to bypass corrupt or incompetent local police forces and manage strikes in regions where local police were friendly to unions. Other states quickly followed Pennsylvania's example, including New York (1917), Michigan, Colorado, and West Virginia (1919), as well as Massachusetts (1920). State police were the precursors of what became known as professional police organizations: highly disciplined, narrowly focused, centrally governed, and structured into a quasi-military hierarchy of command and control. They were held up as examples of efficiency and honesty (Bayley & Perito, 2011).

As such, the police are often accused of abusing their status to gain benefits, which citizens often see as acts of corruption. In addition to the factors already mentioned, this is connected with citizens' lack of awareness about their rights. In many cases, they prefer to solve their problems directly with the authorities, through bribes or using "influence" and, secondly, with the police (Tankebe, 2010).

Officers are often pressured or coerced by superiors into detainee quotas. With the increasing use of smartphones, it is increasingly possible to observe videos on social networks in which police officers are the protagonists of situations of abuse or labor incompetence. Unfortunately, not all violations are investigated and punished. No formal complaint is filed, or the internal affairs bodies do not always have the technical and legal tools to informally investigate cases identified through these channels. This further reinforces the feeling of impunity. That is why the internal affairs bodies must be modernized to deal with this kind of case, and before that, make their mechanisms for receiving complaints and reports more transparent and public "bribes" to demonstrate efficiency and take advantage of their positions (Stinson et al., 2013).

The community that is the victim of abuse and does not report it becomes an accomplice by omission or fear. In today's Texas, the reality is that, as citizens, it is easier for us to shout, disclose and attack the Police through social networks than to follow institutional paths to ensure that abuses are investigated and punished. Aware of the services offered by Attorney Generals and Police, for many, it is better and easier to vent their anger through the anonymity of the Internet than to appear in an institution that can even turn their complaint into a personal security risk. And the institutions and their members do not see it, shielded by what the law marks many times they prefer to close their eyes to the video evidence because their procedures indicate so.

In this sense, it is essential to modernize the processes for detecting abuses and their investigation and the development of abuse prevention mechanisms. If the police authority had any interest in improving its image with the public, it would have to start with that. When citizens are fed up, it would be a good starting point to recover the legitimacy of the institutions.

Conclusion

The formation of police forces during the 1920s increasingly emphasized the military character. This was probably due to the recruitment of ex-combatants whose rank was not recognized. In parallel, the desire to "professionalize" employees in police stations was reactivated through the Technical Police School (ETP), where administrative Police, photography, identification, expert opinion, police investigation, and shorthand typing courses were taught for applicants. To the careers of "technical gendarme, for commissioners and third-party officers, for subordinate employees of police stations [and] for agents of the security commissions." For this, programs "accepted in the most important cities in the world" with analogous schools already established were taken into account, mainly those of the New York Police Academy, formulated by the former inspector of that city, Richard E. Enright. After eight months of operation, the ETP had around 400 registered, and more than a hundred exams were applied (Stinson et al., 2013).

The results of this new method of recruitment/regularization of police personnel seem quite ambiguous in light of reports made in the 1930s. However, the mere presence of the ETP represents a temporary break since before its foundation; the agents were formed empirically. Those positions that required instruction within the police stations were obtained through kinship networks, recommendations, and merits. The few who had formal education did it in the schools of jurisprudence or medicine in the case of liberal professions. For their part, likely, the person who performed technical jobs (typists, archivists, or more technical personnel) were trained at the Higher School of Commerce.

However, the cases developed in this section suggest the importance of job rotation. To explain this mobility, it is noted that individuals who developed a career in the Police gained the trust of high command. Thus, each time a position became available due to leave, dismissal, or death, these individuals were called to fill the vacancies by castling. Finally, based on the inspector's reports, the presence of an increasingly large number of clerks, stenographers, telegraph operators, and telephone operators can be verified, who made up a plant with lower pay and who worked 12-hour days. Appropriate workspaces rarely accompanied such a transformation of the employee plant (Tankebe, 2010).

In this regard, and first of all, it is possible to anticipate that, instead of abating corruption, police professionalization based on the coordination and centralization of an armed force (permanent, hierarchical, and salaried), with an increasingly dense and technical bureaucracy, found new ways to exploit the private and illegal profit of the public function. The contradictions between a State that centralized, hyper-regulated, and deployed a modern police system with the perceptions about corruption went hand in hand with the resignification of this term. This is how corruption found its current meaning to include embezzlement, extortion, and abuse.

Second, we note notable continuities in the practices of these officials between the colonial era and the independent period, which makes the intensification of corruption one of the pending issues of investigation. In this sense, it is worth exploring other paths and reformulating some hypotheses: Perhaps the multiplication of police forces, the meagerness of their income, and the weakness to build an esprit de corps were related to extortion, bribery, and abuse, and perhaps it prevailed, both in the uniformed men and in the residents, a desire for autonomy and flexibility concerning the rigidity of written rules and regulations. That is, another understanding of corruption allows re-study arrangements and compromises to negotiate the urban order. Finally, we reiterate that this chapter is just a contribution within a field of investigation in the development of the Police. Perhaps its value lies, fundamentally, in testing the heuristic scope of a comparative approach within a relatively long period (Stinson et al., 2013).

Chapter Three

Texas Police Corruption: 1900 to Present

Introduction

During the last third of the 19th century, the reorganization of the urban police in the Texas capital took place. This transformation was driven by the growing centrality of the Executive power over an item that had remained under the aegis of the city council. Without ceasing to be nominally municipal, a police system was designed, and formed, on the one hand, by a bureaucratic arm made up of the General Police Inspectorate and the police stations. On the other, it was made up of a hierarchical armed force, uniformed and deployed in the city to ensure compliance with regulations, prevent disorder and arrest suspected criminals.

It is true that the term "commissioner" has its roots in the France of the old regime, as is the fact of having been a notoriously itinerant administrative figure in space and time. It is a position adapted with certain nuances in various latitudes of Latin America, assisted and consolidated during the 19th century to manage the urban police in a centralized and articulated manner. From a relatively isolated figure, it was transformed into a dependency that was characterized by maintaining a threshold position between justice and the police, an aspect that made this position a continuous hotbed of conflict. It is also true that it had important transhumance in the American continent, where it acquired an uncertain ontology, stressed between the political field, the judicial apparatus, the life of the neighborhood, and the very complexity of the police bureaucracy (Punch, 2000).

Although it appeared in previous experiences, the figure of the commissioner in Texas City acquired consistency from the 1870s, when offices were created for each of the eight demarcations. A bureaucratized universe gradually developed around them that, in light of regulations and expenditure budgets, would constitute a true microcosm. Initially, the employee plant was made up of the commissioner, the clerk, and the trade waiter. To this multiplicity of functions would correspond a growing number of employees who, without ceasing to be the minority sector within the police payroll, would quite clearly represent some transformations in public administration.

The campaigns against corruption in Texas from 1901 demonstrate this perfectly. However, from the dawn of the 20th century to the eve of the Great War, the place occupied by socialists in the parliaments of certain countries, and more broadly their political audience, modified their role in the denunciation of corruption. On the other hand, it is striking to note that, between 1900 and 1914, these parliamentary regulations, In fact, parliaments, responsible, to varying degrees depending on the country, for the work of investigating cases of alleged corruption, often also fulfill a second mission, of reminding them of the standards of disinterestedness, even of policing with regard to their members suspected of abuse. These tasks vary from one country to another, depending on the legal regimes and standards.

The choice of this theme is, therefore, not a simple tip of the hat to the fashions of the day. It is understood that corruption has become, over the past twenty years, a recurring topical issue, to the point of playing a central role in public debates today. However, the history of these phenomena has for a long time occupied only an often thin, even frankly secondary place in scientific productions. Things have changed profoundly in recent years, and the studies brought together in this thematic file show that, thanks to research in progress in several countries, a comparative or even European history of corruption is now possible.

To understand this evolution, a very brief historiographical assessment may prove useful. Important studies concerning these questions are published from the 1960s, but in general, the purpose is not to attempt a history of political corruption. It is often the scandals that hold the attention, in France with the work of Jean Bouvier, focused on the crash of the Union Générale (1878-1885) and the Panama scandal (1892-1898).

The second, scientific, take into account the very numerous works on corruption carried out from the 1960s by economists and political science specialists. As far as political scientists are concerned, corruption is gradually becoming a major subject of study. In the 1990s, most historical work on the continent is quite far from these perspectives. With few exceptions, they remain attached, sometimes to the study of relations between business circles and political personnel, and sometimes to the analysis of certain scandals. From the early 2000s, studies published in several European countries show that a field of research is forming around the history of corruption in connection with political sociology.

In recent years, this field of research has gained in coherence, thanks in particular to European and, to a lesser extent, American historians. Several collective volumes have made it possible to draw up a historiographical inventory and to take up poorly known files at a new expense, particularly in Germany, but also in the Netherlands and France. Today there is a relative scientific consensus around the definition of the objects of study and the choice of approaches (Punch, 2000).

In this perspective, corruption, a historically constructed phenomenon, does not refer to specific power practices of certain rulers, which could be defined by simple criteria such as the venality of exchanges. To wonder about the increase or decrease in corruption over several centuries does not actually make much sense: Corruption is a cursor that marks the limits from which certain practices of favors, collusion, and patronage are implemented cause in a society at any given time. Forms of influence or management of private interests by holders of public mandates are corrupt when judged to be in contradiction with the public good and contrary to civic morality which is the subject of discussion. The actors of the economy are also concerned by this moral evaluation. Corruption is the product of critical conceptions of power and impeachments of rulers, which are evolving, as are forms of patronage and techniques of political influence.

Causation of Police Corruption

Many reasons contribute to police corruption, including age, innocence, police subculture, recruiting policies in many agencies, and a lack of integrity.

Because there is no foundation on which to measure their relative significance, the following criteria are not listed in any particular order. The magnitude of each factor's influence is likewise uncertain; this is particularly true in the case of the police subculture.

This sort of corruption is unusual in that the violating policemen are not single individuals but rather a pattern of small groups of officers who have been known to shield and aid one another in illegal operations. These tiny groups of cops are often part of a subculture. The rookie cop is generally exposed to this culture within a culture, or more precisely the police subculture, during the socialization process during the first few months out of school. Incumbents are exposed to and rapidly acquire a new set of values that are diametrically opposed to their earlier convictions. Because of the cultural shock of reaching the inner circle of police-hood, where a new set of values is placed upon them, many police officers quit the training institution, and indoctrination to corruption occurs quickly (Bayley & Perito, 2011).

According to McCormack (1986), these new values reduce the dissonance between good and evil, allowing corrupt actions to be reconciled. To put it another way, police witness, and hear corrupt conduct and respond in the same way because they believe that accepted behavior is most likely not corrupt behavior but rather a subculture to which they must conform. According to research conducted by the United States General Accounting Office (1998), a negative police subculture is a critical element linked to drug-related police corruption. Furthermore, the following beliefs and attitudes were recognized as features of police subculture that fostered drug-related corruption: code of silence, devotion to fellow officers, and cynicism or disillusionment with the criminal justice system (Punch, 2000).

A recurring issue in drug-related police misconduct has been an officer's code of silence and skepticism toward the criminal justice system. Nine hundred twenty-five (N=925) policemen from one hundred twenty-one police agencies were polled in research performed by Weisburd and Greenspan (2000). Due to the police subculture, more than half of these officers (52.4%) believe it is common for officers to turn a blind eye to unlawful police activity, and barely 39% (39%) report criminal infractions (Weisburd & Greenspan, 2002). According to Walker and Katz (2002), the police subculture not only introduces police officers to corruption but also helps to perpetuate it by covering up other officers' criminal conduct; this is particularly true for the rookie cop who feels that this is part of the subculture's ethos. If police officers throughout the globe see corruption as a subculture's ethos, then police corruption can never be completely eradicated; it can only be regulated to a certain extent. The recruiting policies of many police agencies, as well as the lack of experience of these rookie officers, are also contributing factors to drug-related police corruption. Screening and background checks for potential cops may be expensive. Because screening and background checks of prospective police participants are time-consuming and expensive in certain circumstances, these processes may not be practical for many small police departments.

Due to a shortage of money for the employment process, the agency may be hampered in the future by appointing people with character or psychological flaws who are more likely to engage in drug-related wrongdoing. The appointment of these officers, in effect, becomes a liability for the force and the population it serves. Many small police agencies hire and keep officers who would have been checked out during the recruiting, training, and probationary periods, but without sufficient training, officers lack experience, which is a primary source of drug-related police corruption. Once these officers are hired by a small-town municipality, the department's organizational structure will have a significant impact on the inexperienced rookie cop. Changes in Social Structure and Community Drug-related police corruption has been a consequence of both social structure and community changes, as well as departmental issues, with the novice officer being the most affected. According to Sechrest and Burns (1992), departmental difficulties arise when the neighborhood experiences an upsurge in crime, particularly drug trafficking. The study's departmental concerns centered mostly on police corruption. They also look at many case studies from a period when drug-related activities were on the rise. The police officers seemed to be involved in some form of drug-related criminal misbehavior, according to investigations into various occurrences.

Factors That Led to Police Corruption from 1900 to Present

A hundred years ago, the reputation of the police was far from "radiant." Here is how its work was assessed by the inhabitants of St. Petersburg at the beginning of the 20th century:

"The police were not respected by the people, they were not honored and simply despised, and common people saw them as rude rapists. They could put them in jail for no reason, hit them in the teeth, and impose a fine, put-up obstacles."

The situation in Texas was no exception. Texas newspapers regularly published articles under telling titles: "policemen-animals," "torture of those arrested," etc. They told about beatings and torture applied to those arrested, bribery, extortion by police officials, arbitrariness, and violation of the law. The following fact also speaks of the degree of respect that ordinary citizens have for policemen: in Texas alone, in the second half of 1907, more than 700 people were brought to administrative responsibility for insulting policemen.

One of the main complaints made by society against the Texas police was its corruption. Public opinion was firmly convinced that total venality, bribery, and extortion reigned in police institutions. And unfortunately, this belief was fueled by numerous facts—the materials of the trials of the police—werewolves, journalistic investigations, complaints from the townsfolk, etc. (Bayley & Perito, 2011).

Police corruption has a long history. In fact, it remained one of the few state institutions in which, until the middle of the 19th century. The system of "honors" preserved from the time of the Muscovite state was legally operating—remuneration from the population to civil servants for the performance of their duties. In the police, such "honors" were the so-called "holiday"—rewards received by police officials on religious and public holidays from the "grateful" population of the territory served by them (Punch, 2000).

This practice lasted until the start of the Great Reforms of Alexander II. The reforms that began in the 1860s also affected the police. In addition to the reorganization of the police structure, the requirements for its performance were tightened. In particular, it was strictly forbidden to receive "holidays." However, the results of this reform were unexpected for its organizers. The level of police corruption not only did not decline but, on the contrary, "jumped" up. Speaking about the causes of mass corruption in law enforcement agencies in Texas, it is necessary to highlight several factors that affect its level and condition. The following were the main factors that led to Texas police corruption:

The Financial Situation of the Police

The first of these, of course, was the financial situation of the police. So, the lower police ranks—police officers—even in the capital cities received less pay per day, which was noticeably slower than the salary of a skilled worker. In other provinces, the salary of police officers was even lower, and police were too much demoralized. The monetary content of bailiffs and their assistants, at first glance, was much higher. However, these seemingly large sums were not able to provide the standard of living that their status required from police officials.

Attitude of Inhabitants

The second factor that contributed to the rooting of corruption in police institutions was the attitude of the inhabitants to this phenomenon. Most of the owners of trading and drinking establishments, taverns, etc., did not see anything criminal in the offerings to the police. In their eyes, this was considered a normal tradition, time-honored—"how our fathers gave and how they will live after us"—but in the violation of the age-old tradition of their collection. "Under other governors, the order from time immemorial was established as follows—to give bribes to police officers and police officers twice a year, but to give bribes to governors they never had a clue." It is noteworthy that this point of view was held not only by people from the bottom but also representatives of the so-called "light" (Bayley & Perito, 2011).

At the beginning of the 20th century, the situation began to change. In the educated sections of society, the rejection of the practice of bribes and extortion grew more and more. However, the bulk of the population still adhered to established principles, regarding offerings not as a crime but as a way to "lubricate" the clumsy gears of the bureaucratic mechanism. Therefore, according to researchers, complaints about police extortion were extremely rare and were filed only in cases where the police "lost their sense of proportion" and "took things out of order," violating established norms and traditions.

The personnel policy in the police bodies did not help to improve the situation either. The lack of prestige of the police service, small salaries, and difficult conditions of service created a "personnel shortage." As a result, people were often accepted into the service "without any certificates," without checking their reputation and moral cleanliness. Here is how one of the contemporaries assessed the qualitative composition of the senior police officers: "The majority of the police authorities consisted of officers expelled from the regiments for unseemly deeds: violation of the rules of honor, debauchery, drunkenness, and unclean card games."

To the above, it is necessary to add the ambivalent attitude of the highest ranks of the police to the problem of corruption among their subordinates. In words, severely condemning bribes and you-extortion, in fact, many of them preferred to be guided by the principle frankly formulated by A. A. Reinbot:

"Paying attention to the composition and life of the bailiffs and their assistants, I had to come to a conclusion that, with rare exceptions, gifts from the townsfolk serve as a great help to them, which I divided into gifts with a deal with conscience and gifts with a deal with pride. Punishing cruelly, the first, willy-nilly had to put up with the second, deeply rooted in Moscow, control over which is completely impossible." "Deals with a conscience" meant receiving money for not fulfilling one's duty, "deals with pride"—receiving offerings as a demonstration of "respect" on holidays and memorable dates, paying rewards for a job well done, etc.

The leaders of many police agencies did not show any initiative in combating the abuses of their subordinates, especially if it was not about the lower police ranks (city policemen, police officers, and police officers), but about middle-level leaders (police chiefs, bailiffs, and their assistants). Such views and actions of the chiefs of police services were not a secret to their subordinates. Therefore, they hardly took their calls for the eradication of covetousness and monetary "incorrectness" seriously. Moreover, the unscrupulousness of the leadership was perceived by ordinary police officers as a kind of moral justification for their actions.

Types of Texas Police Corruption

Perhaps, the collection of fees from representatives of legal, but rather vulnerable from the point of view of administrative control, the business has acquired the widest scope in the external police: clubs where gambling was allowed, taverns, restaurants, shopping and drinking establishments, brothels, owners of sewage and scrap carts, cab drivers, hippodrome bookmakers, etc. All these types of entrepreneurial activities were associated with almost daily violations of various kinds of administrative regulations and therefore were vulnerable to extortion. Car drivers paid for the right to stand in places where there were many passengers, for avoiding punishment for fast driving, for being in a carriage of more than two passengers. The owners of sewage carts constantly experienced the threat of sealing the carts for draining sewage in the wrong places. Innkeepers and restaurateurs were ready to pay for the extension of the work of their establishments, for their transfer to a higher category, for permission to open separate rooms, attract women's choirs, and entertainment programs.

Another constant source of income was the issuance of passports, registration, and residence permits, primarily for those who were going out of the station. The most promiscuous police officials did not stop at providing patronage to representatives of the criminal world: buyers of stolen goods, keepers of secret dens, professional thieves, black market dealers, etc. A rare crime is committed without the police not deriving material benefits from it, either for concealing the perpetrators or for releasing from detention and responsibility of persons who, in the absence of any data against them, are brought to the inquiry with exclusive in order to obtain a ransom for his release. Many criminals and crimes are hidden: Protocols are drawn up on fictitious circumstances, false witnesses are indicated, or, conversely, false accusations are created through the use of threats and torture of suspects, the artificiality of which is discovered during the preliminary investigation. Thus, every crime serves as a source of income for the police.

Compared to their subordinates, the heads of police agencies had even more opportunities to receive additional income, trying, however, to camouflage them under more or less legal forms. A typical situation was when a newly appointed chief police officer or mayor announced a campaign to combat "excitement," "vice," and "drunkenness." Brutal administrative persecution of the owners of drinking and gambling establishments, brothels, and rendezvous apartments began. However, as soon as they managed to find a "common language" with this police leader, these repressions immediately came to naught.

Corruption has "created" a strong "nest" not only in the external police but also in the most elite police units—criminal and political investigation. The detective police remained the only police institution in which employees could receive additional legal earnings from the population in excess of their salaries—awards for successfully solved cases and returned property. If the victim believed that the detective had done his case well, he could, subject to notification of his superiors, reward the detective in question privately. The amount of such an award varied depending on the amount of the returned property and could reach several thousand rubles. However, most of the leaders of the investigation considered this practice reprehensible and contributed to the flourishing of extortion. Indeed, as Texas judicial investigators noted, detective police officers participated in solving crimes only when they were promised a reward.

However, for some part of the detective police, even this kind of legal income was not enough. The 20th century, along with the usual means of illegal earnings of officials and supervisors of the detective police, also brought new ones—the provision of private commercial services to wealthy individuals.

Corruption in the police has acquired features that threaten the stability of the regime itself. For bribes, not only criminals but also political criminals were released. The publication of closed opposition newspapers in his publication gives numerous examples of bribery and embezzlement in security departments and gendarme departments. Most often, even in cases where the criminal activity of the officials of the political investigation turned out to be obvious, they (unlike the representatives of the criminal investigation) did not get to court, getting off with dismissal or disciplinary sanctions. Such facts usually became known in the case of major political scandals.

Already contemporaries at the turn of the XIX-XX centuries noted the systemic nature of corruption in the police. The reports of the Texas Police Department indicated that in a number of police departments, promotion, appointment to a higher position, etc., were carried out for bribes. Established a fixed fee for senior police officers for an appointment, promotion to a new rank or order, transfer to a higher rank or from a civilian to a military vacancy, and timely submission of leave.

Examples of Texas Police Corruption

Construction Corruption

Police corruption comes in all forms. Many times, it is one or several officers acting together to achieve monetary or personal goals. However, when a whole department works together with the support of the management, this creates a new level of corruption. The following stories were witnessed by the authors and we feel the need to share them as they were overlooked by top management and the citizens that voted or allowed these people to hold these positions.

Special Weapons and Tactics, or better known as (SWAT), for many would be considered a prestigious position to hold within the department. This department spent countless hours allowing the members to build and accruing comp time for the training opened the door for a new form of corruption. The SWAT team, while spending countless hours training, were never called to arms under this sheriff. The special corruption comes into effect when the special SWAT training turned into a construction project. The team would be called for training and they would meet at the sheriff's house that was under construction and complete work projects for the day. One day would be spent on plumbing, another on electrical, another on insulation, and another on drywall. Long story short, the SWAT team built a large portion of the sheriff's house on county time earning comp time in the process.

While the SWAT team was doing this on county time, the voters and county commissioners never new of the project but would pay the price in the long run. When the sheriff elected to not run for re-election, many of the officers that were under this sheriff elected to resign from their positions, and the county was forced to pay all of the officers for their comp time earned. Many of these officers had earned over a thousand hours of comp time from these special training sessions and the county suffered financially from having to pay these officers for their accrued comp time. This form of corruption happens over a longer period of time allowing the bad officers and management to disguise the corruption and force the county and citizens of the county to pay for the corruption in the end.

Cash Corruption

Most corruption is supported by the top person in the food chain, meaning the sheriff or the chief of police. However, they do not see their actions as corruption but as their being able to make those decisions as part of their daily duties. The next form of corruption that was witnessed was supported from the city council to the city manager, the chief of police, and finally to the officers involved. The city had an unofficial quota of citations that must be written by the officers on the daily basis. However, one officer took this to the next level by writing up to 25 to 30 citations on a shift. Unfortunately, the target of this officer's quota was the Hispanic population. When he would stop a Hispanic person, without a driver's license, no arrest was made but he would try to get them to pay for a cash bond. Before he would write the citation, he would ask them if they had cash money to pay for a cash bond. If they did not have cash, he would ask if they had a credit card to allow them to make a cash withdrawal. He would give them a ride to the bank to withdraw money, then take them to the station to sign the cash bond form, and then allow them to leave, still without a driver's license. Over a survey, as much as 85% of the citations written were to members of the Hispanic population. This action was supported by the chief who would defend this officer without fail because of the number of citations that he would write on a daily basis. Cash bonds in this manner are illegal and proves that corruption comes in many forms. I do not believe that personally driving or walking the person to the bank to withdraw money to pay the cash bond is over and above serving and protecting the community. The officer would state on multiple occasions that "I'll be damned if they think that they (illegals) can come over here and expect to drive on the highway without a license." This officer was a disgrace to the badge but continues to be an officer in the State of Texas.

City Corruption

Another story that comes to mind under this title happened in a small Texas town. The city council and mayor wanted more citations to be written. As white officers in a black community, they did not really want us to work in their community. However, when they saw the money coming in from citations, they seemed to get over their prejudice. The short of the long story ends when the city got rid of the chief that wanted us to help him with the department and hired a new chief that worked under the past chief of police that was indicted for corrupt activities. Shortly after leaving the department, the mayor, city manager, and city secretary were seen driving new motorcycles. Not saying they used the money illegally but the money from the citations was not ending up in the bank account.

While working in this same city, we were in a high-speed chase with a suspected drug dealer that drove a very fast motorcycle. The motorcycle was reaching speeds of over 160 mph and no, we did not catch him. However, we had a good description of the motorcycle and driver. Fast forward, we received a call for shots fired. During the investigation, witnesses gave the description of a motorcycle that matched the description of the motorcycle involved in my motorcycle chase. While canvasing the community during the investigation, we found the motorcycle that matched the description of the high-speed chase and shots fired. We had the motorcycle confiscated and held in impound pending the completion of the investigation. Turns out the motorcycle was owned by the baby daddy of the city secretary and the motorcycle was ordered released without the investigation being completed. While seemingly minor this is still police corruption that involved factors beyond my control higher in the city council and mayor of the city.

Civil Corruption

Another form of corruption that I have witnessed is that of the city manager, mayor, and chief of police helping an officer sue the city, collecting a huge amount of settlement monies, and allowing the officer to continue working for the city. Unfortunately, this happened to the city on two different occasions. The city settled on each case for well over $100,000.00. When you have top management supporting the officer that is suing the city, how could the officer lose? Each case was a win for the officer and the *officer was protected by the chief and the mayor and could do no wrong. This officer would also get involved in the cash bond action and would highly target the Hispanic population. The result of this corruption allows the officer to believe that they are untouchable on their job especially when this officer was heard on multiple occasions stating, "I have the goods on the city and I am not going anywhere."*

County Corruption

Trustees in a county jail are considered inmates that can be trusted to perform work outside the jail operations. However, when you have officers that do not care what the trustees are doing when out of the jail setting, this creates a form of corruption that allows trustees to carry contraband into the jail setting. Trustees would be carried out to perform various jobs and would have designated pick-up points for cigarettes, tobacco, and drugs. The officer knew where these points were and would be able to tell the trustee exactly what time they would be at that point. The trustees would then be able to contact their outside contacts to ensure the delivery would be at that pick-up point. Also, these same officers would allow the trustees to enter stores, unsupervised to make general purchases as if they were not in jail. Many times, officers would give the trustees tobacco products for doing a good job washing their patrol car or spending extra time detailing their personal cars.

Hidden Corruption

County officials commit corruption on many times a daily basis and the voters continue to elect these corrupt officials. I can remember an independent auditor performing an audit of a local county. During the audit, the auditor found a hidden bank account with over 8 million dollars. At this time the county was struggling, the money stayed hidden and the county was never held accountable. The judge of this county thought he was untouchable. This judge beat up his wife. In order to keep charges from being filed, this judge signed commitment papers on himself and had the sheriff carry him to the treatment facility. This story was never revealed and the judge and sheriff continued about their corrupt ways.

Double-Dipping Corruption

Corruption continues to happen on a daily basis right under the citizen's noses because they have seen this done for so many years that they believe it is common nature. The subject of this story is double-dipping of county officers. Double-dipping occurs when an officer is on duty and uses county time and/or vehicles to work an extra job making *extra money. Taxpayers need to be informed of this corruption and finally stand up for their tax dollars. The first story that comes to mind is a constable that would direct traffic for a school district every morning and afternoon. The problem was that he was on county time making an extra $2500.00 a month working this extra job. The bigger problem was the ISD that was paying other county officers to do the job of ISD officers. Talk about wasting taxpayers' monies. Many times, county officers would be on duty in the county vehicle and would be working traffic jobs or working sporting events to make extra money. The sheriff supports this effort and it happens all over the State of Texas. Taxpayers need to know that their tax dollars are being abused in this form of corruption.*

Constable Corruption

Constables are a unique breed of law enforcement in that they do not answer to anyone for their day-to-day activities. This is probably the most corrupt area of law enforcement in Texas. They work when they want to and many times choose not to take regular calls from the SO. They will spend taxpayers' monies on working other security jobs.

Constable working extra jobs using county gas and county time and would not take any calls from the local SO. Told them to never call him as he would not go on any calls. Was called by the Sheriff for a call of shots fired and told the sheriff that he was serving civil papers and could not help him.

The constable that was paid by a local ISD to provide security would sit in his truck by the football field and would not go on service calls that he was actually paid to perform.

The constable that spends most of his time escorting funerals for extra money using taxpayers' dollars to pay for his gas to make an extra 60K-70K per year.

The constable and his deputies that was performing extra security for a community and would perform the patrols while they were working on county time.

The ISD that paid a constable 18K for a vehicle. This was the chief looking out for a brother in blue.

The constable that based his promotions on how much money you donated to his campaign fund.

The constable that was paid security for an ISD and would set in his truck at the football field and answer county calls. When asked why he was not in the school performing security, he stated that that was not his job and if anything happened in the school, the local police department was responsible.

Former South Texas Police Officer Gets 14 Years for Participation in Drug Smuggling Conspiracy

U.S. Attorney Ryan K. Patrick said that a former law enforcement officer got a hefty sentence after being convicted of conspiring to possess and distribute more than 1,000 kg of marijuana. Ramon "Ramey" Delacruz, 39, of Rio Grande City, served as a Rio Grande City police officer, a Starr County Sheriff's Office deputy, and a Starr County District Attorney's Violent Crime Task Force investigator. On April 4, 2017, he entered a guilty plea.

Senior U.S. District Judge John D. Rainey sentenced Delacruz to 168 months in federal prison, followed by five years of supervised release, today after a nearly six-hour hearing. The court heard further evidence on the levels of corruption Delacruz reached in his assistance of the Beltran Drug Trafficking Organization, which is centered in Rio Grande City. Delacruz allegedly escorted shipments of marijuana across Starr County while on duty, according to witnesses. He also aided in the theft of marijuana loads from other traffickers by fabricating police reports of bogus law enforcement interdictions that never occurred, as well as the theft of narcotics revenues via phone law enforcement takedowns. He also allegedly gave the group a stolen law enforcement radio and a Starr County seal embosser, as well as guns seized from the Beltran ranch and previously used in prior violent acts, according to the court. Delacruz was compensated with racehorses, cocaine, and drug money for his efforts.

Delacruz had not only engaged in the conspiracy but had also utilized his service-provided handgun and made threats of violence in the conduct of cocaine smuggling crimes, as well as assuming a leadership position in the group, according to the court. Rainey stated, "Today is a terrible day for your family and a sad day for police enforcement." Delacruz owes society a debt as a result of his violation of the confidence placed in him by his community, according to the court.

In January 2013, a Victoria County Sheriff's Office officer discovered nearly 600 pounds of marijuana hidden in a horse trailer, sparking an investigation. That incident sparked a multi-agency, multi-jurisdictional investigation that resulted in the discovery of information and evidence proving the Beltran drug trafficking organization's criminal actions. The network exploited horse farms in Rio Grande City to receive, repackage, and hide hundreds of kilos of marijuana before shipping it north in horse trailers, flat-bed trailers, and trac-tor-trailers. They exploited horse racing as a means of facilitating drug trafficking and laundering criminal funds.

For over a decade, the group used violence, intimidation, bribery, and official corruption to enable and prolong their illegal actions with near-total impunity. The inquiry revealed the organization's ties to the Gulf and Zeta Cartels, as well as the Starr County Chicano Brotherhood. Delacruz utilized his official position, as well as municipal and county resources, to help the Beltran organization transport hundreds of pounds of marijuana into and across the United States. Delacruz also used his peace officer position to harass, threaten, and compel other drug traffickers, as well as to safeguard drug cargoes, in order to maintain his region's supremacy.

The six-year investigation culminated in the arrest and conviction of 23 people, as well as the seizure and forfeiture of Black Patriot, an American Quarter Horse racing quarter horse, and three horse farms. Delacruz was re-manded in detention after his sentence today, awaiting his transfer to a U.S. Bureau of Prison facility to be selected in the near future. The investigation was carried out by Immigration and Customs Enforcement's Homeland Security Investigations, the Texas Attorney General's Office, and the Victoria County Sheriff's Office. The case is being prosecuted by Assistant U.S. Attorneys Patti Hubert Booth and Vincent Carroll.

The Case Study of the Panama Unit in South Texas

The aforementioned factors might act as a catalyst for police misconduct. In-dividually, each variable may not be as effective, but when taken together, they may be disastrous. In any social system where there is frequent change in society, such as in south Texas, there is a strong predisposition for corruption. The Panama Unit was made up of cops from a tiny border hamlet in south Texas. When these young guys joined the police force, they had every intention of becoming excellent cops. When they originally began, they did not succeed or stand out at the academy. Their familial ties, on the other hand, would rocket their prominence virtually instantly. These policemen went from being "decent cops" in a little border town with a lot of promise to becoming the most renowned narcotics squad in Hidalgo County, Texas. The task force's official name was Hidalgo County Sheriff's Office—Mission Police Department Local Level Drug Unit, but they were known as the

Panama Unit on the streets (*New York Times*, 2015). The Panama Unit was statistically the most vulnerable group of officers for corruption, with several of these criteria present, including age, naivety, police subculture, recruiting processes of many agencies, and a lack of integrity.

One of the most well-known flips (slang for trading a small-time drug dealer for a larger fish) netted an estimated $55,000 in filthy money. These commanders, who were in their late twenties, were eager for money, power, and fame. In addition to being hungry, they had strong familial ties, and they lived in a city with all the components for corruption. A bust in 2010, just before Christmas, was one of the first reported instances of corruption (*New York Times*, 2015). Three officers of the Panama Unit pulled stopped a suspected intoxicated motorist around 2:45 A.M. in 2010. The driver had a couple of ounces of cocaine and a bag holding $50,000, which he took and divided among the three buddies; it was easy money. The majority of the time, the search began legitimately, but when no money was available, the narcotics were seized and resold.

The Panama Unit was expected to get $15,000 for a kilo of cocaine, $150 for a pound of marijuana, and $1,000 for methamphetamines (*New York Times*, 2015). Officers progressed from selling to local drug traffickers to co-operating with persons who would transfer narcotics for the cartels as corruption got easier and more drugs became available. They became a "den of thieves," as it were. They began generating an additional $14,000 per month by stealing an 18-wheeler and loading it with marijuana. They were enjoying the high life, with cash, residences, and automobiles, as well as asset forfeiture. The Panama unit's commander always had $10,000 in cash on him to spend. They were becoming much too apparent for their newfound affluence to go unnoticed. By 2012, several law enforcement officials and others suspected the Panama Unit of being corrupt (*New York Times*, 2015).

HSI (Homeland Security Investigations), the Drug Enforcement Agency (DEA), the FBI (Federal Bureau of Investigations), and Texas Rangers began monitoring and mapping the unit's travels and routines in the summer of 2012. The Panama Unit was becoming more concerned about gang members and local drug traffickers rather than cartels at this time. Even before the scandal, the chief of the Panama Unit had been threatened with murder, so he armed himself with M4s and AK-47s. In October of 2012, a Mexican drug dealer approached the Panama Unit, offering to escort narcotics for her, which is a common occurrence in police corruption. During this time, the unit began to hear whispers that they were being observed by the Texas Rangers and maybe other law enforcement agencies.

The team decided to do one more operation and rob a Mexican drug dealer of her cocaine, which had a wholesale worth of $200,000. When three members of the unit met with the drug dealer, they soon discovered the unit had been set up by her and HSI with wire taped affixed to the package rather than a heist. A little battery gadget with cables and a bar code was found on one of the cocaine parcels; it was a GPS tracker (*New York Times,* 2015). The Panama Unit was no longer operational. The Panama Unit's news continues to jolt the community. The nine officers who were part of the squad were indicted, and the Hidalgo County sheriff was eventually fired. It was just a matter of time until his corruption caught up to him since he was the father of the Panamanian Unit's commander. Many reasons contribute to police corruption, including age, innocence, police subculture, recruiting policies in many agencies, and a lack of integrity. All of the variables were present in this case study, and some of them are still present.

Probable Strategies to Curb Police Corruption

Political corruption and state capture are inseparable. For political purposes, police may be used to suppress dissent or to evade laws and regulations in favor of friends and allies. There are a variety of ways in which this might manifest itself, including political intervention in police investigations, the launching of fake investigations, the "framing" of political opponents, and so on. Social and political control measures in non-democratic conditions are commonly used by police to repress dissent and democratic competition. As a consequence of police political interference, political parties may be suppressed, freedom of speech and association restricted, demonstrations suppressed, and political fatalities covered up in certain cases. These sorts of political corruption are connected to human rights breaches because they allow for the discretionary use of force and the development of a culture of impunity.

Corrupt conduct may be prevented by altering the underlying structures that encourage it and by creating an institutional atmosphere that limits the rewards and opportunities that corrupt activity provides. The institution's management systems and organizational culture may be overhauled, as well as efforts are taken to promote integrity at all levels of the police force, develop accountability mechanisms, and involve the public.

Promotions and Recruitment

Appointment procedures must be open, fair, and transparent in order to recruit the best professionals and ethical standards. To ensure that employees are promoted on the basis of their abilities rather than their gender or ethnicity is essential. The rotation of high-risk positions should also be governed by policies. There are several significant personnel considerations to make while reorganizing the police force, including whether to maintain current officers or employ new ones. Lessons learned from South Africa suggest the need for a combination of both strategies, including reselection/vetting corrupt police officers and a systematic approach to new recruitment (Bruce, 2003).

When it comes to employing new officers, selection procedures and policies are critical components of police reform. Police officers may be unable or unwilling to uphold high ethical standards because of a lack of rigorous criteria for selecting new hires. South African police reform, for instance, included a new selection method implemented to enhance the quality of police recruits, with basic acceptance standards including a minimum level of education and the absence of a criminal record, for example (Newham G., 2002). According to the belief that women are less likely to tolerate corruption, female traffic officers have been deployed in countries such as Colombia, Peru, and Mexico. According to reports, these initiatives have had some success in reducing bribery claims.

Benefits and Salaries

For the sake of public safety, it is imperative that police officers be paid a living salary on a regular and consistent basis. Measures to eliminate corruption in Singapore, for example, include raising the salary of government personnel and political leaders so that they are more competitive with those in the private sector. Reducing the number of senior police officers and using the savings to increase pay for rank-and-file officers are part of Afghanistan's police reform efforts (USAID, 2007). To be sure, the majority of research agrees that increasing compensation is unlikely to eliminate corruption unless accompanied by effective systems for monitoring and implementation of sanctions (Chêne, 2009).

Inmate Work

One police officer used inmates to build BBQ pits and would sell them for profit.

Another officer used inmates to build a huge trailer BBQ pit and later tried to sell it on an actual television show that would buy strange items from individuals.

One officer would bring all of the trustees out to the shooting range for a BBQ and would invite their family members out as well. Many of them were allowed to have sex in the shoot house.

Turn-the-Other-Cheek Corruption

Several officers would use their work at the department to aid their security company to make money.

Several officers use the resources of the department to aid in their private investigations company.

The county judge that would use county money to travel to Austin to spend time with his boy toy.

Development and Training

As part of efforts to build professional and merit-based career standards, police officers must be taught to be able to perform their jobs in a professional, impartial, and ethical manner. To achieve this goal, police departments should have access to training and development programs that promote professionalism and ethics. Human rights-based policing capacity building is included in this endeavor to help police personnel recognize wrongdoing and equip them with measures to fight back against attempts to corrupt them. In South Africa, for example, the training curriculum for new recruits was reworked to teach democratic police ideas and practices. Additionally, managers must get training on how to develop an ethical culture and how to act as role models. In order to motivate their staff, managers, in particular, need to be well versed in management skills and strategies that recognize and reward moral conduct and exceptional performance.

Proper Administrative Systems

In the past, police investigations and actions have been undertaken without the public's knowledge or participation. Current investigations must be protected from criminals, witnesses must be protected, and swift action must be taken without waiting for approval from the right authorities. When it comes to the institution's long-term reputation and accountability, it is possible that a lack of transparency might lead to an organizational culture that is filled with secrecy and corruption.

The public's faith in the police may be increased if all parts of the organization's governance and administration, including budgeting and expenditures, are made public. Transparency may be improved by making police performance and statistics publicly available on a regular basis, as well as by maintaining meticulous records. Increasing the effectiveness of audit and inspection capabilities, improving procurement and resource management systems, and modernizing personnel records are some other solutions. Implementing effective recording systems, such as detention records that include the names, badge numbers, locations, and reasons for the arrest of police officers, may help limit the risk of police power abuse in the community.

It is clear that open government, inspection, and proactive disclosure principles may meet public expectations and restore public trust in the institution as shown by the United Kingdom's experience. Freedom of information requests, public meetings, and public inquiries of the success or failure of police programs and operations are now routine in British police services after the passage of laws on human rights, freedom of information, and whistleblowing in the late 1990s and early 2000s (Sturges P. and Cooke L., n.d.). In order to minimize conflicts of interest and illicit enrichment, Interpol's global guidelines for combating corruption in police forces include adopting and executing rules for the declaration and registration of income, assets, and liabilities of police officers and their families. According to these standards, employees should be forced to disclose their income upon being hired and at periodic intervals afterward, including upon retirement (Interpol, n.d.).

County Cover-up

I remember one story of a county investigation that never existed. During an investigation of a local county official, it was determined that this county official voted in both primaries. When the injustice was brought to the attention of the higher management, the file was requested from the investigating officer and was then discarded. The investigating officer was told this investigation never existed and was to be dropped. This form of corruption happens in local politics on a regular basis and is used by officers and management as a form of ransom. They hold this incident over the head of the person until a time when they are needed by the officer or department. Until then the person sits on pins and needles wondering if they make the wrong person mad causing the case will raise its wicked head.

Leadership Development

In order for anti-corruption measures to be effectively implemented, it is critical to have a strong organizational and political commitment to anti-corruption policies. If there is political will, an anti-corruption message may be explicitly defined in operational policies and vigorously promoted at public events. Integrity in police management and supervision is a primary focus of anti-corruption measures based on experience, according to the authors. Officers in the police department must be willing and competent to enforce rules and use the official disciplinary system to guarantee that their subordinates adhere to those restrictions. Police chiefs and managers should lead by example by exercising authority, adhering to the highest standards of rule and procedure compliance, and creating an environment in which individual police personnel may work honestly.

Community Policing

Citizens' trust in the police is being rebuilt, and community support for police reform is being gained by presenting crime prevention and victim empowerment projects in the framework of democratic policing, community-based policing, and community-based policing (CBP). The goal of community-based policing is to bring together the police and the people they serve in order to find solutions to community issues and make the police more responsive to public needs. For example, the establishment of forums for community input may be beneficial in this regard.

Strong Internal Accountability

As a part of improving internal accountability, police supervisors should have the authority to impose disciplinary measures and be held accountable for doing so. Since enforcing fundamental discipline may annoy senior and lower-rank commanders or be regarded as motivated by other considerations, many police supervisors lack the will or expertise to do so ("scapegoat syndrome"). Disciplinary actions in South Africa, for example, must be initiated by supervisors who must deal with a complicated and detailed system that managers may not understand properly. To put it another way, front-line managers do what their superiors tell them to do, which leads lower-level managers to regard themselves as closer to their subordinates rather than as part of a unified management system (Newham, 2002).

There are several approaches to improve internal accountability, including enhancing internal investigations, conducting random integrity checks, and establishing early warning systems. In order to ensure that public officials are not corrupt, random integrity testing places them in situations where they may be offered money or gifts. According to some authors, this is "the only approach to establish a broad deterrent impact on police agencies that will be meaningful and durable" as part of an anti-corruption effort (cited in Anozie, V.; Shinn, J.; Skarlatos, K.; Urzua, J., 2004). Additional internal accountability measures include conducting regular station and unit inspections, having an effective auditing and asset management capacity, or establishing transparent custody and file management systems.

Conclusion

Recent events in Texas once again denote a very serious situation of the practice of corruption at the highest levels of the officials in the police. We are referring to the well-known events related to the irregular and corrupt provision of security services by the National Police, apparently to a character prosecuted and at the time convicted of crimes of corruption, involved at the time with the organized structure during the disgraceful decade of the 1990s. These events allow us to understand a little more how routine or usual it is to find. For example, various Traffic Police officers who are bought in their public function in order not to fulfill their duties of imposing ballots for traffic violations or making them.

All the commentators agree in emphasizing how complicated or almost impossible to reverse the aforementioned police situation. A series of well-intentioned ministers of the interior, despite their best will, have not been able to alter this situation or, worse still, have been tarnished in their clean professional careers. Faced with this unfortunate scenario, a series of unavoidable questions come back to us: What to do with so much police corruption? Is it possible to reverse this situation? And if this is not possible, why don't we ignore the matter and turn a blind eye and act as accomplices—active or missive—of corruption?

Chapter Four

Texas Police Brutality

Texas Demographics

The State of Texas is home to more than 2.8 million people, with a median age of 38 and an average income of $59,206 per household. Over the course of its history, the State of Texas has seen its population rise from 27.9 million to more than 2.8 million residents. This indicates a 159-percent increase in overall median income from $56,566, or around a 4.5-percent gain over the previous record high. The previous record high was set in 2005. According to the census completed in 2010, white people make up 42 percent of the population, while Hispanic people make up 39 percent, and African-Americans make up 12 percent. It is estimated that 35.5% of the population of Texas is able to speak English, while the remaining population does not (Campney, 2021). According to a recent survey, Asian workers in the State of Texas received the highest earnings. They were paid more than one and a half times as much as the workers of the ethnic group that held the position of the sec-ond-highest pay in the region, which was white workers. According to the computation of the GINI wage index, the degree of income inequality in Texas was approximately 0.5 percent in the past, but it has since climbed to above 0.6 percent. At the present time, the poverty rate in Texas is higher than the estimated percentage for the entire country, which sits at 16 percent of the population. The majority of Texans living in poverty are women between the ages of 25 and 35, followed by young adults (18 to 24 years of age). In order to obtain accurate data, the Census Bureau employs a set of income standards that are mostly determined by the size of the already disadvantaged household. White people make up one of the largest known ethnic groupings that have a population that is well over the poverty threshold. This is the case when looking at poverty in relation to race (Crenshaw, Ritchie, Anspach et al., 2015). The national census assigns a person's level of material hardship according to the size of their family unit as the criterion. If the total income of a family is either less than or equal to the threshold for the family as a whole, then all members of the family are regarded to be poor and are included on the page that lists the poor. When compared to earlier records, the percentage of individuals holding jobs in the State of Texas has significantly increased, reaching a new high of 2.2 percent (Nelson, 2001). In Texas, two of the most popular professions are those related to teaching elementary school students and serving as principals of elementary schools.

Police Brutality

The 911 caller states that there is a man with a gun. Of course, the adrenaline rush hits, and every officer wants to get involved in this call. The video footage shows a man standing in the front yard when police officers arrive. The man is unarmed and holds his hands above his head when the first officer is running toward him. The officer runs up to the man and starts wrestling with him to slam him to the ground. Shortly, other officers arrive and help the first officer at which time the man is on the ground. The officers that were second on the scene started beating the man in the head and face with the butts of their AR-15 rifles. This goes on for several seconds as the man is struck multiple times in the head and face by the officers. While the call was a man with a gun, the first officer that arrived on the scene did not assess the situation but instead ran in like a bull in a China shop. The second officers were unable to control their emotions or adrenaline and started beating the man with the butts of their AR-15 rifles. The situation could have been controlled much differently but the lack of experience, education, and training coupled with the officers' lack of mental control caused the incident to become out of control. The officers were not disciplined for the incident even though the video showed otherwise. This incident proves that once the officers have a badge and gun, they believe that they are above the law of the average citizen.

Death at the Hands of the State

A month after the passing of his daughter, Marquis Jefferson was murdered by law enforcement officers in the course of a mass shooting. A recent incident took place in the neighborhood close to the intersection where residents of the black community live. The man's daughter had passed away, and he wanted answers about what had happened, but he ended up passing away himself. The fact that the police went on a shooting spree in their neighborhood, which resulted in the deaths of a large number of innocent people, including the young girl and her father, is evidence of the violence and cruelty with which they carry out their duties. The police officers at White Fort who were responsible for the murder of Jefferson's daughter and who left her family in anguish are the ones who are to blame for her passing. The spokesman for the family tells how the tragedy took place in their homestead, where the police carried out a wholesale killing without giving any thought to the protection of innocent Americans. The death of the father's only kid has left him inconsolable, but since he is a member of a marginalized group, he was not given the opportunity to voice his concerns about the manner in which justice is carried out. As a parent, he adds, "I had to go through a lot in order to make sure that the family felt his efforts in fighting for justice in the loss of their only daughter." He says this because he wanted to ensure that the family felt his efforts in fighting for justice. In spite of Mr. Jefferson's greatest efforts, he was unsuccessful in changing his course of events. The family was greatly impacted as a result of this. The police brutality in Texas, which resulted in the deaths of several of the family's loved ones, has caused the family to suffer from post-traumatic stress disorder (PTSD). Mrs. Jefferson ultimately passed away as a result of her wounds not long after the deaths of both her husband and her daughter. After her next-door neighbor discovered that all of her doors were wide open and phoned for assistance, a security officer who was summoned to check on her home for a non-emergency purpose shot and killed her when he arrived there. She was killed by a gunshot in the middle of the night at her house while she was interacting with her nephew during a game. Her passing signals the end of an entire family, which was brought about by the brutality of the police. As seen by the murder of a Texas family, the use of excessive force by law enforcement has resulted in the deaths of a disproportionate number of unarmed civilians.

A Southern Culture of Violence

There have apparently been seven incidences of mass shootings in the State of Texas over the course of the past decade, which has prompted a public discussion on how to prevent and eliminate such occurrences. Despite the growing body of evidence, those responsible for the brutality of the police toward African-Americans continue to avoid punishment. The state government of Texas continues to disregard the problem of racism in the state's judicial system, which has led to unfair trials for people of African descent living in the state. In recent years, Texas has seen an increase in both the practice of racial profiling and the level of police brutality. African-Americans have been forced to contend with racial discrimination in the legal system, as well as social and economic exclusion (Holmes, 2000).

African-Americans have been unfairly accused of crimes and sentenced to jail terms without receiving a fair trial due to the bias that exists in the judicial system. In Texas, racial bias and violent police tactics have resulted in the incarceration of a significant number of black Americans, and there is no clear path forward to address these problems. The problem of police violence against African-Americans has been made significantly worse by racism. For years, it has been tolerated for someone to judge another person based on the color of their skin, which is a violation of human rights (Embrick, 2015).

If the state government of states like Texas does not pass laws that protect its citizens from being subjected to racial discrimination, then the problem of police brutality will continue to be a problem in places like Texas. The State of Texas is seeing a rise in the number of African-Americans relocating there, and as a result, the city of Dallas is experiencing an increase in the prevalence of discrimination and police bias. African-Americans are regarded as a risk by law enforcement officials when they are on the job, and as a result, they constantly carry firearms. There have been a number of documented incidents of police officers going through African-American neighborhoods with their guns drawn and ready to strike, and these events have been chronicled by the media. Every time a police officer comes into contact with a Black American civilian, regardless of the circumstances, they will unconsciously put their weapons down (Embrick, 2015). However, there are some situations in which the conditions are more precarious. As the level of violence in Dallas increased throughout the course of a single year, there were reports of more than three officers being shot.

Ending Police Brutality against the Black Citizens of Texas

After learning that yet another African-American man had been killed by police in Texas, a number of Democrats put pressure on Governor Abbot to convene a special session of the Texas legislature to examine ways to reduce the incidence of police brutality against African-Americans. The purpose of this session is to look at ways to reduce the number of deaths that are caused by police brutality against African-Americans. On the other hand, Governor Abbott did not answer the request since he did not make the information available to the broader public. They have been going door to door in their community to garner support in the hopes of bolstering their position to push for improvements in the organizational framework of the criminal justice system. Cassandra asserts that they are in favor of reallocating monies from the department of public safety so that they can be used to enhance the quality of social services (2020). There has been an increase in the number of demonstrations taking place in Texas and other states ever since an African-American man was brutally murdered by a police officer in Minneapolis. The topic of discussion is likely going to center on the kinds of bills that members of Congress will be required to tackle during the upcoming session. There is a good likelihood that this will be the case (s). In addition, Governor Greg Abbott came under fire for his choice to leave African-American elected officials out of conversations about the prospect of making revisions. This decision was criticized as racist. After the governor of Texas and the black caucus participated in a virtual conference in which they discussed the possibilities of adjustments to police processes and legislation pertaining to criminal justice, a quarrel erupted between the two groups after the conference ended. According to the findings of the research, powerful police unions present a substantial obstacle to the introduction of any reforms that have the potential to make society more equitable. Recent months have seen a significant uptick in the number of communities across Texas that are working to bring about these reforms (Chatillon & Schneider, 2018). Instead of cutting funds for law enforcement, lawmakers want to increase spending on social programs such as affordable housing, mental health treatment, job training, and food assistance for the poor. They also want to avoid cutting funding for juvenile detention centers. This would come at the cost of decreasing the amount of money allocated for law enforcement.

Texas Shooting Case

On December 2nd, Mr. Carmen DeCruz, a police officer in Temple, Texas, shot and killed a man named Michael Dean, who was twenty-eight years old and unarmed. According to media sources, which stated that the incident took place seventy miles northeast of Austin in Texas, there is no clue as to why Carmen opened fire on January 1. Following the event, DeCruz was placed on paid administrative leave, which infuriated Mr. Dean's loved ones as well as those who were close to him emotionally. The police who detained this man described him as "evading," but that was about all the officer would say while speaking to the reporters. The man was a father of three children. According to Dean, his mother told News One that "Things simply don't stack up," and he believes that she is correct. It is not lost on him that he shouldn't be going at this time.

When he is sitting still in his automobile and waiting, it was said that witnesses saw a law enforcement officer take Dean from his vehicle. The footage from Carmen's body camera shows that he was already holding his gun as he approached the vehicle, and he pointed it toward Dean as he got closer to the window of the vehicle. Why did the police officer shoot him in the head while he had his pistol in his other hand when he pulled him over for speeding? The officer wasn't even holding his gun at the time. Officers are trained to know where to point their weapons in order to slow down a suspect who is fleeing the scene. Nevertheless, Mr. Carmen shot Mr. Dean in the head, which is a particularly brutal act that is undertaken by murderers and other individuals who have no respect for the lives of other people. Even though it was a brutal killing, Mr. Carmen had no right to take Mr. Dean's life. As a direct consequence of this, three additional black children will have to grow up without a father, and a further black mother has suffered the loss of a son due to the brutality of the police. However, in reality, it is the veteran cops who are more likely to use force and make arrests. Many people have the misconception that newly hired officers are the ones who are willing to make arrests and use force, but this is not the case (Ritchie & Mogul, 2007). My opinion is that before you pull the trigger on your firearm, you should first ascertain whether or not the individual in question poses a risk to your wellbeing.

Many individuals believed that DeCruz ought to have been sentenced to manslaughter because of the location of the bullet wound in the victim's skull. Manslaughter is punishable by a term of imprisonment ranging from five to ninety-nine years and a fine of no more than ten thousand dollars, whereas murder is punishable by a term of imprisonment ranging from five to ninety-nine years and a fine of no more than ten thousand dollars. But DeCruz didn't have a fine, and his bond was just $500,000, so what exactly did he get for his money? Furthermore, if he had been arrested, why was he still on paid leave? Although he was found guilty of involuntary manslaughter, the judge did not impose any prison time on him for the crime. Officers of the law are obligated to do so.

It's possible that DeCruz had a difficult day, but does it excuse him for shooting an unarmed man in the head? Because of the recent history of racial tensions, a white police officer who pulls over a black person needs to exercise extraordinary caution in both what they say and do when they interact with the black person. Because the lives of all people are equally essential, law enforcement officers have the authority to stop anyone, regardless of race or gender. The black community was driven to organize the march after a string of instances in which white police officers killed black men and women and mistreated black people. These incidents occurred over a period of more than a year. People of African descent had the impression that the people who were supposed to be protecting them were the ones who were killing them because it was so easy for those people to do so. Because of this, the expression "Black Lives Matter" came into being; nevertheless, I believe that every life should be treated as valuable because you never know who you are killing or how their death will impact the people who knew them in the past.

At a traffic stop, it takes some force to bring a driver to a halt; the question is, how much force? If the subject refuses to obey, you have the option of using a taser rather than a pistol. I'd rather incapacitate someone by shocking them or piercing their tires than take their life. It is impossible for them to comply while they are still alive, and the police need to be aware that when they pull someone over, that person is highly terrified, regardless of race, because of what the media portrays. It is impossible for them to comply while they are still alive. I wish there was a way to stop police brutality, but unfortunately, there isn't one as long as the justice system continues to reward the officers who commit the crimes. I wish there was a way to stop police brutality. To me, it doesn't seem fair that police officers can just be released on bond, go home to their families, and go about their everyday lives while the family of the person they killed is left to grieve in silence. This doesn't seem like it should be the case.

During my investigation into this incident and others like it, I gained a lot of knowledge about police violence, and I came to the conclusion that it had a particularly detrimental impact on the African-American community. I've been a witness to several incidents in which police officers have abused their power and neglected their responsibilities without facing any consequences. I am of the opinion that there will never be any consequences for the activities of police officers when it comes to wrongdoing in the police force. Because members of the black community have had loved ones slain by police officers throughout the years, they have a deep-seated mistrust of the police. People automatically think that you are going to cause problems if you are black, live in the "ghetto," or drive a particular automobile. This is not acceptable, and no one should be singled out because of the way they look. The frequency of unprovoked shootings of unarmed black men and women has gradually increased over the course of the past decade. Following an occurrence such as this one, police personnel ought to be fired from their employment. In my opinion, if your acts are motivated by racism or any other purpose other than protecting yourself, you should not be permitted to wear the badge and call yourself a police officer. You should also not be able to call yourself a police officer. When a suspect disobeys an officer's commands and refuses to comply, police personnel need to be better trained on how to use their firearms, tasers, and other types of weaponry. They should also go through psychological training that teaches them not to be so biased against the black community due to the way black people look or for other reasons. Instead of breaking down and destroying the faith that their community has in them, police officers should work to build it up. Ultimately, at the end of the day, you want the community to have trust in you and support for you since you never know when you'll need them. As a consequence of this, everyone must work together to hold police officers accountable for their behavior in order to bring closure to the loved ones of the deceased and to enable the black community to continue on with its lives.

Amendments and Public Opinion

For far too long, there has been far too much violence committed by cops, and it is just growing worse as time goes on. As a result of the brutality and injustice committed by police, the State of Texas has been negatively impacted. The number of people killed by law enforcement officers in Texas is the second-highest of any state. In addition to this, the rate of homicides committed against black people is the third highest in the country. Twenty percent of the people who were killed in the State of Texas in the previous year did not have any kind of weapon on them. According to the findings of a study conducted by Amanda Woog at the University of Texas, between 2005 and 2015, there were 1,118 African-Americans who passed away while incarcerated in the State of Texas (Campney, 2021).

Due to the fact that this issue has persisted in every state across the nation, it should be considered a national rather than a state-level concern. Despite the fact that state governments also have a part to play in this situation, the federal government ought to move to take action on this problem. Among the amendments that would be in breach of the constitution are amendments 4 and 8. The Fourth Amendment makes it clear that unreasonable searches and seizures are not permitted under any circumstances. In the court case known as Kaupp v. Texas, which was filed against the State of Texas for allegedly breaching the Fourth Amendment, Texas law enforcement agents showed up at Robert Kaupp's home around midnight. He was roused from his deep sleep by the sound of handcuffs being placed on him and the sound of being led to the police station for questioning. Any confession that was made as a result of this unconstitutional seizure should have been suppressed in accordance with the precedent set by the Fourth Amendment. This would have reinforced the view of the court that citizens are protected from unjustified searches and seizures (Baenziger, 1969). People are wrongfully detained by police officers in the vast majority of situations involving police brutality, and officers rarely or never provide a valid reason for their actions. According to this amendment, the 8th Amendment's prohibition against cruel, unusual, or excessive punishments, as well as the imposition of excessive penalties, does not apply to anyone. Every example of police brutality contains at least one violation of the Eighth Amendment. Because of this, the government is prevented from imposing severe punishments on criminal defendants who do not merit such a course of action. The punishment that the victims get at the hands of the authorities is severe, but in the end, it is completely without purpose. The rioting that took place in the downtown area of Los Angeles for five days is documented in the history of police brutality. The assassination of Rodney King sparked a frenzy of fury among the general population. An unarmed African-American man, who would later be identified as King, was subjected to vicious beatings by four police officers, which were seen on body cameras. After the judgments and body camera footage were made public, there was a massive outpouring of protesters in Downtown Los Angeles. They also plundered businesses while the road was blocked by them. When they originally started, these riots were right up there, with the most significant civil unrest that took place in the twentieth century. Protests and looting broke out in Houston, Texas, where George Floyd was born and raised, after the news and video recordings of his death were made public. However, the title of "most hated city in America" did not last long. Demonstrations against the police that involved hundreds of people were stopped by the police. They opened fire on the protesters with pepper spray and rubber bullets, causing dozens of people to sustain injuries.

The deaths of three of the most high-profile victims of police violence, including Jonathan Price, Tony Timpa, and Darrell Zemault Sr., round out the top three. During the incident, Jonathan Price was shot and murdered by Texas Rangers. According to them, the officer's actions did not appear to be "objectively reasonable," so they decided to shoot Jonathan as a result. There is still an investigation being conducted into the behavior of the officer, Shaun Lucas, who has been placed on administrative leave until the results of the investigation. Tony Timpa was being held down by a Dallas police officer, and the officer heard Tony Timpa yell for help. He screamed, "You are going to put an end to my life!" As he passed asleep, the officers laughed and made jokes about how they would have to wake him up for school in the morning. His body-worn camera captured footage that showed him being restrained for a period of fourteen minutes. There is one thing that all of these predicaments have in common, and that is the fact that they are all connected. This is because none of these individuals possessed any kind of weapon whatsoever. Nobody else was getting hurt, and nobody else was putting the community in jeopardy because of them. Due to the fact that their ages ranged from 46 to 12, all of them experienced it, and this demonstrates that it did not discriminate based on age. The police officer is the only person of another race among them; the others are all black (Peeples, 2020).

Every single member of the police force is held accountable to the same standards and regulations that have been established by the government. As a direct consequence of this, analogous instances of police violence have been documented in a variety of locations around the nation. Numerous reports of cases that are virtually identical to one another have been received. More than half of the time, a police officer will shoot and kill an unarmed African-American man or woman. In these cases, the victim was not armed. However, despite the fact that police brutality is a nationwide problem, there are differences from state to state. Another illustration of how racial and ethnic differences influence police brutality may be found all around the United States.

When compared to Wichita, Kansas, Chicago, Illinois, has a rate of police brutality that is twenty-two times higher. Protests and rioting have broken out across the country as a direct result of the high number of unarmed minorities who have been killed by police. These events have an impact on minority groups. Indeed, this is a problem that is experienced by families with lesser incomes. Because of this, the police have a different perspective on people like them than they do on more affluent segments of society. Regarding my problem, the opinion held by the vast majority of people is that this is not correct. The problem and the growing trend of police violence are both well known to the general population. Nothing had changed about it for decades at that point. As a direct consequence of this, there have been no advancements made in either the legislation or the training for law enforcement. As a part of the Black Lives Matter movement, a half-million people participated in protest marches across the country in response to the killing of George Floyd, as well as the killings of hundreds of thousands of other African-Americans who have been failed by the judicial system and the police force. Recent research on police brutality and African-Americans have shed light on the attempts made by the police to both maintain white supremacy and control the growing black population in American cities. Some of the most recent works on the topic of police brutality and African-Americans center their attention on the efforts made by the police to uphold white supremacy and regulate the growing population of African-Americans in the United States. Republicans are too accountable for the political views on police brutality since Texas is a Republican state, and Republicans are to blame because Texas is a Republican state. Recent protests against racial inequality have led to the declaration by Democratic leaders that the Republican idea for policing is "not salvageable." This statement was made in response to the recent protests. The Texas House Chamber voted yes on a number of different reform measures for the police department. In addition, officers who violate the terms of their employment will be subject to stricter disciplinary measures. In the case of Williamson County Sheriff Chody, Javier Ambler was stunned five times before his body became limp and he passed away an hour later at a hospital. In the case of Williamson County Sheriff Chody, Javier Ambler was shot by Williamson County Sheriff Robert Chody. Democrats have made it clear that they want Texas Governor Greg Abbott to take note of the current situation and make a public demand for Officer Chody's release (Bryant, 2021).

The resolution of this issue would require participation from the local police department, the state legislature, and the judges of the Supreme Court. Both the presidential branch and the legislative branch need to give some thought to the issue of police brutality, which is one that is very close to my heart. The rights of the states, as outlined in the 10th Amendment, are applicable to the degree that they are not specifically ceded to the federal government. It's possible that there's a government agency that acts as a go-between for the community and police enforcement. It is possible that this agency may propose a new law or bill that will assist minimize police brutality not only in Texas but also throughout the rest of the country. The task force also acts as a guide for law enforcement officers to follow when they are confronted by an unarmed criminal. It is possible to stop police brutality by providing officers with specialized training and giving them opportunities to act out different roles. Officers hold a significant amount of influence, but what if they were to lose it? In the vast majority of the cases, police officers do not lose their jobs immediately. It is not unusual for them to take a break of a few weeks to a few months before coming back. If we want to find a solution to this problem, it may be necessary to treat these officers the same way we would treat anyone other who abuses another individual. They are not able to get any advantages due to the fact that they are a member of the police force. "It is just as vital for the government to bring prompt justice to its citizens as it is for private citizens to do the same." The safety of the general public, the prevention of criminal acts, and the preservation of legal norms are the primary responsibilities of police officers in the United States. Because it is the role of the police to ensure the public's safety, the public should not be fearful of the police. Sadly, the next decade will see no letup in instances of police brutality. This pattern, however, ought to begin to reverse itself as more individuals become aware of the aforementioned problem. Indeed, there are a number of bills in the legislative pipeline that are still awaiting action. Especially when considered in light of the extensive history of police abuse, I have faith that it will be codified into law. Alteration is necessary. Lawyers that specialize in human rights issues are taking action and speaking out on behalf of individuals who are unable to speak for themselves in order to facilitate the achievement of a solution. Reading, listening to, or watching movies are all excellent ways to educate oneself about the history of police brutality. in order to have a deeper comprehension of the growth in the use of force by police. The general populace has a legal obligation to be informed of what is occurring and why nothing has been done to stop it. People who have been wronged in any way can also get their voices heard by signing petitions and speaking out for them.

Conclusion

Since the beginning of the industrial revolution, there has been a steadily increasing problem of police brutality in the State of Texas. The majority of the cost is shouldered by minority groups in the United States, primarily African-Americans and Latinos. A hard and excruciating existence, including the loss of some of their loved ones, has been inflicted upon racial and ethnic minorities as a direct result of the excessive use of force by law enforcement. As a consequence of the attacks on members of these minority groups, members of these groups who were attacked now have social difficulties, such as a fear of being attacked at any time. There have been allegations that law enforcement in Texas, notably African-Americans, has a bias against minority groups and sees them as a threat to public safety. As a consequence of the existence of such legal evidence. This minority group struggles with feelings of discrimination and hostility as a direct result of the majority of Americans' persistent perception of them as disruptors of the peace. The history of racial oppression in the United States contributes to the formation of a negative picture of the entire police force whenever these kinds of operations are carried out by law enforcement personnel. There have been other occurrences involving the way the police have treated members of minority groups, and this has become a national issue that the federal government needs to address in order to preserve the safety and quality of life for all Americans. Many people view the excessive use of force by police officers in Texas as a sign of the injustice and racism that has played a role in the plight of many members of minority groups in the United States. Every American citizen needs to demonstrate love and support for one another without displaying any signs of discrimination in order for Texas to become a better place for everyone, and they also need to work together to ensure that law enforcement conducts proper investigations and punishes those responsible for police brutality. Only then will Texas become a better place for everyone.

Chapter Five

Sexual Misconduct within Law Enforcement in Texas

Introduction

Like many organizations, the Texas Department for Criminal Justice faces issues of sexual harassment and sexual assault. But it's time for the department leadership to take this seriously. Sexual harassment and sexual abuse undermine the integrity, professionalism, and effectiveness of the country as a whole, not just the victims. One of the main findings of the External Reviewing Body (ERO) is that there is a culture of sexualization within law enforcement agencies in Texas. This culture is hostile to women and LGBTQ people and encourages serious cases of sexual harassment and sexual assault. Therefore, cultural change is needed. It is not enough to revise policies or repeat the "zero-tolerance" mantra. Leaders must be aware that sexual harassment is a serious and very real issue for Texas law enforcement and must be addressed personally, directly, and continuously. Implementing cultural change is an important task. Texas law enforcement has many measures in place, including policies, training programs, disciplinary and military justice systems, and victim support services, but these measures will only be effective if they are strengthened. This report presents REA's findings from an analysis of policies, processes, and programs related to inappropriate sexual behavior, as well as methods that the Texas law enforcement department can use to reduce incidents of sexual harassment and sexual assault, as well as recommendations for a preferred approach.

Background

As sexual assault is a serious crime, awareness needs to be raised regarding the code of conduct and policies that exist in case someone faces such a scenario. If people are aware of the laws available for the victims and criminals of sexual assault, only then they would be able to avoid the repercussions. But a point to ponder is that if police and law enforcement agencies are themselves involved in such criminal acts, the surrounding people would be in extreme pain. Sexual offenses include but are not limited to acts of a sexual nature committed under duress and/or against the will of another person. If the victim is unable to consent, do not coerce or submit to the will of the person. Or illegal and optional sexual intercourse ranging from a misdemeanor to a Class C felony. Victims of these crimes must report the crime to the police. UTA medical services assist victims by providing direct advice or referring them to an appropriate facility. The main task of victims of sexual violence is to find a safe place and then get the treatment they need. In addition, time is an important factor in the collection and storage of evidence. In the event of an attack on the campus, report it to the UTA police immediately. Dormitory staff and other campus personnel, such as counselors, can help report sexual harassment to the police. If the attack happened off the UTA campus, they need to contact the local police station where the attack took place. The UTA Police Crime Victim Service can be used to help victims connect with other police agencies or community services (Chen et al., 2021).

Reporting Sexual Violence

Filing a police report with UTA does not require the victim to be prosecuted and does not subject the victim to police control or sentencing. Reporting to the police can help survivors of sexual assault get the treatment they need, get tested, and keep them penniless. Provides an opportunity to collect evidence that is useful to the prosecution but cannot be obtained later (ideally, victims of sexual assault should wash or bathe before medical/legal examination), provides victims with access to free, confidential counseling by specially trained consultants in the field of intervention in crisis situations due to sexual violence. Victims are asked to go to the hospital emergency room for testing for sexual assault after they have been reported to the police. A friend of the victim can take him/her to the hospital, or a police officer can provide transport. The police should receive a statement detailing the attack. Whether the attack happened on campus or the victim wants to report a crime, you can ask the victim's attorney (contact the UTA police station) to take the victim to the hospital.

Victims of sexual assault have the option to choose a pseudonym (not their real name) and address to maintain their privacy. Aliases are assigned at the request of the victim. Victims of sexual assault who live on campus may request changes to their living and learning environment. If these changes are reasonably available, every effort will be made by the department to comply with these requests. If the victim has filed a complaint, the UTA police will conduct a thorough investigation. If the case goes to trial, court testimony may be required. If the defendant is a UTA student for a sexual offense that has been reported to the UTA police, the case will be referred to the student's dean, and the charges will be reviewed. Victims and defendants have the same opportunity for others to be present during a disciplinary hearing on campus.

Incidents

The RER Council, on the other hand, is characterized by frequent blasphemies, highly snarky references to the female body, sexual jokes within the department, especially among recruits and non-commissioned officers, and a tendency toward sexualization has also become apparent, suggestions or discriminatory comments about female skills and unwanted sexual contact. Complaints were primarily about this atmosphere of sexualization, which makes the work environment hostile, but REE also reported instances of receiving sexual favors in exchange for favors. Some participants also mentioned the situation of sexual violence, including cases of suspicious relationships between women of lower rank and men of higher rank and date rape. In the most serious reported cases of sexual abuse, the use of sex emphasized the intensification of power relations and the desire to punish and expel members of the unit. REE has found that as the army rises in rank, it seems to get used to this culture of sexualization. For example, both male and female non-commissioned officers tend to appear insensitive to the culture of sexualization.

Officers, on the other hand, tend to tolerate instances of inappropriate sexual behavior because they believe Texas simply reflects the private sector. Some members are convinced that senior non-commissioned officers are imposing a culture of silence that discourages victims from reporting sexual harassment. Faced with this attitude, many subordinates believe that members of the chain of command are tolerant of inappropriate sexual behavior or willing to turn a blind eye to related incidents. Therefore, a complete cultural change is needed and cannot be carried out without the active participation of senior Texas law enforcement leaders. Senior leaders, especially those in charge of general oversight, recognize that the military has problems with sexual harassment and sexual assault, make it clear that sexual harassment is unacceptable, sexualization, and, above all, successfully integrate women into the army by appointing more women to top management positions.

Unreported Cases

During the counseling session, it quickly became clear that a large percentage of cases of sexual harassment and sexual assault go unreported. First, interviewees said that fear of career advancement, such as moving to a new unit, was one of the biggest reasons military personnel did not report such incidents. Victims mentioned a fear of appearing unbelievable, of being seen as weak or a troublemaker, of receiving retribution from peers or superiors, or of being classified as unemployed. Many in the military are convinced that a complaint does not guarantee confidentiality. These concerns reflect deep concern that a number of commanders have not taken their complaints seriously. Sexual harassment in situations where many believe that military personnel may view the female body as a thing, make one-sided and hurtful jokes about sex with military personnel, question the capabilities of military personnel, and be reluctant to report attacks. Such behavior, even if inappropriate, is usually ignored by the chain of command and discourages many victims from reporting the inappropriate sexual behavior they are targeting.

Accountability of the Cases

RER has repeatedly heard from participants that the only way to increase accountability is to create an accountability mechanism outside the chain of command. In fact, many other military agencies (e.g., U.S., Australia, and

France) receive reports of sexual harassment, provide victim support and reasonable driver training, and have independent offices to track data. In most of these offices, victims can choose whether to formally file a complaint and investigate it. Victims are provided with treatment and support, regardless of their decision. REE is responsible for sexual harassment and sexual assault independently of Texas and is responsible for receiving complaints of inappropriate sexual behavior, as is done in other countries and at the request of many Texas law enforcement members. We recommend the establishment of a responsibility center. Not only to provide prevention, support for the victims, data collection, training, and follow-up of the results of incidents. The complaint must allow the victim to decide whether to formally investigate the complaint but must always be entitled to treatment and support services.

Policy changes may not be enough to eliminate cases of inappropriate sexual behavior, but policies are still an essential tool for guiding the behavior of Texas law enforcement members. Unfortunately, RER has discovered that prohibited behavior is not properly defined in the current policy. Specifically, some interviewees have shown that they cannot accurately explain what constitutes sexual harassment, sexual misconduct, harmful relationships, and friendships. Especially when it comes to sexual harassment, the definition of Texas law enforcement is not only too complex but too narrow to capture the various behaviors that make up inappropriate sexual activity. The definition of sexual harassment should include not only harassment itself and the acquisition of sexual services in return for goodwill but also unwanted sexual behavior that contributes to the building of a hostile organizational culture. Making comments and jokes that create an unhealthy climate of sexualization is part of these actions, although not necessarily targeted at a particular person.

Suggestions for Improvement

The current process of identifying, reporting, resolving, and investigating cases of sexual harassment is complex and not producing the desired results. Therefore, it is not surprising that an impressive number of victims prefer to remain silent. Specifically, parties must go through three stages before a sexual harassment complaint is finally resolved, during which they seek to reach a settlement. Using Alternative Dispute Resolution, conduct an administrative investigation with the responsible officer, and file a complaint. This process is too long and tedious. In addition, there is a problem with introducing self-help methods and focusing on resolving grievances at the lowest level. Victims generally do not want to be able to confront the persecuted person. Especially if the person is taller than the victim. In addition, some interviewees who complained to their boss stated that their complaints were not taken seriously. RER concludes that pressure on parties to resolve complaints at the lowest level discourages victims from filing and threatening complaints. This pressure has the opposite effect of what a zero-tolerance policy should achieve. Victims also have the option to choose the official ADR. However, REA concludes that this approach is not generally acceptable in the case of sexual harassment.

Duty of RER

RER also seems to generally scoff at the sanctions imposed, even if the complaint of sexual harassment ends up being well founded, "hands-on," and an effective deterrent. This was not the case. To simplify the process, people need to eliminate the first two steps of resolving the complaint and go directly to the complaint. The Commanding Officer (CO), acting as arbiter, can always initiate a harassment investigation as part of a complaint. This streamlined process reduces unnecessary delays and pressure on the victim and quickly brings the issue to the attention of the CO. It is possible to continue to provide victims with the opportunity to go through mediation or alternative dispute resolution, but this opportunity is special. In addition, if the CO concludes that the complaint is legitimate, it should recommend to the CO that appropriate sanctions be imposed. More serious problems have been reported related to the investigation of cases of sexual harassment. RER is particularly concerned about the testimony, which highlights the inability of the gendarmerie to resolve this issue. She has met with many constitutional soldiers, many of whom do not fully understand the relevant directives, are unaware of the issue of sexual assault, and are an integral element of the crime (such as legal consent).

In addition, she heard testimony that those that did not cause minor attacks and physical injury were often ignored. Victims concerned about how they will be treated in the military judicial system often choose not to report sexual harassment for one reason or another. In addition, many of the victims who reported the attack described their experiences as "unbearable." In order to restore confidence in the system, complainants must reassure Texas law enforcement of their commitment to ensuring that complaints are properly investigated. This goal can be partly achieved when victims can request that their cases be referred to civil authorities. Finally, RER found that Texas collects very little data on cases of sexual harassment and sexual assault. The military has incident tracking mechanisms in place, but they seem to be used infrequently, and most incidents go unreported anyway. Without data to track the incident, it would be difficult to hold the chain of command or members of the gendarmerie accountable, and Texas has no information to prevent further incidents.

Current Texas Law Enforcement Practices

It appears that Texas law enforcement offers many programs and services to help victims of inappropriate sexual behavior, but in reality, these services are only available in certain locations and are ineffective because they do or do not fit the needs. In addition, many participants stated that they were not aware of available services and noted that there is no centralized source where victims could find all available support services. Overall, RER is the most important resource for nurses and social workers who may be victims of inappropriate sexual behavior and sometimes for those who are questioned or criticized when they are helpless. However, the role of nurses and social workers is inevitably limited. This is because they are usually only asked to intervene if the victim is in severe distress, and their medical department recommends this. Many victims avoid seeking medical attention because they feel that the confidentiality of their case is not protected. In addition, many of those interviewed had had the difficult experience of reporting sexual harassment to their doctors. Finally, although nurses and social workers play an important role in helping victims, they have a duty to protect victims and advise on various legal procedures and ways of proceeding.

Texas law enforcement members must regularly complete mandatory training, including prohibited sexual behavior. However, in reality, such training does not seem to be very effective. Many participants showed that the course was not taken seriously. Teaching about harassment is ridiculed, the course is too theoretical, and part of harassment is "drowned" in all subjects of education. Preparation: The presentations in the form of PowerPoint presentations are called "Death by Slow Fire with PowerPoint," and online learning has been heavily criticized. Many interviewees also expressed skepticism about the training provided by the unit. By all accounts, those who provide such training often engage in prohibited acts. Participants stated that the CO was not well trained and unable to identify, evaluate and deal with sexual harassment. Overall, the RER has found that the training currently offered fails to educate members about what constitutes acceptable behavior and instills an ethical culture within Texas. In fact, this training is unreliable and furthermore supports the notion that Texas does not take the issue of sexual harassment and sexual assault seriously. Courses focused solely on inappropriate sexual behavior should be taught in small groups by trained professionals using interactive methods. In-unit training should be limited, and online training should only be provided to non-commissioned officers if they also include interactive components. Leaders must also be regularly trained in their responsibilities in accordance with the policy related to inappropriate sexual behavior. Military police training should emphasize the concept of victim support, interview techniques, and consensus (Wood et al., 2020).

Examples

Three detainees at the Immigration and Customs Enforcement Authority (ICE) data center in El Paso, Texas, said they had been sexually assaulted or harassed by security guards, and their lawyers are demanding an investigation. The horror at El Paso's local ICE facility has become a new landscape of horror. Over the recent past, there have been victims of sexual abuse and harassment by guards at this detention facility for women and men. There has been recorded a very disturbing report by a lawyer at the Las American Immigration Center in El Paso. ICE spokeswoman Leticia Zamarripa said the agency does not tolerate any form of sexual abuse or assault on detainees and takes all allegations of misconduct by employees very seriously. As a civil servant working in law enforcement, ICE employees must maintain the highest standards of professional and ethical behavior (Franklin et al., 2020). Illegal cases are treated with the utmost seriousness and thoroughly investigated. Once this is proven, appropriate action will be taken. Las Americas sent a letter to the State Department of El Paso explaining the allegations. The first woman said two guards forced her to kiss and touched her private part several times. According to the complaint, the attack occurred between November 2019 and June 2020 in a location not accessible by surveillance cameras. She told her that hopefully, he would help her get out of her detention, but she refused to move forward, said one of the guards. Both guards reportedly said no one would believe her, and there was no evidence as her incident happened in the "camera blind spot." According to a Las Americas investigation request sent to an investigator, the woman filed a complaint with the ICE against the first guard in December, but the captain "despised and responded to the complaint." She hadn't seen the first guard for several months, but he returned in March and said that she had become more and more aggressive and intimidating against her. Immigrants, what he said to her again. She said she lived in a constant panic, saying she might do something. The second woman said she had repeatedly been sexually harassed by two guards in March and April. One told her he has been fascinating, and she should "play with him."

The second guard was equally successful and advised her to buy medicine for anxiety and depression "so they could meet at night and have sex." She was released in April, and after her release, she received a message from one of the guards through two women detained with her. In these reports, the policeman again tried to have sex with her, the complaint says. The third case cited in this complaint concerned a man who claimed he was the victim of sexual harassment and retaliation at the El Paso Data Center (Davis et al., 2021). The man said guards saw him and other men showering in July. The immigrants told the guards not to look at them, and the guards retaliated by rubbing their genitals, the complaint says. He reported the incident, but the captain told the guard that he was "just doing his job." The immigrants were taking a shower in mid-July when the guards entered and demanded to leave. The police officer yelled at him and pressed his face against his face until another guard pulled him away. The immigrant said he was put in a cell for five days after he complained about the second incident in the rice field. According to the complaint, he went on a hunger strike and was transferred to the Otero County data center, located about 20 miles away.

The final agreement to vote on the bill is a result of the Me-Too movement, which has uncovered a series of sexual abuse scandals in different sectors of the country and also rocked Capitol Hill this year. Minnesota Senator Al Franken resigned after being accused by several women of sexual misconduct. In the House of Representatives, several congressmen, such as Blake Farenthold of Texas, used public funds to forge settlements with victims of harassment. It is worth recalling, at the outset, the factual elements and the judicial process that gave rise to the decision of the U.S. Supreme Court in the Lawrence case.

With another man, the two individuals were preventively arrested and later convicted under the Texas law that represses the practice of sodomy between two people of the same sex in June 2003. The Court, on that occasion, puts before itself three questions to be decided whether the appellants' conviction under the Texas law criminalizing same-sex sexual practice violates the Fourteenth Amendment, which guarantees equal protection of laws; whether the conviction of the appellants for having had private and consensual sexual relations violates their vital interest in freedom and privacy protected by the regular legal process [due process clause] of the Fourteenth Amendment if the precedent of the Bowers v. Hardwick should be revised (Teague, 2018).

Roadside Rape

This story blew me away and when I saw the actual video, I could only shake my head wondering how stupid could the officer have been. During a traffic stop, two females were in the vehicle in question. A male supervisor ordered a female officer to perform a body cavity search on both females. The female officer put on rubber gloves and proceeded to perform a vaginal and anal search on the first female occupant of the vehicle. You can hear the female jump, wiggle, and voice her concern about where the officer was inserting her fingers. The second female was then searched by the female officer wearing the same pair of gloves. A vaginal and anal search was performed on the second female while she was voicing her concerns. No matter how you look at this situation, it is sexual assault by the officer. Both the male supervisor and female officer were suspended for this action but the female was later allowed to return to work because she was following the instruction of a superior officer. This is yet another example of officers abusing the power of the badge and thinking they can do whatever they want since they have a badge and gun.

The next example involves two male officers. After performing a traffic stop, the officers suspected the female driver of having illegal substances on her person. The officers requested that the female submits to a roadside cavity search and the female refused. The department had policies in effect that required the person to be brought to the station and placed in an x-ray chair to determine if drugs were being transported in body cavities. The two male officers did not follow policy and physically started performing a body cavity search on the female. The altercation ended with the officers having the woman on the ground, forced halfway under her vehicle performing cavity searches on her. Again, this is a roadside sexual assault as the woman tried to get them to stop verbally and physically. The officers should have been fired never to work in law enforcement again.

Setting for Promotion

I know people want to set the stage for them to be successful and achieve promotions when entering a new job. In this situation, a female officer was setting herself up for promotion before being hired. As a cadet, this female officer was outgoing and let it be known that she would be willing to do anything within her power to graduate from the academy and set herself up for promotion within a local agency. During drills in the shoot house, this female officer could be found sitting in the laps of current officers and supervisors allowing them to have their hands under her shirt and rubbing her breasts. Being easy does not set you up to be an outstanding officer. This future officer made herself available to other officers before she became commissioned and to many more after becoming an officer.

Obeying a Senior Rank

It is a proven fact that sex within a department is an epidemic and at times it seems to be a challenge for male officers to sleep with female officers of females that work in dispatch. One would be amazed at the foul language that is used between officers of the same and opposite sex. In this incident, a female officer was placed on patrol for a local agency and her male whore of a sergeant went on his own patrol. Understand this sergeant was married and had children, but this did not discourage him from trying to conquer the new female officer. They worked the night shift and the new female officer was placed on his shift. It was only a matter of time before the female officer saw the opportunity for promotion and the male sergeant saw the opportunity to finish his mission. While on patrol one night, they were caught in the action of a sexual encounter. The sergeant had the female officer bent over the hood of the patrol vehicle sexually interrogating her in an attempt to get a confession. They were both given the opportunity to resign instead of being fired. They both resigned and moved to other agencies. However, the female officer ended up pregnant and one is to speculate who is the father. The sergeant is still married and his wife is none the wiser. Unfortunately, this sergeant was constantly in an unfaithful state as he had sex with several of the female dispatchers as well. Funny thing is that everyone thinks this sergeant is a good officer even knowing his transgressions. You know this would have been a Kodak moment of seeing both officers with their pants and duty gear around their ankles doing the dirty-nasty with her bent over the hood. Talk about "deer in the headlights" look from both of them.

Supervisory Shock

While in the law enforcement field, I was constantly trying to better myself by attending additional training and development. The agency offered me the opportunity to attend a two-day training along with a sergeant of the agency. Understand, I had the utmost respect for this sergeant as he went out of his way to mentor and train me. Once we arrived at the town where the training was to be held, we checked into the hotel. At this point, I saw the familiar face of one of our dispatchers. Turns out, she was there to spend time with the sergeant. I would not have suspected this from the sergeant, as he was married with children. He ended up spending both nights with her allowing me to have a room all to myself. I was shocked by the actions of this sergeant but was not sure he would tell his wife. I am assuming that he did not as they are still It was my understanding that this particular dispatcher was quick to give of herself to officers that showed interest in her. Not only was she married, but was married to an officer at the same agency. Talk about keeping it within the family.

Role of the Supreme Court

The Supreme Court will justify its change of position in the Lawrence case on the basis of an interpretation of the Fourteenth Amendment by virtue of which no State may deprive a person of his liberty without due process clause, nor refuse everyone under their jurisdiction the equal protection of laws. Justice Kennedy, who drafted the Court's majority vote, stated that the point of the question is whether the majority [that is, the legislature] can use its state power to impose a moral conviction on the whole society through criminal law (Davis et al., 2020). Their obligation here consists in defining freedom tout court and not in enforcing our particular moral code. The Lawrence case thus raises the question of the existence, at the center of this "regular legal process," of a right to private life, in the sense of intimacy of sexual life, which could be claimed by homosexuals. By a majority of six to three, the constitutional right to respect for private life, including sexual intimacy, was recognized for adult homosexuals engaged in a freely consented relationship.

Justice Scalia, the author of one of the Court's minority votes, refused to recognize the Supreme Court's power to intervene and take a position on issues that shake American society and on which the federal states do not agree. If Justice Stevens, a minority vote in the Bowers case, were true to say that the fact that there is a ruling majority in a state that has traditionally made homosexual practice immoral is not a sufficient reason to pass a law banning this same practice, then, under these circumstances, majority rule would be suspended. Now, if the state can no longer, by the majority, legislate on moral matters; consequently, all legislation incriminating fornication, bigamy, adultery, incest, bestiality, etc., would be abrogated. Said [in the Bowers case], it is constantly based on notions of morality, and if all laws essentially representing moral choices are to be invalidated under the Due Process Clause, the courts will be very busy indeed. More than taking a stand in the moral debate, the Court should impartially ensure and observe that the democratic rules of the majority are observed. That homosexuals seek to persuade citizens that their way of life is the best, continues Justice Scalia, does not authorize them to impose their own point of view in the absence of a democratic will.

NFL quarterback Deshaun Watson on Friday gave his most blunt and forceful denial to date of allegations of sexual misconduct leveled against him by two dozen women. The Browns traded for the 26-year-old quarterback last week, sending the Texans a package including three first-round picks and giving Watson a five-year, fully guaranteed $230-million deal that set a new record for the NFL for the guaranteed money. The team made this pledge to Watson as 22 women alleged in civil lawsuits that Watson engaged in sexual misconduct during massage appointments by exposing herself, touching them with her genitals, or, in a few cases, by forcing oral sex. Two grand juries in Texas dismissed ten criminal charges against Watson this month. Watson declined to address specifics of the allegations, citing the civil cases, but he claimed the civil and criminal complaints filed by a total of 24 women are not true. He added that it is "not my intention" to settle the civil suits against him. "I've never done the things these people claim, and I'm going to keep fighting for my name and clearing my name," Watson said. Yet he has settled with almost all of the civil cases.

Andrew Berry, the Browns' general manager, said the team embarked on a "five-month odyssey" to feel comfortable pursuing a trade with Watson, a three-time Pro quarterback, but he confirmed that the process did not include speaking to any of the women who sued Watson. He said lawyers consulted by the team had indicated that reaching out "could be seen as interfering with a criminal investigation" (Goodson et al., 2020). Additionally, NFL investigators have already conducted interviews with at least 10 of the complainants. Berry said the team used "independent investigative resources" in Houston's "law enforcement community" to gain a "big-picture and holistic perspective" on the allegations against Watson. Berry did not respond when a reporter asked if those investigators had spoken to any of the women who filed the complaint.

Tony Buzbee, the attorney representing the 22 plaintiffs, said no one affiliated with the Browns or any NFL team contacted him or asked to speak to any of his clients. A lawyer for another woman who told *Sports Illustrated* her account of Watson's inappropriate behavior during a massage appointment in 2019 also confirmed that the Browns did not contact her or her client. Washington Commanders owner Daniel Snyder is under investigation by the NFL after allegations of sexual harassment were made against him by former employees. In July, the league fined the franchise $10 million after investigating allegations of harassment within the team's front office. The Houston Police Department has not discussed its investigation of Watson, and a spokesperson said Friday afternoon he could not say whether the Browns had contacted the agency. In search warrants that were part of the police investigation into Watson, one of the officers who worked the case for nearly a year described the women who filed criminal complaints as "credible and reliable."

Watson suggested their easy access via social media was a factor in why he used them but declined to elaborate. He said he, his agents, and the Browns would "come up with a plan" to find massage therapists in the future. Watson said he'll have to earn the trust of the Cleveland community and that "there's a stain that's probably going to stick with me for a while." He bristled when a reporter asked him if he wanted to consult, saying, "I have no problem. I don't have a problem, and that's what I've been saying since the beginning." Berry was asked if he and the Browns organization believed Watson had committed any wrongdoing. In response, he expressed the team's confidence in Watson and the positive impact he will have in Cleveland. A team public relations officer then wrapped up the press conference and asked for a photo. Watson stood between Berry and Brown's head coach Kevin Stefanski, holding a No. 4 jersey for the team he now represents (Santana, 2018).

Unwanted speech based on age, race, color, religion, gender, sexual orientation, gender, gender identity and expression, country of origin, ethnicity, disability, predisposition to genetic information, and targeted veteran status or a form of discrimination that is a physical act or (a) exposure to or experiencing any of the foregoing ineligible activities related to education, academic background, work, or participation in a program or activity. Other categories or benefits provided by law, if directly or indirectly related to the condition: The allegation or denial of such adverse conduct is directly or indirectly related to education (e.g., admission, academic background, grade, job), employment (e.g., employment, promotion, job) or participation in the program, an activity or interest that is used to make decisions that affect an individual. In the context of work, such repetitive activities unreasonably interfere with the performance of a person's work or create an intimidating, hostile or unpleasant work environment. In an academic context, such repetitive activities may be so severe, persistent, or debilitating that they unreasonably interfere with students' ability to participate in or benefit from educational activities and programs. For the purposes of this section, for an act to be considered "unacceptable" or "unreasonably interfering" with a person's activities, such an act must be more than subjectively offensive or harmful. Indeed, it must be objectively offensive or offensive to a rational person with a similar identity.

Suggestions

Texas Law Enforcement department needs to take the following actions intentionally or deliberately. Intimate activity, including, but not limited to, undressing, sexual activity, using the restroom, bathing, or other activities normally considered private, without the knowledge or consent of others to control or observe others involved in the activity (sometimes referred to as voyeurism). People who are victimized are also the ones whose recordings, photograph, transmitting, viewing, live streaming images, video, or audio has been done without their knowledge and consent (Cross et al., 2019). They should exceed the consent limit (for example, allowing others to hide in the closet to see sexual activity or distribute sexual images without the consent of the person taking the picture). Also, the ones who have sexual intercourse with another person and intentionally infect them with the human immunodeficiency virus (HIV) or a sexually transmitted disease/infectious disease (STD/STI) without notifying others of the illness or exposure are the criminals. The ones giving alcohol or drugs (such as "date rape drugs") to others without your knowledge or consent and showing their private parts in a nonconsensual situation are also considered victims.

The law enforcement oversight body has a special duty to report suspected violations of this policy. Therefore, if a supervisory authority receives a report of an action that may violate this policy, or if there is reason to believe that a violation of this policy has taken place, the supervisory authority will contact the OIE and report the action or possible incident. Authorized or reasonable attention may be aware of any violation of this policy by an authorized or controlled person and may not take appropriate action. Individuals considered confidential resources are exempted from this obligation if they receive the information in the context of providing professional services to students. For purposes of this policy, Confidential Information is an employee of the University who may maintain legally protected confidentiality at the department with respect to the person providing the information. Employees of the following universities act as confidential resources: Licensed Mental Health Professional at Counseling Center. Confidential Counsel; minister of the department, ordained in the position of religious and spiritual life. Qualified sports medicine physicians are also a confidential resource for student-athletes to receive information in the context of professional services.

Sex Parties

There was an officer that worked for an agency that would go to the dark side and cause himself to be removed from law enforcement. This particular male officer was married to a beautiful lady and gave the impression that he was happily married and loved his wife without question. I worked with this officer on several occasions and he was very knowledgeable in law enforcement. Unfortunately, this officer developed a fetish that would prove detrimental to his career.

The officer developed a fetish for drugging his wife to allow uninhibited sex with her. He decided to take this even further by drugging his wife and allowing other people to have sex with her. This fetish spread and he moved to allow other officers to take part in the sexual parties. This would include male and female officers. At one point he even started allowing his own father to take part in the experience. His father was an officer as well. The unique part was that the officer would not only allow these other officers to enjoy his wife, but he and others also recorded the experiences on their cell phones. After his wife learned what he was doing to her, she filed for a divorce. Upon review of the cell phones of the officer and others, a statement was made by an investigating agency as "the worst spider web of police officers they have ever seen." We need to understand that during the investigation a sergeant would keep the officer informed of the ongoing stages of the investigation. There were times the sergeant was able to inform the officer in time for him to microwave his cell phone to destroy evidence that could be used against him.

This is part of the brotherhood looking out for another officer. But we must understand that the sergeant and his girlfriend, a dispatcher, were allowed to participate in the basic rape of the officer's wife. The officer in question moved to another agency, and the dispatcher became an officer at the agency but moved to another department during the investigation process. The sergeant left the agency and got out of law enforcement altogether. This investigation was kept quiet and did not go public.

The Evil Rises Again

The officer that was allowing his wife to basically be raped moved to another agency where he would start a new chapter in his illegal digression. This time he had sexual misconduct with a minor female. This would happen several times over the course of her childhood. This female minor had two sisters and this officer did the same with the other two sisters. He would threaten to harm their parents if they would not let him do what he wanted with them. Once this was brought to light and the investigation began the officer even got rid of his vehicle to help hide DNA evidence. The investigating agency confiscated the vehicle from a dealership when they found out about the officer trading in the vehicle to get another. At this point, the officer has not been officially charged, and looks like the charges are going to be dropped. Had this been an average citizen, they would have been tried and convicted for having committed such a horrible crime. At this point, I do not believe the officer has even surrendered his peace officer's license.

Jailer Troubles

Once I heard this story, I was in disbelief at the outcome. Several male jailers and officers had a party and invited a female jailer. Drunk and passed out, the male jailers and male officers decided to have their way with her. They recorded the experience on their cell phones as they thought this would be fun. The next day the female officer learned what happened to her and filed a complaint. The agency made it out that she was the cause of the incident and forced her to resign from her position. The officer was given the opportunity to resign as well as the male jailers. The officers went to another department and worked for several other agencies after committing what would be equivalent to rape. The male officers were not charged with any crime. Should law enforcement officers be given such free passes when the average citizen would be in prison?

Brotherhood and Agency Disrespect

This story is funny in that it involves an officer from one agency and the chief of another agency. The officer was brave in that he was having sex with a woman in her driveway. The problem was that she was the wife of a police chief and he was in the house at the time of their escapade. While they were in the vehicle having sex the chief came out of the house and caught them. The officer from the local agency took off running and the chief fired several shots. The interesting thing is the incident went away as fast has it happened. The incident was never investigated nor was the chief accountable for firing shots at the officer. The officer was asked to resign from the agency and the chief stayed employed. Not sure if the marriage survived but this would be a dealbreaker for me.

Ranger Romping

This story involves a Texas Ranger that was initiated to investigate a murder case. The case was of a prominent Texas businessman that was murdered. After, supervisors discovered the Ranger was engaged in a sexual relationship with the estranged with of the murder victim. One could easily see how this could jeopardize the murder investigation. Unfortunately, this officer's integrity in the courtroom was determined worthless and the department even questioned as to whether or not the officer led the investigation away from the widow. Once again, we see how officers are protected in that the Ranger was demoted to Trooper and would be up for promotion back to Ranger in a year. Even though this officer put his integrity, honor, ethics, and professionalism to question, he still was able to keep his peace officer's license.

Conclusion

It is imperative that Texas changes its policy to address issues of sexual harassment and sexual assault. However, they must go further. First, cultural change is needed. Policy changes are only likely to be effective if they are part of the implementation of major cultural reforms. For this, Texas law enforcement has a low rate of sexual harassment, such as against women and LGBTQ, as well as serious cases of sexual harassment and sexual assault. Second, reform must be led by leaders with strong leadership. Without a deep, honest, and specific commitment from senior leaders to develop programs that really impact the organization, to send clear messages to law enforcement members that inappropriate sexual behavior is unacceptable, and to senior members. Thirdly, in order to carry out cultural reforms, it is necessary to improve the integration of women among other senior officers (Bracewell, 2018). It is true that addressing the general issue of achieving the desired level of representation of women in Texas is not part of the mission of the RER, but is the presence of a hostile organizational culture characterized by contempt and the existence of women's integration into the organization. Increasing the number of women representatives in Texas law enforcement, including in the highest positions among senior leaders, is an important condition for cultural change. Fourth, Texas law enforcement must convince its members that it takes the issue seriously.

Establishing an independent organization to receive reports of inappropriate sexual behavior and provide assistance to victims is an important step, among other things, to improve the process of handling cases of sexual harassment and sexual harassment, as well as a way to demonstrate Texas law enforcement to members. People ought to take the problem of inappropriate sexual behavior seriously. Similarly, by allowing victims of sexual violence to file complaints with civil authorities, Texas sends a clear message that the needs of victims are a priority. As part of the independent review contained in this report, the law enforcement department's willingness to critically examine its practices and processes indicates that it is focused on the issue of inappropriate sexual behavior. It is not easy to achieve cultural change, improve women's integration into Texas law enforcement, restore the members' trust in the chain of command, and eradicate the epidemic of harassment; achieving these goals requires strong leadership and sustained efforts. However, cultural change is necessary for the development of modern military organizations that adhere to the principle of respect for human dignity and, in addition, can optimize their work thanks to the skills and talents of all members.

Chapter Six

The Exploitation of Women in Law Enforcement

Introduction

This chapter examined the exploitation of women in law enforcement. The emphasis is on issues like household obligations put on female law enforcement personnel and job discrimination. This study also looked at why female police officers made the decision to advance in their careers in spite of the added demands and challenges they faced. Although this issue has been covered in some prior studies, most of them concentrate primarily on female law enforcement personnel in Europe and offer little insight into the experiences of women in the United States. The need for this inquiry is still present even though women have been working in law enforcement for more than a century, and there are still big gender gaps in employment and leadership roles. The most recent statistics show that just 3% of U.S. police officers in positions of authority are women, who make up 16% of full-time police officers. Compared to other sectors like commerce and public relations, the percentage of women in senior positions in law enforcement was much lower.

Women make up two out of every five business owners, 63 percent of public relations employees, and 59 percent of managers in the corporate world, according to the Bureau of Statistics. Statistics also reveal that, despite the recent growth, males still make up the majority in federal law enforcement, just as they did throughout the Clinton administration. About 14% of the national federal law enforcement agency's work in 1996 was performed by women. Only 15% of the population are women now. If things continue as they are, it will take women 700 years to hold half of these positions (Stratton, 1986).

Understanding why women are not as appreciated in law enforcement and what can be done moving forward to address this gap is crucial, given that women hold authoritative positions in other fields. This study is being done to determine why, in light of the gender disparity that still exists, women are still so devalued in law enforcement, especially in their high positions. The need to do so was crucial. Examining the obstacles that female police officers experience, particularly if these obstacles prevent their permanent employment or promotion, is crucial to adequately understanding these inequalities.

The work-life balance that female law enforcement officers manage while juggling obligations like parenthood, family commitments, and other caregiving jobs are also covered in this chapter. The results of this investigation have given important information about current female police officers, raised awareness of their professional and personal struggles, and assisted police leaders with guidance on how to maintain and improve the representation of women in the workforce, particularly in leadership positions. This is because there is a dearth of information on this topic.

It has long been believed that men predominate in law enforcement since the profession is regarded as an "All Boys' Club." This idea could be true, according to recent statistics. Only 13% of U.S. law enforcement officers are women, according to recent figures. This underestimate is reflected in the general position of women in other professions and American society, despite the fact that women are the primary wage earners in four out of ten homes and account for over half of the U.S. workforce. But women are still largely underrepresented in law enforcement. Gender discrimination may be a potential factor in the development of substantial gender disparities, according to a preliminary evaluation of the research. Although gender discrimination was made illegal by the Civil Rights Act of 1972, several police agencies seemed hesitant to adapt to the shift. Additionally, a lot of this prejudice is accidental or indirect, such as when women are given fewer demanding duties, elevated to management positions, or only allowed to work in certain sorts of cases as officers (Harrison, 2012).

Many women felt discriminated against when it came to departmental missions and promotions, according to a 2015 Pew Research Center poll. 7917 female police officers participated in a study, and 43 percent of them said they thought men in their department were given precedence when it came to missions and promotions. The investigations carried out pushed female police officers to work more than male police officers to acknowledge comparable accomplishments and were frequently confined to specialized responsibilities, notably secretarial ones. This highlights discrimination in police stations. Other women who were questioned stated that the department lacked a mentor or role model and that they were more likely to experience physical constraints in comparable roles than male law enforcement employees. In addition, several female police officers noted that domestic and parental responsibilities frequently act as significant roadblocks to job progression. Further research will be done to see whether there are additional external variables that should also be addressed as possible hurdles since discrimination and internal accountability have been highlighted as key repercussions of gender discrepancy in law enforcement.

Entrance of Women into Law Enforcement

Women started entering the traditionally "males-only" sector of law enforcement around the end of the 19th century. Six women were employed by the New York City Police Department (NYPD) in 1845. These ladies were employed to pay the earnings and benefits of these widows as an allowance to the deceased NYPD officers. In reality, they were the widows of slain NYPD officers. These six women initially worked with runaways and unstable youngsters at small social events and in nightclubs since women were recruited more for formalities than for their qualifications. Law enforcement didn't grasp the necessity to raise the number of women until the then-rare female convicts were committed in the jail, which would allow them to hold male and female prisoners separately in the future.

In the early part of the 20th century, the police officer's original moniker, "Matrona," gained popularity. The Oregon Police permitted Laura Baldwin to actually arrest a man in 1908, marking the first known appointment of a woman to a senior position in law enforcement. Other female guards soon followed, and the Los Angeles Police Department (LAPD) watched Alice Wells become the first all-around police officer in 1910, capable not only of making arrests but also of questioning suspects. The next year, Margaret

Adams took oath on behalf of the LAPD. However, unlike contemporary agents, Adams's primary responsibility was handling evidence, and her record-keeping reflects the early "badged mom" police station for women. Many supervisors place restrictions on you (Jurik & Halemba, 1984).

Women in law enforcement enjoyed respect from the late 19th to the early 20th centuries, but they also received lower pay and were assigned to more stereotypical roles. Nevertheless, people paid attention to their authority, and their respective police departments valued them until the end of the 1920s. Women in law enforcement were quickly let go after the stock market fell, or if they were permitted to maintain their employment, they were transferred to secretarial roles. The remaining women frequently worked as clerks and dispatchers. A stance that endured for a very long time after the Great Depression. Some women attempted to challenge the status quo because they were unhappy with their jobs in law enforcement. Women are gaining ever greater responsibilities, pay, and profits in other industries around the nation, and they believe they should be given the same chance. In the majority of the nation, male bosses and coworkers actively opposed the movement.

Female law enforcement officials didn't get more authority or more access to non-clerical tasks until the late 1950s. The demand for disguised policewomen grew during this period as prostitution and drug trafficking became increasingly common. They were granted a little lenient opportunity because only women could help the probe in this manner. Women will have difficulties when working alongside men, despite the fact that there are now many more female deputies. Since the practice of male domination had been entrenched for many years, rejection by male coworkers was one of the most visible issues. Due to the longstanding misconception that law enforcement was a "men-only field," women experienced significant prejudice. Women who wanted to become police officers had to adhere to stricter standards of police work, were limited to certain units and bureaus, and worked mostly in administrative, juvenile, and security tasks. Additionally, they were entitled to lesser pay, were not eligible for advancement outside of designated women's units, and were not permitted to obtain the same promotion rate as males. Whilst women seemed to be accepted by law enforcement men by means of special assignments and hiring, they continuously faced more severe challenges and standards due to their gender (Zappia, 1996). Females were held to higher standards of qualification than males, even though they were offered more opportunities. These took the form of a strict dress code, which included high heels, a business suit, gloves, hats, and necessitated excellent physical appearance, people skills, and a college degree (Russo, 2019).

Women in Modern Law Enforcement

Only approximately 16 percent of law enforcement officers in America are women, despite the fact that women today make up roughly 47 percent of the workforce. Only around 7% of state police employees and 14% of municipal police officers are women, respectively, according to statistics on the representation of women in police departments. In other professions like business, science and technology, and marketing, where women normally make up roughly half of the workforce, these percentages are much below the national average. Since women are still underrepresented in law enforcement, as was previously indicated, these statistics have not increased in order to better address the difficulties faced by women in law enforcement.

Exploitation of Women

Women in the law enforcement field are slowly making a turn. In the days of old, management would not try to hide their discrimination of allowing women to work patrol. I have witnessed a sheriff that stated that he would not allow women to work the streets. Why would a male have this thought process, the answer is simple in that he is prejudiced against women working the streets. He thought that women could not hold their own on the street and the male officers would be placed in the protective role of watching over the females. When I worked on the street, I had a female partner and trusted her to the end. I knew that she had my back and I did not worry about her when she was handling a situation. In a domestic situation, we could de-escalate both parties with no further incident. More agencies need to understand the importance of having women on the street and not just there to look pretty or place them in non-contact positions. The above-mentioned sheriff would only allow women to work animal control, warrants, or civil process. Unfortunately, women in uniform are targets for the male officers to express and show their dominance over women with the end goal of getting in their pants. On the other hand, I have witnessed women officers play the female card to get the male officers to do their bidding or get them to do the dirty work. It works both ways, but women still do not get a fair shake in working the streets and allowing their knowledge and experience to come into play and not what they are willing to do sexually for the management to get them promoted.

Lack of Upward Mobility and Discrimination

At all levels of law enforcement, gender discrimination—the idea that one gender (often female) is inferior to the other—is extensively documented. Gender discrimination is the predominant form of prejudice experienced by women leaders, according to a prior study. The analysis revealed that high levels of sexism at each institution were the most common complaints made by female law enforcement employees at all levels. Additionally, it has been said that this kind of sexism may be seen in many of the political and procedural rules that female officials must follow on a regular basis. Female officers' physical deficiency compared to male officers prevented them from doing activities that required physicality as well, according to the majority of the women who acknowledged that they were aware of the pervasive discriminatory practices at their institution.

Because male managers believe that women cannot handle the physical demands of succeeding in a variety of well-known professions, women are frequently tracked into clerical, social service, or other desk jobs rather than the patrol assignments they desire. Discrimination against grooms in policies and procedures is also affiliated with a special role. Women must pass the same physical fitness exams as males, dispelling the myth that they can't withstand the physical exertion required for success. Because they never acquire the job experience required for promotion, taking care of women in administrative and other leadership roles may have long-term effects. An encounter.

The widespread sexual harassment in their separate workplaces is another issue that female officers have raised, and that has been well documented. Female law enforcement officials are aware of the stereotypically super-masculine behavior that male and female police officers find uncomfortable and dissonant at police stations. These behaviors include offensive jokes, frequently made fun of by female cops, wild parties and drinking, jokes and statements against homosexuals, and widespread racism, and the women who participate in these behaviors "earn public approval." Many women who work in law enforcement find this sort of workplace culture poisonous, and if a woman refuses to participate, it may hurt her chances of getting promoted, getting the employment she wants, or getting future services (Harrington & Lonsway, 2006).

It is sometimes difficult to believe that female police officers are truly regarded as serious contenders for advancement, given the prevalence of sexism and sexual harassment in the legal profession. According to a poll done by municipal, state, and federal agencies, the majority of female respondents were not inclined to contemplate getting promoted, especially if it meant competing with their male coworkers and superiors in "pay program" advancements. Otherwise, he claimed that the options are scarce. Because male coworkers and supervisors think women can't successfully perform the duties, they need to play a decent role as police officers; women are still in leadership positions, etc., just as in earlier generations. Even though female police officers frequently establish their physical competency to carry out police duties, they nonetheless frequently encounter challenges and criticism as they work to advance their careers (Williams & Kleiner, 2001).

Most institutions are based on gender stereotypes since police work has always been seen as a male-dominated field. When reviewing women's prior roles in law enforcement, evidence is evident. Early police missions included keeping tango dancers at least 10 inches apart by patrolling the dance hall and stopping covert operations by patrolling the seashore. Research indicates that female police officers are frequently removed from the streets and placed in divisions that conform to traditional gender roles, such as those dealing with teen runaways, demonstrating the persistence of this practice today. Female police officers frequently lack experience as female police officers since they are given roles in many institutions that urge them to be moms or women. Women may be discouraged from quitting the police service or aspiring for senior positions because they feel unwelcome as a result of this dissatisfaction. Only 25% of women in management and leadership roles think they have the same chance to advance within the same amount of time as their male colleagues in the same job.

The failure to recognize equals is another kind of prejudice experienced by women in the legal system. One of the biggest pressures in a police organization is the desire to be seen as a good policeman. Female police officers must overcome the societal stigma of being seen as the weaker sex, making it harder to accomplish, and failure to get this job may be demoralizing and upsetting. Many female leaders frequently believe they must step up their efforts in order to establish themselves and get acceptance. Peer recognition issues in other job fields were also covered by the Pew Research Center poll. According to their study findings, half of Americans hold women to higher standards than men, and four out of five Americans believe that men and women are equally adept at running successful businesses. Because they had more work and a leadership role, these representations are well known, according to research. Even after managing education and job experience, there is still a disparity in promotions. Women perform as well as males do overall and in leadership roles, according to data, but opportunities for leadership and representation do not correspond to these skills.

Removing the Obstacles, Having More Women in Supervisory Roles

According to data that has already been mentioned, female police officers may first find it challenging to develop their careers in law enforcement. Only one in ten leaders of law enforcement agencies are women, according to data. Compared to other fields like public relations and technology, this figure is much lower. Sixty-three percent of public relations professionals are women, and 59 percent of women are in leadership roles, according to statistics published by the Bureau of Statistics. Women progressively overtook males as the primary proprietors of small businesses, and they achieved success in hitherto male-dominated fields. This fact demonstrates how, given a chance, women may be successful in fields that were previously only open to males. The following numbers corroborate this truth further: In 2016, there were 2.8% more companies that were owned entirely or primarily by women. Additionally, the 2016 annual income is $318,156,186, greater than the 2015 annual salary of $293,079,225 (Parker, 2016).

The achievement of women CEOs in various fields was also demonstrated by a 2008 Columbia University business school poll. Firms with women in top management outperformed males, according to their assessment of 1,500 American companies. This was particularly true when the business adopted what the researchers refer to as an "innovation-intensive strategy" that placed a strong premium on teamwork and originality. According to studies, women frequently outperform males in terms of performance, but law enforcement doesn't seem to notice this trend. Even the savviest businesswoman may find it challenging to succeed in a number of other businesses that are still "good old networks." Although it may take additional skills like networking, breaking into a male-dominated business is not impossible. One of the key areas of this study's attention is the Wolf point. Despite the fact that the police force is predominately male and that women are rarely in senior roles, some women have managed to break down these obstacles. This study attempts to learn how women thrive in law enforcement and the strategies they employ to achieve a more favorable work-life balance.

Enhancing Women's Success in the Workforce

As was previously indicated, research reveals that while women face challenges in leading law enforcement, these challenges are less frequent in other occupations. Women outnumbered males in the workforce in 2010 for the first time in U.S. history. According to statistics demonstrating why women currently make up the majority of managers, the fields of long-term care, home help, childcare, and food preparation have the most potential for growth. The capacity to sit still and focus, social intelligence, and open communication are among the most desirable qualities in a worker. Women are more likely than males to have any symptoms. Male physical fitness and aggressive impulses are increasingly out of place in the white-collar profession. Men and women both possess equal amounts of raw intellect, which is highlighted by the white-collar industry. Numerous studies also call for social intelligence and communication abilities, where women have a modest edge. Women have all the necessary abilities to succeed, but as with many popular studies, they are still disproportionately underrepresented in leadership roles, particularly in law enforcement.

Women's Accuracy and Recruitment to Law Enforcement Agencies

Many women select careers in law enforcement in order to better understand if these hurdles are evident when choosing a job in law enforcement since there are several barriers that women must overcome to develop in their careers. Knowing how they market can be useful. Similar studies are used by many law enforcement organizations to examine hiring procedures for programs at various levels, including local, state, and federal law enforcement programs.

Institutions tend to attract idealized women. After the employment of women, many departments' values don't appear to align with the idea that female leaders should be strong, daring, and capable. Women are frequently represented as being at their best and capable of handling the mental and physical demands of the work. Additionally, the majority of personnel documents demonstrate that male and female executives collaborate and appreciate one another. It is advised to post recruitment flyers and material in locations where girls "with atypical hobbies or interests can be located." Locations include high school workshops, auto body shops, gyms, and sports clubs. With a greater number of qualified candidates, job advertisements will be seen more frequently by women who are typically more assertive and macho.

There isn't much proof that women intentionally misinterpret recruitment materials, but when it comes to authentically portraying the workplace, this kind of recruitment material might be difficult for women to accept. There is a chance that this will occur. Various of the aforementioned barriers. Additionally, this kind of recruitment drive may potentially deter other cohorts from applying and consequently getting hired. It is logical to believe that the work culture of law enforcement will not alter when this occurs. It is doubtful that a German work culture will emerge if recruiting processes consistently favor men and women who value masculinity.

Gender-Specific Inequality

There is no denying that women have advanced significantly within the police department, yet there is still male hostility to their hiring. The subordination of female officers is still promoted through barriers put up by male officers. Because they had not yet been acknowledged as officers and the atmosphere was extremely hostile, female officers said that after six years in the forces, it was simpler for them to be among criminals than it was for male cops. Gender components of professional behavior or "appropriate" behavior undoubtedly cause numerous issues for women wishing to join the police. These behaviors are socially determined standards that arise or are put into practice during contact. As female officers try to fit into traditionally male-dominated fields, the symbolic standing of women in police organizations is under a lot of pressure. Women are under tremendous pressure to excel, and accepting female leaders is not simple (Davis, 2005). Many female police officers have made specific decisions in the hopes of assimilating into police culture as a result of their symbolic standing. Female police officers are compelled to adopt or reject the standard police role and establish their own subculture. When women take on conventional responsibilities, they adopt a non-professional police approach that emphasizes the "pansies cop" age of public service and eliminates the chance for advancement. When women try to fit into the stereotype of the male police culture and combat crime, they are adversely referred to as "men" or "mounds" and are not seen as women by other officers. Regardless matter their decision, they will struggle to fit in. The idea that women are largely in charge of taking care of their families also has an impact on the opposition of male officers to the inclusion of women. Male police officers believe that, aside from possible personal obligations and family commitments, women are not capable of carrying out police duties. Due to the apparent conflict between their familial and professional obligations, female officers are assumed to be less dedicated to their police employment.

Sexual Harassment against Women in Law Enforcement

Women have been victims of degradation and victimization for a long time. Even with everything and the precarious conditions in which the police live and work. Despite the fact that today, the position of women in society has evolved considerably, we cannot say that they are not relegated or marginalized from positions that, in general, are for men. Taking into account in general that police officers are relegated and mistreated, women suffer even more, and all for the simple fact that they are women. Within police forces, women are forced to live in vulnerability; Common Cause carried out a study called "Being a Policewoman," which seeks to make visible the defenseless situation in which women find themselves within police corporations.

INEGI reported that, in 2021, police personnel consisted of a total of 75% men and 28% women. Therefore, this tells us about a system that is very culturally established. Police institutions survive with hierarchical structures, in which discrimination is tolerated and even promoted and even, in more extreme cases, sexual harassment and abuse. The survey "What Do the Police Think?" also carried out by Common Cause in 2019, reveals that 5 out of 10 women had suffered discrimination in their corporations and, in addition, 35% of policewomen highlighted that many of their colleagues had received compliments offensively that has to do with their appearance or are sexual in nature (Appier, 1998).

Bearing in mind that the majority of police officers, whether they are men or women, enter the police force by vocation, it is natural to think that they are treated equally among themselves. However, already being inside the corporation, women must face precarious conditions and, in addition, the discriminatory treatment they receive either from instructors or coworkers. The Common Cause survey reveals a pretty harsh reality, especially if a policewoman faces that. In 2021, 68% of women received compliments or comments that insulted their person. We could think that, in institutions of this nature, this type of aggression would be denounced and punished; however, this is far from the truth. While 83% of women do not report this type of offense, more than 50% of the time, the institution does not take any type of action for those who do report it.

Security institutions could be defined as those organisms that are part of the system of protection of the community itself against the risks of work and of existence in general. Therefore, we can ask ourselves, if the objective of security institutions is to seek and protect the community, how is it possible that this type of attitude and treatment continues to be so present within them? Having put all this on the table, we can ask ourselves, what can we do to try to eradicate this type of behavior? In the study of "Being a Policewoman," they were asked what kind of actions could be taken to improve the situation. Sixty percent of the women said that they would like workshops and courses with a gender perspective to be implemented. This is relevant because the objective is to achieve equality in terms of rights and freedoms within the institutions.

Being a policewoman implies facing the difficulties in which policemen survive, but also marginalization, offenses, and even abuses. Being a policewoman is a challenge that definitely has many obstacles where you have to face the macho ideas that are so ingrained, especially in the popular culture of Mexicans. Therefore, we must try to find ways to find equity so that women can work in the most harmonious way possible. Few women reach high ranks (general commissioners or inspectors); only three run a superintendence (of a total of 32 departments); and the violence they suffer, together with strenuous and poorly paid workdays, leads many to "hang up their uniforms"; more and more women occupy administrative positions or directly request leave.

A 34-year-old sergeant, who asks that her name be withheld, tells her story. At 19, fresh out of college, she was assigned to an anti-drug commando in a suburb far from her home. She left at dawn and waited for the bus in uniform and alone. "I felt gifted to be killed," she says. One day, a boss who was taking her by car unexpectedly put her in a hotel for hours to have sex. As she refused, she assigned him training routines further still; she traveled so much that she didn't sleep. She ended up on a psychiatric license and traded the gun for office work. "But I studied to be a police officer," she laments.

A 42-year-old deputy commissioner who suffered sexual harassment, pressure to be a mistress of the bosses, and discrimination in all her assignments for two decades says, "I carry a gun, and I have the same training as men, but we always have to prove more." Added to this was the domestic ordeal: Her ex-husband, also a police officer, beat and raped her. "I will never forget my tears falling on my pregnant belly and the abuse I suffered myself when I reported it to the Women's Police Station," she adds. Complaints of injuries, threats, and homicides of women break into these police stations 24 hours a day. The norm says that they must be received by sensitive and trained professionals. However, one of them, a psychologist with 20 years at the Buenos Aires University, says that this is not always the case and that these units are usually a "punishment or discard" destination. Many police officers also live on both sides of the counter: They must act in cases of violence, and at the same time, they are victims. "But their cases do not come out on social networks, as if they were not women," says the psychologist (Newbold, 2005).

Family Abuse of the Badge

In our small town, we had a police officer who wore the badge for years, but no one knew what went on behind closed doors in his house. He regularly assaulted his wife, even after she was diagnosed with cancer and began chemotherapy treatments. As her weight dropped down to nothing and she lost her hair, she had to walk on eggshells around him in her own house, trying not to set off the rampage that she knew was eventually coming. Since her husband wore a gun and a badge, she feared that no one would believe her if she filed a report. He also let her know that since he wore a gun and a badge he would be above the law. Especially since he had a spotless record with the agency.

Twenty years ago, the applicants still had to parade naked before evaluating doctors in silent harassment. Today, the gender perspective has come down to schools and training centers, both to review internal logic and to improve the response to the huge population that they must protect. General Commissioner Jorge Figini, deputy chief of the force, says, "We are in the process of transformation, accompanying social change. You don't change an institution overnight. We fight against the uses and customs of closed organizations and with a lot of discipline, especially with the older staff. There are behaviors that were allowed to pass before, and now they are not.

Advantages and Disadvantages of Women Going into Law Enforcement

- Women working in police departments face the following disadvantages:
- Emotional overstrain.
- Irregular working hours.
- Obligatory obedience to the Charter.
- Lack of free time for the family.
- Following the orders of management.
- Prohibition to show initiative.
- Wearing a uniform.
- Filling in many documents and preparing reports.
- Participation in inspections.
- Nagging from male employees and superiors.

Despite the above disadvantages, policing has the following advantages for women:

- High-profit payment.
- Free travel and medical care.
- Appointment of a pension for 20 years of activity.
- Obtaining a subsidy for the purchase of living space.
- The reduced interest rate on loans.
- Long vacation.
- Provision of compensatory payments for processing and irregular working hours.
- Opportunity to rise in rank.

Females That Have Had Relationships with Inmates

With prison as the background, it is a common theme in adult films to start the forbidden "connection of love." If this happens in real life, many problems will arise. A few days ago, in the Fresno County Jail, California, a terrifying love affair between a female prison guard and a male inmate occurred, which attracted international media attention (Matusiak & Matusiak, 2018). According to foreign media, the protagonist is a 26-year-old female police officer, Tina Gonzalez, prison guard. She admitted in court that she had sex with a male inmate and even especially changed into a prisoner. Pants with holes to facilitate sex.

It is absurd that the "connection of love" between the two was still in the public area of the prison. Eleven inmates witnessed the farce, and it was rumored that Gonzalez did not hesitate to smuggle contraband to the male inmate. Use to make him "better" in prison. After the incident came to light, Gonzalez was arrested in May last year and sentenced to seven months in prison. Gonzalez' boss, Steve, who is also an assistant sheriff, said that he has been in this industry for more than 20 years and has seen many disgusting things in society, but he has never heard anything more than Gonzalez and an inmate happen to him. The relationship is even more surprising; probably only the evil and depraved people can think of it.

Another incident in which the love escape of prison guard Vicky White and inmate Casey White was abruptly ended after 11 days. The two were stopped by the police. The policewoman committed suicide with a pistol shot while the inmate was returned to prison. The woman had helped White escape on his last day on the job. The escape of a prison guard and an inmate from Alabama was halted after about a week. Vicky White and Casey White fled Lauderdale County Jail together on April 29. The 58-year-old prison guard had worked out a plan with 38-year-old inmate Casey White to get out of the facility without arousing suspicion. On her last day on the job, she had managed to break him out of the cell first and then the prison. The two fled for 11 days before being spotted by police in Indiana. The woman shot herself shortly after being stopped and died in the hospital. Inmate Casey White, on the other hand, was reintroduced to prison.

The 38-year-old was charged and then arrested in 2020 for the murder of 58-year-old Connie Ridgeway. The man already had pending sentences for other crimes committed in 2015, including burglary and resisting a public official. In Lauderdale prison, the 38-year-old met guard Vicky White, who had never had a criminal record until ten days ago. The two had started a relationship, and for months they planned to escape from the facility. To allow Casey to escape, Vicky White had chosen the last day of work before her retirement. Time before her, the woman had told her colleagues that she wanted to spend much more time on the beach and, according to the police, the 58-year-old wanted to leave with her boyfriend to reach an exotic destination. The two were stopped before they could leave the country aboard the Ford Edge on which they had escaped from prison. Casey White escaped from Lauderdale prison shortly before being tried for murder. At first, the man had confessed to the crime, but he had later retracted by claiming that he was incapable of understanding and wanting. He's now at the risk of the death penalty.

Prison Love

Having worked on both sides of the criminal justice system, I have seen the turds going to prison and seen them in prison. What is it about female officers that fall in love with prisoners? The two incidents I was able to witness personally. The first is a long-time state and local female law enforcement officer that fell in love with a male serving life in prison. She would later marry this prisoner. I find it confusing that she was an intelligent person but chose to fall for a prisoner that could never give her anything in life. The funny this is that another officer that worked with her performed the ceremony. The second was an officer working as a jailer that chose to have sexual interactions with a turd on the local jail. This officer was married but chose to jeopardize her job and social standing by having relations with a prisoner. On the other side, security guards are constantly having sexual relations with prisoners. This was not only guards but ranking officers as well. On that comes to mind is a kitchen boss that was retiring from her position and gave herself a going-away present. She allowed all of the inmates that work in the kitchen to have their way with her in the kitchen. Not only did they have their way with her but she allowed them to record the incident on their cell phones. A lieutenant was caught with a prison field minister by her supervisors. She was bent over a desk in the gym office by the inmate but was caught in the action and walked off her job. Not only did she lose her job of 20 years in the free world, rape charges were filed against her.

Conclusion

Despite the increased strain and challenges they encounter, policewomen continue to rise through the ranks. Despite the fact that there have been women in law enforcement for more than a century, there is still a sizable gender imbalance in employment and supervisory roles. Compared to other sectors like commerce and public relations, the percentage of women in senior positions in law enforcement was much lower. Through this analysis, we have been able to more clearly define and comprehend the unique difficulties that female police officers have while applying for promotions. Law enforcement organizations and management are learning important lessons about how to more accurately recognize this issue and if current harassment, discrimination, and stigma rules are enough to minimize these concerns. The findings of this study may potentially be a sign of problems with criteria for promotion, advancement, or recruiting.

Chapter Seven

Police Abusing Their Powers while On-Duty

Introduction

The problem in Texas is very clear in that when multitudes of people that decide to become law enforcement officers, they feel that they are now above the law. There is something about having a badge and gun that makes many people forget their purpose in society. It seems that the badge and gun give them the feeling of being bullet proof and that they are above the average citizen. Unfortunately, I have seen officers that do not respect their position nor do they respect anyone that they come in contact with while on duty. I have seen officers disrespect citizens in the area they patrol and far be it to respect someone that they have arrested. Being a police officer should be a position of great pride, honor, and ethical standing but many officers forget the reason they became officers and turn to the dark side of law enforcement. We will focus on local law enforcement but branch to a larger scale to allow the reader to better understand that the problem is epidemic and steps need to be taken to bring the honor and respect back to law enforcement throughout the United States.

The United States is engulfed in mass protests, and people around the world, despite the pandemic, took to the streets to support Americans in their speech against police violence and arbitrariness. Why is the social explosion in America happening? How do American law enforcement agencies differ from State to State? How acute is the problem of police violence in our country? These questions are answered by political scientists, sociologists, and human rights activists.

When Policing Goes Bad

Police violence in the United States is a systemic problem. In part, it stems from the peculiarities of the structure of police work: In the United States, each state, city, and municipality has its own police force, which is subordinate only to local civil authorities. This is generally good because it is local, serves the local community, and should be easy to change by default if something is wrong. And since, in most places, people are satisfied with the work of the police, it is difficult for Americans to decide to change the system as a whole because of individual excesses. But there is a problem: These excesses are not accidental. There are thousands of police organizations in the country, and the ability of each of them to change depends on the quality of local authorities. Because of the two-party system in the United States, there are places like Texas, where representatives of one party rule for 50 years, and each successor is not interested in dealing with the sins of his predecessor. And despite the fact that in the American civil sphere, there are enough mechanisms of external control—independent opposition, courts not inclined to play along with the police, the press, and social networks—with such a huge number of police organizations, there is always a risk that in some of them the control mechanisms will not work in time, and the corruption will go too far (Ristroph, 2017). The U.S. police, and indeed throughout the world, are very bad with self-cleaning mechanisms from the inside. It's a closed institution, made up of people who can make trouble for anyone.

By the way, in Texas, this is even worse. Because our police force is a single cumbersome organization employing a million people, it is a federal hierarchy, independent of any public control from civil local, and federal authorities. The only body to which the board or commissions report is the councils or advisory committee, not even the governor. All this means that the Texas police are even more closed. And its leadership is very bad with feedback from below. The only thing that will make the federal government pay attention to the problem in a provincial town is a federal-scale scandal to the level that few can reach. Our other problems—

the incapacity of the courts, and the prosecutor's office, which is trying to control the legality of the actions of the police and at the same time is accountable for the performance of their work—there is a conflict of interest. Therefore, the processes of decomposition in the police in Texas have been going on for decades. No one remembers the last time the law enforcement agencies in Texas really shook up (Brice, 2012).

The problem of police violence in the United States is difficult to solve because it is connected with the structure of American society and with the Second Amendment, which allows people to own, and in some states carry, weapons. The number of weapons circulating in the country is incomparable to the situation in any other state. Police officers in the U.S. risk their lives much more than in Russia and Europe, and they are always ready to shoot and use brute force. With racism, it is even more difficult because it is not so much a matter of whether a particular police officer is a racist but that there is institutional racism in the country. African-Americans as a whole live worse and poorer; they are less educated than whites, and, in fact, crime in this environment is higher. Racists attribute these statistics to the natural propensity of black fellow citizens to crime, while modern theories attribute them to the injustice of society and the legacy of slavery and segregation.

By the way, in Texas, the problem with police violence looks different—due to the fact that people have fewer weapons, and most of our protesters are law-abiding and disciplined. Although, judging by the technique of our National Guard, one gets the feeling that they are preparing for the American scenarios of other states. We also have fewer murders during detention, but in Texas, police violence is systemic; we see regular reports of torture in police stations (Staudt, 2009). And it is much easier to hush up these cases here than in any other state of the U.S.A. Two Texas police officers and a former police officer, Ryan Mabry and Melvin Williams. were indicted on felony charges accusing them of using excessive force against demonstrators protesting against police brutality in 2020, and no one took to the streets again. In general, people in our country are less ready to climb on the rampage and face the police, not only because of the legislation tightened in recent years but also because they remember that the state exists to kill citizens.

Running on Empty

An officer responded to a theft in progress at a local business. Upon arriving at the location, the officer witnessed two male subjects stealing gas out of tractors at this business. The officer confronted them and they stated they were needing gas for their truck. The officer had gone to school with the one subject and told them to take what gas they had already gotten and leave the premise. My question is if this was a judgment call and would the officer have arrested the subjects if he had not known them. I know officers must make subjective decisions in the field but allowing one that was so cut-and-dry is beyond question. This officer would later run for sheriff in the local county and the question is, how could you trust someone to run the office when they would not uphold the law as an officer?

Badge of Dishonor

This story brings to a story of officers that used their power and authority to turn to the dark side of the badge. One thing that must be remembered is that this officer's father was a county sheriff. The young officer was placed in charge of a newly created narcotics unit. It was noted that this unit was making over 30 narcotics arrests a month. As the story goes, the unit made a bust that found cocaine and a bag with 50,000 dollars. This opportunity allowed the unit to turn to the dark side as they agreed to take some of the money that was split between the unit members giving each around 3,000 dollars each. Once the officers got a taste of the high life, they started using their badges to escort drug shipments, which led to stealing drug money and to stealing the actual drugs. The operation of the unit would identify a person trafficking drugs, bust the stash house, confiscate the drugs, check part of it into the evidence room and sell the remainder to another drug dealer. The temptation of money and power fueled by the badge leads them to prison. In the southern part of Texas, the opportunity to smuggle narcotics, cash, or weapons can generate large sums of money and when a police officer has this opportunity, they can hardly resist, especially when they are under the protection of the sheriff or in this case father as well. The sad part is the officers were making over $70K per year with overtime but could not resist the temptation to live in the world of what would be a drug lord. Unfortunately, the officers flaunted their riches with expensive meals and trips to the casinos, which caused rumors of their lifestyle to float around the community. Based on the rumors a sting was set up in which a tracking device was placed on a large amount of cocaine and hired a private informant to smuggle it. She contacted the police unit to provide protection on the highway and the unit could not resist and this turned out to be their demise. Busted and prison time was served by the officers and the sheriff. While these officers got caught, many continue to perform illegal operations on and off duty. This *gives a black eye to the law enforcement community but gets overlooked as many still believe that cops can do no wrong.*

Policing Abuse

In another famous case in Texas, a white police officer, 41-year-old Eric Casebolt, quit his job after a video leaked to the Internet showing his rough treatment of a black girl. The incident occurred on June 5 in the city of McKinney (Texas) during the dispersal of a party at the city pool. Police Chief McKinney said, "The actions of Casebolt, which we see in the video filmed during the riots at the pool, cannot be justified and are inexcusable. Our policies, training, and practices are contrary to this behavior. He came on a call and no longer controlled himself. And during the incident, he did not control himself." Eric Casebolt, along with other law enforcement officers, arrived at the pool after the police received a call complaining about a noisy party. The officer roughly knocked a 15-year-old black girl in a swimsuit to the ground. The policeman also threatened her friends with a gun. In just a few days, the video was viewed by 7 million people. Hundreds of demonstrators took to the streets of McKinney on Monday. They demanded to put an end to police arbitrariness to make the work of law enforcement officers transparent and accountable (Olzak, 2021).

The most vulnerable to police violence in Texas are people from socially disadvantaged groups who do not have certain resources—for example, they cannot afford a good lawyer, have no connections, have recently migrated, or lost their permanent place of residence. And the main problem of police violence in Texas, in my opinion, is that confession is the queen of evidence. You need to get it in any way, and then you cannot work, hence the threats of both psychological and physical violence. At the same time, law enforcement officials evaluate the real risks for themselves by looking at the official statistics of police convictions in the state. So, judging by the statistics, we register only 700 sentences per year under the article "Abuse of Power" (article of the Criminal Code), which includes violence by police officers, employees of the Federal Penitentiary Service, and military personnel. According to statistics, out of 700 verdicts, 4% are acquittals, which is significantly more than in general for other offenses (less than 1% there). And if the verdict is guilty, more often, the policeman faces only a suspended sentence. And this is just the tip of the iceberg because most of these cases simply do not reach court.

Often in such cases, criminal proceedings are denied. For example, they interrogate the victim and the employees about whom he complains; they deny everything—it turns out that the word of the police is against the word of the victim. Qualitative inspection of the scene and the interview of witnesses are often simply not carried out. There are many delays and videos that they categorically do not want to show. Based on my own experience, I will say that in cases on charges the police always go with a creek, and the investigators also show little interest. Sometimes, even in the presence of video recordings and witnesses, cases are not initiated. For example, they refused a participant in the Texas rally who had a broken leg after his arrest. Another example is a person who participated in the rally and complained about torture by the police. Doctors recorded 80 paired and symmetrical marks from a stun gun on him, but the investigator said that these were insect bites, such as bedbugs, and refused to initiate a case. Regrettably, these arguments were considered sufficient by both the Court of First Instance and the Court of Appeal (Hamilton & Foote, 2018).

Protests in the United States can be attributed to extreme forms of the political process, and one of the fundamental questions now is whether the violence used by the police is legitimate—how much do the people agree with it? In the case of the murder of George Floyd, I clearly disagree. However, it is necessary to distinguish between protests in the form of processions, speeches, statements, and outrages of those who rob shops and engage in arson. These are outcasts who, taking advantage of the tense situation and the uncoordinated actions of the police, commit pogroms and loot. But for others, the murder did become an occasion to assert their rights. Behind this lie, on the one hand, the accumulated problems in the richest country in the world, and on the other hand, the use of the situation by certain political forces in the power struggle. Social stratification in America occurs not only along the rich-poor line but also along the white-black line. A significant part of the black population is socially unsettled, marginal, and ready for illegal actions (Applewhite, 2021). It is clear why the murder of Floyd was the occasion for mass riots of such magnitude and provoked a social explosion.

Ranger Rudeness

This Ranger was on duty and a driver of a vehicle flipped the officer off, shot him the bird, or told him he was number one. While letting his emotions get the best of him, he pulled the vehicle over and pulled his gun on the driver. The driver asked for a supervisor but was refused. The incident was kept on the low until a lawsuit was filed bringing the erratic incident to light. Just another example of police protecting their own at the risk of injury to a citizen. While the investigation proved the officer did not act within policy and conducted himself in an unprofessional manner, the officer is still on the street. What people need to know is that it is not illegal to flip a bird at a police officer nor is it illegal to use your First Amendment rights when talking to a police officer. The problem is that most police officers think that they are above the law and have more rights than a citizen. Simply put, call a police officer a "dumb ass" and that is perfectly legal. Please understand that you may suffer from POP, "Piss Off Police," but you will come out on the good side. The saying by police officers is "You may beat the crime, but you can't beat the ride." This is the perfect example of someone hurting the officer's feelings and the officer getting mad, unable to control his emotions, and making a decision that could come back to haunt him.

Many believe the police world that produces bad cops is a systemic problem, top to bottom, and senior ranks have allowed these negative cultures to flourish within law enforcement. Far too many times, young, uneducated, inexperienced, and arrogant officers let their emotions take control of their actions and they believe their actions are justified because they have a badge and gun. Withing law enforcement agencies there are constantly hundreds of allegations of discrimination, harassment, sexual harassment, and retaliation by law enforcement officers. Many go unreported because of the fear of retaliation from the law enforcement world between agencies. I have seen this where officers hold grudges and will harass the citizen and even their family members. Reports show that since 2013 there have been nearly 500 allegations of harassment, discrimination, and retaliation just in the Texas Department of Public Safety. Something must be done to keep these bad cops off the street and not allow them to be protected by the agency.

Mob Boss Cop

A Texas cop was arrested after being accused of stealing from businesses over a course of at least seven months. The officer was visiting several businesses while in a marked police unit and in full uniform and was demanding money from the businesses. During the course of the seven months in question, the officer had demanded and stolen over 5,700 dollars from the businesses. Another officer working for an ISD was arrested on charges of his many-pronged briberies scheme. Officers get brave but the arrogant attitude that "I can do whatever I want since I have a badge and gun" is a way of the past, but veteran police officers instill this arrogant attitude in them and send them off to protect the community. In the end, the officer is only looking to protect themselves allowing for this unprofessional and illegal activity.

Policing Blunders

To warm up the situation, "warming up historical memory" is used. Footage flashed on TV screens—a dark-skinned girl of 5-7 years old was marching in a column of demonstrators and chanting slogans about the oppression and lack of rights of African-Americans. And a blond child of about the same age with a microphone in his hands in another plot asks for forgiveness for the horrors of colonial policy. Of course, the fundamental process of reconciliation between whites and blacks in America is to be welcomed, but it somehow "unfortunately coincided" with the presidential race and was stimulated by the murder of blacks. In general, this is a deeper political process than it seems. European and American politicians have reason to seriously think about adjusting migration policy and social adaptation of migrants. Undoubtedly, what is happening in the United States is a spontaneous process, and it can be dangerous if it falls into the general channel of inter-civilizational contradictions and conflicts when the former colonies begin to settle scores with the former owners. I don't think it will come to that, but a "divided" America with its military power can be a terrible danger.

Official figures for the past four decades on the number of police homicides in America have been underreported by more than half, according to a new study by scientists at the University of Washington that reveals a lack of reliable national accounting. It is reported by *The New York Times.* The study, published September 30 in the British medical journal *The Lancet,* is one of the most comprehensive studies of police violence in America. The scientists compared information from a federal database that collects death certificates with the latest data from three organizations that track police homicides through news reports and requests for public documents. A striking discrepancy was found: About 55% of deaths from clashes with police between 1980 and 2018 were listed as other causes of death. The publication notes that these results indicate the concealment of the real extent of violence by the police, as well as the lack of centralized national data (Nuriddin, Mooney & White, 2020). Private non-profit organizations and journalists have filled this gap by studying news reports and social media. Between 1980 and 2018, a period of the war on drugs and rising mass incarceration, researchers estimate that about 31,000 Americans were killed by police officers, with more than 17,000 deaths not included in official statistics. A sharp racial gap was also found: African-Americans were 3.5 times more likely to die at the hands of the police than white Americans. Data for Asian-Americans were not included in the study, but Hispanics and Native Americans also suffer more police violence than whites.

Out-of-Control Officer

Recently, a 20-year veteran of a local sheriff's department responded to a call of a man walking down the middle of a road. The officer ended up at a house and the residents stated that they had not seen anyone on the road. The officer jumped the fence of the residence and started demanding the identification of a male on the porch. The female owner of the property asked the officer to leave their property. The incident ended up with the officer getting into an altercation with two females. He dragged one to the ground and while holding her arm, punched her in the face and head multiple times. When the mother of the mother of the woman that was being struck in the face approached the officer, he punched her in the face and knocked her out. Several arrests were made but this is a clear example of an officer that placed himself in a bad situation and thought that as a cop, he was the one that had all of the power in the situation. The officer should have never placed himself in the situation and could have been better trained in handling the situation to avoid confrontation. This is yet another example of a person with a badge and gun abusing their power to try to intimidate citizens.

Constable Power

The conduct of a constable in Texas was first drawn into public scrutiny. A Texas constable and two of his leading law enforcement officers within the department were arrested and accused of stealing makeup, ammunition, an Apple Airpods box, sunglasses, cash, and other items from a home where they were serving eviction papers. They were charged with Official Oppression and Abuse of Official Capacity. The incident came to light when one of the three appeared to mistakenly turn her body camera on while thinking she was turning it off at the time when the thefts were allegedly being committed. The cameras were later handed over to a separate law enforcement agency where the discovery was made.

In the six months since the incident, the constable has remained in office, collecting a $74,000-per-year salary, while criminal charges remain active against him. Since

May 13, Traylor-Harris has been in the Gregg County jail for violating bond conditions after the initial arrest.

Police Brutality with Impunity

The police in any state, by virtue of the obligations assigned to them, are responsible for ensuring public order, the safety of citizens, and the fight against crime. Meanwhile, in the United States, the police have become a tool to undermine public safety and intimidate the population. Of course, the historical record of American police behavior suggests that police violence is not a new problem and that some U.S. police officers have always been prone to excessive violence. However, with the development and expansion of the use of information tools and audio-visual recording devices among the public, especially with the increase in the use of mobile phones with video cameras, public opinion began to get a better idea of the violent and discriminatory behavior of the U.S. police much more than in the past.

The growing violence in U.S. police behavior can be seen as a reflection of institutional violence in American society. In other words, as violence increases in society, especially among armed citizens of the United States, the police also increasingly use firearms to fight suspects, including saving their own lives and killing any suspicious person immediately after the danger arises or severely beaten. Thus, American society suffers doubly from violence in the sense that violence by criminals provokes police violence, and as police violence increases, criminal elements resort to increasingly brutal methods. Meanwhile, most victims of violence are ordinary citizens who die at the hands of criminals, mental patients, armed and enraged people, and, in addition to this, the police.

In January 2018, the U.S. Violence Tracking Center reported that 1,147 people were killed by U.S. police officers in 2017. According to a study by the center, 48 police officers who committed violence against citizens in 2017 had previously killed at least one person, and 12 had a history of multiple murders on their record (GBD 2019 Police Violence U.S. Subnational Collaborators, 2021). It is extremely unfortunate to see these statistics. During police training in 2017, training in the shooting was spent 7 times more time than training in friction relief in difficult situations. Such a situation can in no way be in favor of American society as a whole. The police repress representatives of racial and ethnic minorities and people from poor and low-income families primarily.

Against this background, of course, the events that took place in August 2014 in the City of Ferguson stand out in particular in Missouri, which raised a number of important issues related to the problem of police abuse in the United States. Just before the lamentable occasions in Ferguson, a stupendous jury of 12 hearers totally cleared the cop who shot African-American Michael Brown at short proximity. This choice prompted a flood of fights and exhibitions, which later transformed into serious conflicts with the police and later with the U.S. National Guard.

The case against the policeman fell apart. The prosecutor proved that Michael Brown disobeyed police officer Darren Wilson and posed a threat to his life. At that moment, burning aggression was written on his face. I can only describe it like this: He looked like a demon; he looked so evil. The officer said that Michael Brown hit him and tried to take his service weapon from him. All these indications, coupled with the reality that Darren Wilson used a weapon on a person for the very first time in his whole service, led to a release. But one thing must not be forgotten Michael Brown was 18 years old only, and he wasn't armed. It is worth noting that related cases of the usage of weapons by police officers against U.S. nationals are far from isolated cases, and they take place pretty often. Similar cases with African-Americans who are killed by law enforcement agencies occur time and again. Under American law, such conduct of the police is totally acceptable. Peace officers possess the right to utilize weapons if the suspect poses a danger to him or any U.S. citizen, and even if the suspect tries to hide from view, the policeman has the ultimate right to stop him in any possible manner. And this not only applies to armed suspects but, as in the case of Michael Brown, to all unarmed suspects.

In the year 2013, there was a case in the city of Santa Rosa when a police officer opened fire on a 13-year-old teenager, considering his toy plastic AK-47 to be real. Law enforcement officers were not embarrassed by either the age of the "suspect" or the fact that he was easily controlled with a "real" machine gun. In the same year, in November in Cleveland, Ohio, a 12-year-old teenager was shot dead, this time just because of a toy gun (Lysiak, 2013). The same police officers will most likely not be charged even if they were proved guilty. Another case that stirred public sentiment in the United States occurred in the year 2012. Eight policemen fired a total of 46 bullets at a psychologically unwell African-American, calling his actions a hazard. All the above cases are the blatant use of power by U.S. law enforcement officers.

Each time, prosecutors said at the start of a case that race didn't matter, but it all boiled down to disobedience to "honorable" police orders.

Recently, a Dallas police officer was arrested for disorderly conduct by displaying a firearm in public. The officer was taken into custody by a neighboring police department after a heated argument between the officer and another man. The officer went to his vehicle and grabbed his AR-15 rifle and was approaching the other man when the local police arrived. This officer has been with the Dallas police since 2013 and has been placed on administrative leave pending an investigation. In April 2020, this same officer was arrested on charges of assault by strangulation and unlawful restraint. He pled to a charge of disorderly conduct and the grand jury declined to indict him. After completing three months of deferred-adjudication probation the officer was free to go about his brutal was of enforcing the law. This is yet another example of an officer not being held accountable for his actions causing harm to another person. The future will be bliss if officers are not held accountable by the court system.

Police Militarization Leads to Rising Trend of Violent Law Enforcement

The U.S. federal government has successively taken several measures to strengthen the militarization of the police. The militarization of the police not only includes the application of the concept of war to the practice of anti-criminal law enforcement but also includes the provision of militarized weapons and equipment for the federal, state, and local police agencies at all levels establishment of heavy weapons and ammunition depots. The National Defense Authorization Act passed by the U.S. Congress in 1990 clearly stipulates that the military can transfer outdated weapons and equipment to local security, but only in special areas such as drug control. In 1997, the field of allowing the use of weapons and equipment in the United States expanded to many law enforcement fields such as anti-terrorism and drug control. In June 2014, the American Civil Liberties Union released a special report titled "War Is Approaching: The Extreme Militarization of the American Police." This 96-page report revealed that in the 1990s, the U.S. federal government began to implement a code-named "Project 1033," the program authorizes the Department Of Defense to transfer surplus weapons and equipment to local law enforcement agencies for use in anti-drug operations. Between 1998 and 2014, the value of military equipment received by law enforcement surged from \$9.4 million to \$776.8 million, a cumulative total of more than \$5 billion (Lawson, 2019).

Another prominent manifestation of police militarization is the militarization of SWAT teams and their overuse. In the 1970s, there were only more than 300 special police raids per year in the United States, but in 1980, the number of special police operations increased sharply to more than 3,000 times; in 2005, it increased to more than 40,000 times, and in 2015, it reached 50,000 times. Not only do cities with a population of more than 50,000 have SWAT teams, but more than 90% of cities with a population of 25,000 to 50,000 also have SWAT teams, more than four times the number in the mid-1980s. Although it is necessary for the police to use SWAT teams in high-risk situations, today SWAT teams are often used to handle ordinary cases such as drugs and even participate in routine cases such as operating barber shops without a license and selling alcoholics beverages to minors (Kraska, 2007). SWAT teams often use some weapons and equipment that were originally used in military operations in peacetime law enforcement. Such violent law enforcement operations can easily lead to tragic casualties. Like the ram and flash bombs that are often used by the SWAT team, the ram will cause injuries to people indoors when breaking walls or doors, and the flash bombs temporarily blind people in the house. Although these special weapons are not lethal weapons, they can cause damage when used improperly. Indoors were injured or even killed. For example, Tarika Wilson is a 26-year-old black mother in Ohio. On January 4, 2008, her boyfriend was arrested by the SWAT team on suspicion of drug trafficking. During the arrest, the SWAT team broke in and fired into the house, killing the innocent Tarika at the scene and seriously injuring her one-year-old son.

Police Accountability Mechanism Is Not Perfect

New York Times reporter Sheila Dewan once pointed out that there is an unspoken rule within the U.S. police system. When investigating complaints about police enforcement behavior, the internal supervision departments of each police department tend to deal loosely. Outside the police system, there is a Citizen Review Oversight Committee, but the agency lacks enforcement powers on police complaint findings. The committee makes recommendations for disciplinary action following the conclusion of an internal police system investigation, but many times it is not adopted by police system leadership. Dewan believes strong police unions are also hindering police system reform. The task of police unions is to keep police jobs, which to a certain extent has also contributed to repeated police brutality. According to the data from the "Police Violence Map," 98.7% of police officers in the United States were exempted from prosecution after violent law enforcement caused death, only 1.3% of police officers were prosecuted, and only 0.33% of police officers were eventually convicted. From 2013 to 2017, there were 7,666 cases of police brutality recorded in the United States. Of these, only 99 cases of law enforcement officers were prosecuted, and only 25 cases of law enforcement officers were convicted (Rios, 2016).

Violent Subculture within the Police System

Professor Paul Buckley of Middlesex University in the United Kingdom has conducted an in-depth investigation and research on the violent law enforcement problem of the Texas Police Department in the United States. Through research, he found that the Texas Police Department has long adopted a laissez-faire attitude towards police brutality, which to a certain extent contributed to the formation of a police culture advocating violence, which also makes most police officers instinctively choose violent methods with law enforcement because they believe that even violent law enforcement will not be punished by laws and institutions (Barak, 2015). Since the 1960s, the Texas police system has nurtured a police culture that advocates violent law enforcement, which advocates and encourages police to use extremely violent law enforcement methods. Influenced by this culture, five precinct police officers in Texas' South Public Community formed the "Round Hat Gang." In order to successfully arrest criminal suspects or make criminal suspects plead guilty and serve the law as soon as possible, they will use all necessary extreme violent means in law enforcement. In addition, they often abuse the police force against residents of black communities as a psychological deterrent. Due to the use of extreme force or illegal arrests in law enforcement, members of the Round Hat Gang have complained about 128 times but have received little legal or disciplinary action. According to the statistics of the American Citizen Police Database, the core member of the "Round Hat Gang," Robert Steigmiller, has been sued 62 times for improper law enforcement, more than 98% of the overall police officers; the number of written inspections due to the use of violence reached 13, far higher than the overall 88% of the police. He was supposed to be the focus of the Texas Police Department's oversight, but in fact, the police only launched investigations into two of the complaints. Robert did not receive any disciplinary action; instead, he received 159 awards, higher than 97% of the overall police officers. The above data is enough to show that as long as the suspect can be caught and pleaded guilty, the Texas Police Department will firmly support Robert's law enforcement. This practice of the police department makes the police officers believe that the use of extreme violence to enforce the law will not only be praised but not punished and gradually strengthen these bad police subcultures. Due to the extremely fast pace of police enforcement work, police officers are often forced to make decisions in a very short period of time, and they must rely on the subculture formed collectively within the police or the experience accumulated in their own careers. The police subculture is in the process of police enforcement. Quick decision-making plays an important role, so a subculture of violent tactics continues to drive police brutality (Chaney & Robertson, 2013).

After the repeated incidents of police violence in law enforcement were exposed by the media, it seriously damaged the public image of the American Police and greatly reduced the credibility of police law enforcement, which directly led to the increasingly tense relationship between the police and the people, and even caused violent assaults to occur from time to time. After some vicious police violent law enforcement cases were fermented by the media, large-scale public demonstrations and even violent protests were triggered, resulting in continuous conflicts between the public and the police. Sometimes, in order to disperse the demonstrators, the heavily armed police will take some extreme violent measures, which further aggravates the occurrence of police violence in law enforcement, thus falling into a vicious circle of violence and violence.

Ways to Reduce Police Violence

Given the serious problems of excesses of the police with the protest and the demonstrators, it is relevant to ask what policy alternatives serve to reduce police abuse and violence. Recurring incidents of violence by the police affect their trust and legitimacy, which, in turn, makes it more difficult to fulfill their mission (Ristroph, 2017). Many countries in the world today face a similar problem. We analyze the empirical evidence on different options to reduce violence in exchanges of civilians with police officers, as well as the lethality of situations that can inevitably be violent. We review alternatives that can be implemented at the operational level and without major legislative changes, which are those for which there is good empirical evidence. This does not exclude more structural reforms, which are crucial. An ideal reform requires both structural and operational changes. We present some of the most relevant results.

To begin with, we find that more and better information reduces violent encounters between police and citizens. The evidence shows that the collection of information on police actions is, in itself, an incentive to transform behaviors that result in abusive use of force. For example, asking police officers to report cases in which they point their gun at a person, even if they do not shoot, substantially reduced civilian gun deaths by police in the United States. In Texas, the existence of systematic and complete information on the actions of the police would allow a better understanding of what works and what does not work.

A second issue is the demilitarization of the police. The evidence shows that militarization—the use of military tactics and equipment, the creation of military-style task forces, and military training, among others—is associated with a higher level of police violence. In 2018 in the United States, a study with data for all 51 states found a causal relationship between the greater militarization of police agencies and a higher number of deaths attributable to the use of force by their agents. Although it may be necessary that, in specific contexts of organized crime, the police use military weapons and techniques on an exceptional basis, these strategies must be exceptional and be regulated, focused, and supervised so that they result in a lower rate of violence (Lowande, 2021). In addition, for the Texas case, it is necessary to reflect on how the police presence can be guaranteed in territories where illegal armed groups persist.

The third is the creation of skills and environments to prevent the use of force. Human rights training programs are insufficient to prevent the excessive use of force. Evidence shows that it is crucial to develop de-escalation and emotion management skills. One of the most widely applied programs in the United States is ABLE (Active Bystandership for Law Enforcement), which consists of preventing the escalation of violence in confrontational situations. The application of procedural justice strategies in the interaction with citizens, in which agents are trained in techniques to interact with citizens and in explaining to civilians the characteristics and motives of their contacts, significantly reduces the chances that the interactions result in aggression (Mesloh, Henych & Wolf, 2008). This can cover different measures that affect the physical interaction of the police with the community. Thus, for example, in the United States, preventing police officers who are pursuing a suspect from managing the situation once they are captured reduced the use of force by 23% and injuries suffered by officers by 11%.

In fourth place is a better formation of police units. The age, gender, and history of police complaints are highly relevant individual factors in forming and managing police teams and their functions. Various studies show that policewomen receive fewer complaints, represent a lower risk to those arrested than their male counterparts, and tend to use physical violence and firearms less. Those young police officers and those who enter the institution at a younger age are more prone to violence (Zhijie, 2015). And that the history of complaints against the police is a good predictor of the use of firearms. Relationships with fellow police officers are also relevant factors in minimizing the likelihood of violence: Officers who are accompanied by officers who have been involved in excesses of violence in the past are more likely to abuse force and use firearms, and fire in confrontational situations. This evidence indicates that institutional arrangements, failed solutions to prior police abuse, and how the institution manages the risk of these individual and contextual factors influence the prevalence of police abuse.

Fifth is the exceptional and restricted use of "non-lethal" weapons. "Non-lethal" (or "less-lethal") weapons are those that seek to control or disable people while minimizing the probability of causing permanent damage and include a huge variety of means. However, any of them, even correctly activated, can lead to human rights violations, serious injuries, or even death (Jussila, 2001). A public report for the UK Home Office on deaths of people in police custody recommends, based on the available evidence, minimizing the use of mobility restriction mechanisms—including the use of "less-lethal" weapons—to situations strictly necessary and as a last resort. Other studies show that for this to be possible, it is necessary to expand the state's response possibilities in protest scenarios, predominantly without the use of weapons, and to regulate in detail the use of "non-lethal" weapons.

Conclusion

Finally, despite the existence of mixed evidence on its effects, the use of body cameras has been gaining popularity in recent years as a control mechanism in various police forces around the world. The logic is that the cameras increase transparency in the interactions between police and civilians: Everyone knows they are being watched and acts with restraint because of it. However, although some studies have shown that the use of body cameras reduces violence, others have not identified effects, mainly because they are not applied correctly. We conclude that it is worth implementing the use of cameras under guidelines to increase their effectiveness, at least in reducing some violent excesses and, at the same time, to minimize the risks to due process and the right to justice.

Chapter Eight

Texas Police Abusing Their Powers while Off-Duty

Introduction

In the context of police, views of organizational unfairness may be linked to acts of retaliation directed at the agency, but they may also give rise to beliefs about the illegitimacy of management authority (Manzella & Papazoglou, 2014). There is a strong correlation between the disobedience of organizational norms and regulations and a lack of legitimacy (French & Raven, 1959; Lind & Tyler, 1988; Tyler, 2006). Therefore, police officers who believe that their agency engages in unfair management practices, unequal distribution of resources, or disrespectful interpersonal treatment may be more likely to violate agency norms and regulations by engaging in unethical behavior. This can take the form of committing acts that are in violation of agency norms and regulations. Even though procedural and distributive justice have been studied, most notably in the context of law obedience (Reisig, Bratton, & Gertz, 2007; Tyler, 2006; Tyler & Huo, 2002), satisfaction with the police (Reisig & Parks, 2000), and satisfaction with the courts (Higgins, Wolfe, & Walters, 2009), and its relation to criminal activity (Fagan & Piquero, 2007). Examining the organizational correlates of police misbehavior, as some critics have suggested, unfairly lays responsibility on police supervisors while, in fact, individual officers must choose to participate in the activity independent of any other variables that may be present (Manning, 2009). This critique is reasonable, but it does not change the reality that police personnel and the company that employs them are intertwined in one another's actions. It is impossible to divorce the actions of a single officer from the larger social environment in which they take place (Smith, 1986). More importantly, identifying the organizational correlates of misconduct does not absolve the officer of responsibility; rather, it draws attention to the ways in which organizations can improve their operations and policy in order to eliminate circumstances that make it easy for individuals to engage in misconduct. Armacost (2003), for example, argued that officers "are embedded in an organization that makes them more likely to frame their judgments in terms of role-based obligations and expectations than according to a simple cost-benefit analysis of their potential actions" and that placing blame for misconduct solely at the feet of individual officers (for example, by using the "rotten apple" explanation) is simply "a search for scapegoats." Armacost (2003) also argued that officers "are embedded in an organization that makes them" (p. 493). Recent studies have revealed that organizational justice components are linked to work stress, organizational commitment, and job satisfaction among correctional officers (Lambert, Hogan, & Griffin, 2007; Taxman & Gordon, 2009). It was also shown that officers' perceptions of procedural and distributive justice were connected to their levels of job satisfaction, organizational commitment, and work effectiveness. This was the case for police who were assigned undercover duties (Farmer, Beehr, & Love, 2003). Additionally, officers' satisfaction with the process was linked to the perception that investigations of complaints against officers were carried out in a procedurally fair way regardless of the result of the investigations (De Angelis & Kupchik, 2007). There have been studies that have looked at organizational justice and employee deviance individually; however, there has not been a study that links the two theories in an effort to explain police misbehavior. In Texas, police have been observed to violate their powers and status to confront others. This chapter will explore and discuss various factors which are associated with the violence against citizens' rights and expectations in Texas (Mullen & Monin, 2016).

Off-Duty Police Work

The one thing that I get tired of hearing from cops is that "I am a cop 24/7." News break, you are not a cop 24/7. That thought process is what gets cops in trouble when off duty and when they are working an extra job. The State of Texas is very lackadaisical when it comes to letting off-duty police officers work extra security jobs.

Security companies must jump through hoops to meet the requirements and standards in the State of Texas and off-duty police officers have free rain in working these jobs. Security companies must be licensed and insured before placing their security officers in the field. Police officers work these security jobs without insurance and without knowing the rules and regulations that govern them. All police officers that are working extra security jobs are not police officers when in this role. While they wear the uniform and equipment of the agency that they work for, they are in the role of a security officer at this stage. The arrogance of police officers in the security role is one that will get their agency tied up in a lawsuit. Unfortunately, many of the agencies do not know nor do they keep track of or monitor officers working off-duty jobs. Many times, the officer is using the equipment and vehicles that the citizen's tax dollars are paying for to make extra money. For the most part, this is illegal, and the taxpayers need to be informed. Also, when things go bad for an officer working an off-duty job the agency will not back or support them as the agency's insurance does not cover an officer working an off-duty security job. Ask any officer working an off-duty security job wearing the uniform of their agency and they will tell you that they are a police officer.

The information that I am providing is from experience. Understand I have been a Texas Peace Officer for over 13 years as well as my wife. We decided that there was a gap between off-duty police officers working security jobs and actually licensed security officers. During our training, we both concluded that we did not understand why we had not already been sued for working off-duty jobs wearing the uniform of our agency. That is when we took a hard look at ourselves and stopped working off-duty jobs as police officers and began doing the job legally as commissioned security officers. We determined that it would be easier to follow the law and not have our names attached to case law.

Officers working off-duty jobs need to be educated, licensed and insured to work off-duty jobs. The venues that hire these off-duty officers need to understand that they are not licensed nor insured to work these jobs and if something goes wrong the venue will be held responsible. An off-duty police officer working a security job does not have the rights of a commissioned security officer in that same role. The commissioned security officer can check IDs, check backpacks, and even frisk for weapons or contraband without cause. The off-duty police officer cannot perform this same action. Also, many need to understand that an off-duty police officer does not have the authority to arrest anyone. When the public starts to realize these rules, more off-duty police officers and their agencies will get sued. Just like commissioned security officers the off-duty police officer only has the right to detain. They must call the local law enforcement agency to follow up and complete the investigation. For example, I have witnessed many off-duty police officers working in clubs make an arrest for public intoxication while the person is still in the club. First, the off-duty police officer does not have the authority to make the arrest, and secondly, the person in still in a private club and not in public. Unfortunately, many believe that is a police officer is wearing the uniform and badge they have the right to act in that capacity. They do not and the public needs to understand this rule and law. The arrogance of the police officer working off-duty security jobs is the same arrogance and attitude they have when working their on-duty police duties. Note, if you are in a private club and feel that you have had a little too much to drink, please get someone to get you home safely. But, if an off-duty police officer asks you to come outside the club so he can talk to you, do not go outside because at that point you will be detained until the local law enforcement arrives and you will be arrested for public intoxication. If the off-duty police officer forces you outside, contact your attorney and let them handle the situation. This is illegal, the off-duty police officer knows this but expects you to comply because he is the Po-Po.

Examples of Police Involved in Power Abuse

After Brandon Brooks uploaded a YouTube video showing McKinney Police Cpl. Eric Casebolt trying to detain a group of black adolescents at a neighborhood swimming pool, the nation's attention shifted to the Dallas suburb of McKinney, Texas (Brooks, 2015). When Dajerria Becton, 15, was taken to the ground and kneeled on her back as she screamed, "Call my mama!" Casebolt was a 10-year veteran of the police force and a white 10-year veteran of the force. As soon as the video was shared on Twitter, the hashtags #blacklivesmatter and #mckinney started trending on Twitter as people began to talk about the event there. People using the hashtag #blacklivesmatter tweeted about the #mckinney incident to raise attention to police misconduct charges around the country in 2014 and 2015. Alicia Garza, Patrisse Cullors, and Opal Tometi started the movement by creating a hashtag and starting an online debate about police brutality. The campaign went on to hold over 1,000 demonstrations (Garza, 2014). Using the hashtag #blacklivesmatter, people on mobile devices and social media such as Facebook and Twitter submitted footage they had taken. As a result of this interaction, social media users are given the option to contribute to the news by providing their own perspectives of events (Springer, Engelmann, & Pfaffinger, 2015).

During a traffic stop in March 1991, four Los Angeles police department officers were seen on camera by citizens beating and kicking a motorist named Rodney King. An important text in studies of the social construction of police brutality is the video footage, which was viewed by both the jury that acquitted the policemen and the American public. This case revealed to many members of the public that even the most "obvious" and "condemning" video evidence may be used to support competing arguments. More and more police-citizen encounters have been recorded and shared on social media in recent years, with the videos being seen and analyzed by a worldwide audience within minutes. After being approached by Staten Island police, a spectator captured the last moments of Eric Garner's life in a chokehold in July 2014 (Baker, Goodman, & Mueller, 2015). #Blacklivesmatter protesters used his dying words, "I can't breathe," as a rallying cry to express their disbelief at the grand jury's decision not to prosecute the cops involved. "The case," as some on social media have dubbed the killing of Eric Garner, has apparently indisputable proof of excessive force by police (Freelon et al., 2016, p. 31).

Mabry and Williams were charged with several felony charges of aggravated assault by a public official and deadly behavior, according to a news statement from the Dallas County district attorney's office. They were indicted for their role in the demonstrations. Privitt was indicted on a single felony count of aggravated assault by a public servant for his actions while on duty as a garland police officer. According to the press statement from District Attorney John Creuzot, the charges are the result of an investigation that lasted over two years.

According to part of Mabry's charges, he is accused of threatening or shooting so-called less-lethal missiles at three victims.

The missiles are intended to harm rather than kill people as a crowd control tactic, but its slang moniker recognizes that they may kill if they strike someone in the right place. And they've hurt people badly.

Prosecutors said they have "solid evidence" and "statutes that enable cops to use force [when] dispersing a disturbance." Protesters who blocked roadways and sought to "inspire a riot" were greeted with missiles by police, he said, despite the fact that many demonstrators were peaceful. He described the scene as "a ruckus." Looting was taking place. Some people had already begun to gather, and they were calmly protesting. Fortunately, no one was harmed in the process. Many demonstrators would leave if requested to do so. People who did not participate in the protests are to blame for the violence and property destruction that ensued. The alleged acts they conducted toward demonstrators were not described in the news statement announcing the charges. In February, warrants were issued for the arrests of Mabry and of Williams. Each of them is also accused on three counts of official oppression Williams is also suspected of using less-lethal missiles in his attacks.

In the meanwhile, William's lawyer did not reply to a message seeking comment. A lawyer for private was not immediately available for comment. Protests against the excessive use of force by police and the abuse of people of color broke out throughout the nation after the death of George Floyd by a Minneapolis police officer, including in Austin, Houston, San Antonio, and Fort Worth in addition to Dallas.

During the day demonstrations, 19 Austin police officers were charged with using excessive force. According to Travis County charges, nine people, including Texas house candidate Justin Berry, are accused of firing lead-pellet beanbag rounds at the same victim. Williams was dismissed in late January for a different incident in which he violated the department's use-of-force policy during a July 2021 encounter that was recorded on film before he faced charges for his role in the 2020 demonstrations. During a fight, Ellum and Williams can repeatedly be seen striking a guy in the face. According to the Dallas Morning News, he was already the subject of two separate use-of-force investigations (Morris & Deshon, 2002).

The Commission to Combat Police Corruption (CCPC) presented a thorough report on the wrongdoing of Texas Police Department officers in August of 1998. The commission determined that a considerable percentage of instances resulted from off-duty wrongdoing by the police. Over 80 percent of the 163 Texas Police Department officers detained last year were charged with off-duty misbehavior and criminal offenses (CCPC, 1996). Most of these incidents included police who threatened or fired at civilians with their service weapons while not on duty, as well as cops who participated in domestic violence or other off-duty acts of violence. Additionally, the paper emphasized the pervasiveness of alcoholism in off-duty indiscretions. About a third of the incidents of off-duty violence investigated by the commission involved intoxicated police officers (CCPC, 1998). Mollen commission (1994) and Fyfe's (1980) prior study on off-duty police firearm abuse were mirrored by the CCPC's report. When off-duty Texas Police Department officers robbed drug traffickers and then sold the stolen goods to their friends and neighbors, the Mollen Commission looked into this. One example featured off-duty police who shot and killed his wife with his service pistol, while another involved an alcoholic off-duty cop who was thrown out of a pub and opened fire on the patrons. According to Fyfe and Kane (2006), off-duty crimes perpetrated by Texas city police officers are just as diverse as those committed by more ordinary offenders. Research of off-duty Texas Police Department misconduct is hampered by the fact that most extant data depict the wrongdoing of Texas Police Department officers. Both independent commissions tasked with investigating Texas city's police corruption and a dataset on career-ending misbehavior among Texas Police Department officers between 1975 and 1996 are used to compile the statistics (Fyfe & Kane, 2006). Even in Texas cities, local "blue ribbon" committees are seldom formed, and police departments rarely release agency data on wrongdoing, whether it happens on or off the job, to outside inspection. Existing studies have covered Texas Police Department officers' off-duty misconduct, but the lack of data from other jurisdictions raises genuine questions about generalizability. Off-duty police misbehavior has been hindered by a controversy in the academic community about whether studies of "police deviance" and/or "political crime" should include crimes performed when an officer is off duty. There are several instances of off-duty offenses when police participate in "acts that have nothing to do with their work" to support the case for exclusion.

However, some, such as Fyfe and Kane (2006), make a strong case for including off-duty offenses since it may be difficult to tell the difference between police activity when they are on duty and when they are not. So far, no empirical study has been conducted on the off-duty crimes committed by officers outside of Texas city because of intellectual bickering and constraints on the availability of official data. More data on off-duty crime cases might assist settle this argument. The need for greater research extends beyond academic concerns about the generalizability and conceptual clarity of scholarly research. Off-duty misbehavior by police officers poses a significant liability risk for agencies, making it a pressing concern for police chiefs. There are various areas of legal responsibility for law enforcement in cases involving off-duty officers, including physical altercations and detentions, the extent of secondary employment, searches and seizures, and individual behavior. Off-duty misbehavior has the potential to harm the public's trust in the police and the legitimacy of the police organization. Corruption, mismanagement, and cover-ups are common in situations of off-duty crime and misbehavior, and media portrayals of significant or violent police crimes are not likely to concentrate on whether an officer was on or off-duty. Off-duty police officers were arrested between January 2005 and December 2007 in order to conduct a content analysis of media stories about their arrests, with the ultimate goal of better understanding the characteristics of off-duty police criminality in the United States. We refer to police crimes as those perpetrated by sworn law enforcement officials who have universal arrest powers at the moment of the incident. For these instances, we give statistics in terms of the: a) officers arrested, b) crimes committed, and c) or her respective agencies. In addition, the research contains metrics to examine whether or not arrested off-duty police officers committed the crime while working in their official position(s). Methodologically, our approach allows us to study off-duty police crime in many locations throughout the United States, as well as to enlighten arguments regarding whether off-duty police activities should be included in research on "police deviance" and/or police crime.

Night Club Arrest Trouble

I have witnessed many off-duty police officers get into trouble because of their police arrogance and attitude. One story comes to mind when a prominent NFL running back was arrested in a club by off-duty police officers. They made an illegal arrest, got reprimanded, the story was covered up, and the charges were dropped as fast as they were made. Another story is of an off-duty police officer following a female out of a store due to suspected shoplifting. As the woman drove away, the off-duty police officer shot through the back window of the vehicle and there was a two-year-old child in the vehicle. The woman was right in suing the police agency and the store that hired the off-duty officer. I could go on for days of the illegal actions of off-duty police officers working in the role of a security officer, but this action will continue because the public will not stand up and fight back. The State of Texas, licenses, and commissions security companies and security officers to perform security jobs professionally. The State of Texas does not, let me repeat, does not license police officers to work off-duty security jobs. Hearing that the way it has always been done does not fly with me and should not fly with the public. Venues need to understand the liability of hiring off-duty police officers. They mess up and you pay the price. Is it worth the chance?

Off-Duty Murder

A North Texas officer was charged with murder after shooting two teenagers while off-duty. One of the teenagers in question died and the other was hospitalized after the incident. The off-duty officer chased the teenagers in his personal vehicle and rammed into them breaking agency protocol. Investigations were initiated after the incident but the question still remains is that we have not heard the outcome of the investigations and whether the officer was convicted of murder. We must still remember that an off-duty officer is not a cop at that moment. Their attitude and arrogance make them think they are but they are nothing more than a citizen. While many agencies have different rules and policies for their off-duty officers, they need to reel in their attitudes and realize where their duty begins and ends. Most agencies do not want their officers to be cops when off-duty, but how is this culture developed? We are left with no choice but to believe that the culture is groomed by experienced officers that continue to work outside the realm of their job duties. If you are confronted by an off-duty officer they must remember this can be a tense situation because the off-duty officer will be arrogant and most likely will have an "I am better than you" attitude. The best advice is to go to a public place and dial 911 while you are moving to that public place. Record the incident because you will most likely be involved in a heated argument that the officer does not know what he or she is doing. I have been involved in incidents where off-duty officers will be in clubs drinking and, in a tense moment, pull their badges and try to abuse their authority. One such incident that occurred with me involved two females that were starting to engage in an altercation. Remember, I was the hired security working at the club at the time. When I approached the females in question, a badge appeared in front of my face. The man was drinking himself and I informed him to remove the badge from my face and put it back in his pocket and that it meant nothing to me and I better not see it again or I would drag his ass out the front door. There have been multiple times that officers entered the club in which I was working and tried to exercise their role of a cop while engaging in drinking alcoholic beverages.

Challenges, Issues, and Reported Evidence

Is the police's power excessive? In the United States, the police's principal role is to protect civilians and make them feel safe. Nevertheless, why is it that so many people are afraid of police officers? There should be no cause for civilians to feel frightened if the police's system for policing is fair. When it comes to the police's authority, there has always been a debate. For the simple reason that we've heard of so many instances in which police officers went too far and innocent people were punished or murdered for no reason at all. As an example, police personnel have been unfairly tried in court, racially discriminated against civilians, and assaulted defenseless citizens. Because of these reasons, it is clear that the police in the United States are abusing their power when it comes to civilians. Citizenry should be informed of several instances in which police officers have abused their power. For instance, a number of police agencies do not permit the arrest of their personnel (Kane & White, 2009). Police officers in the agency have the ability to commit crimes while on duty. In the United States, police officers should be subject to the same standards of accountability as any other citizen. These corrupt police officers will be emboldened to continue abusing their positions of power if they are not held accountable. Police personnel no longer have any boundaries as to what they may or cannot do. A further instance of police overstepping their bounds is when they treat residents unfairly based on their race. As an example, white Mayfield teenagers had fewer issues with police officers and a more favorable image of them in the white area. Residents in this community who identify as white said they have no complaints about the way police officers treat them. In contrast to white youths, black teens in Barksdale, a mostly black community, have a more negative perception of the police. A number of black teenagers have also claimed to have watched or experienced police officers abusing members of their own community (Brunson & Weitzer, 2009). As a consequence of cops not being limited in their authority, this is a perfect illustration of what happens. Officers begin to abuse their position of power. Those who despise the race they dislike utilize their power to attack it. To put it another way, they are not enforcing the law and prosecuting individuals who pose a danger to the nation. Their authority is being used instead to target a group of individuals for no other reason than that they have different personal opinions. An example of police officers abusing their position of power for their own personal gain. As an example of police abuse of power, unarmed citizens are shot and murdered by police officers. It was found that 85.4% of people slain by police officers were armed, according to the research done by Nix, Campbell, Byers, and Alpert, yet just 9.4% of individuals killed that year were unarmed (2015). Even though the number of unarmed people is fewer than the number of armed citizens, there have been instances in which individuals without weapons have been shot. When police officer fires their weapon, they should only do so if the other individual poses a threat to themselves or other civilians.

Since the cops easily outnumber a person with no weapon, they are not in danger. Police officers have unrestrained power, resulting in policemen going above and beyond the law. On the opposite side of the discussion, many people believe that the police do not go too far with their authority. Opponents may argue that police officers are held responsible for their acts. Disciplinary action against a police officer even after he or she has been found not guilty of a crime is one such case (Kane & White, 2009). As this case indicates, law enforcement officers who commit crimes face consequences. They will, however, never be imprisoned. Suspension or termination from the firm would be the worst penalty. In the case of a murder, a police officer should be jailed, not simply fired. In terms of punishment, losing their jobs isn't enough to hold them accountable for their acts. It is also said that police officers do not misuse their position for personal benefit or in line with their own beliefs and opinions. Police officers shoot black suspects with weapons more slowly than white suspects with weapons; Thus, police officers are less likely to shoot an unarmed black person than an unarmed white person. To establish that race is not a role in police shootings, this study found no evidence of a link. Another study asked police officers to click a button next to photos of people they would shoot if they had the chance to do so. When it came to shooting a black suspect, police officers were more inclined to do so because of their race. There should be an equal amount of white and black police officers pressing the "shoot" button in the second study, according to the findings. This is consistent with the findings of the first study. They were just interested in how the suspects looked in these photos, not what they could have done wrong. According to the findings of this study, a police officer is more likely to shoot a black suspect than a white suspect just because of the latter's race. Finally, those who believe that police officers do not abuse their power claim that officers only use their authority when it is really necessary. The use of fatal force by police officers, for example, is not seen as excessive. These measures are, instead, necessary to ensure their own safety and the safety of any surrounding civilians who may be at risk (Miller, 2015).

Face the Facts

This brings me to another point, schools developing law enforcement agencies on their campuses. With the number of school shootings that have happened across Texas and the nation, having untrained or retired police officers working in these positions is a waste of time. The schools need to look at hiring licensed security companies to perform the duties. Security officers can frisk, look through backpacks and inspect vehicles without cause. Police officers cannot do this action. When hiring security officers to perform security actions, civil rights are far less of an issue. Once a school mandates a policy, the security officer can act on this policy without cause. Metal detectors need to be set up at schools and the schools should have security officers that can perform inspections and investigations to prevent future school shootings. Far too many school resource officers are old, retired, or closing in on retirement and couldn't care less about performing their position to the highest of standards. Parents need to be aware of their kids' rights that are being violated by these resource officers daily. Why would you want a police officer guarding your kids when you could have an experienced commissioned security officer that could do a more proficient job at protecting your assets?

Missing in Action

This story is about a school resource officer that failed at the greatest heights. This officer was the only officer employed by the school district. However, every day from 11 A.M. to 1 P.M. the officer could be found in the nearby town having lunch with his officer friends. The officer was hired to protect the students of the school but left the school unprotected every day for two hours. Understand that these two hours were during the lunch periods of the school when guests were on campus having lunch with their children. It does not take a rocket scientist to understand that the lunchtime is the time of mass movements on campus. If something was going to go wrong, this would be the time for something terrible to happen. But we have to understand that this officer was retired and rehired and did not truly care about his job or protecting the students. The worst point is that the school district allowed him to perform his duties in this manner. This tells me the school district was not really concerned about the welfare and safety of the students or staff. Another example of how important it is for school districts and agencies to hire people that have a desire to perform their duties at the highest level.

Many people on both sides believe those police officers will use their power and force when necessary to protect themselves or someone else's life. The police officers themselves, on the other hand, are human beings, and people ought to keep that in mind. There is no guarantee that they know what is correct in every instance, just because they are police officers. When it comes to risk, a police officer's perspective may be quite different from that of the general public. Because the public places such a high value on the activities of police officers, the latter might profit from the former. Despite the fact that they are surrounded by civilians who are willing to defend them, police officers begin abusing their positions of power. Consequently, it is imperative that residents who do not think the police misuse their power open their eyes and realize the wrongfulness of the police to reform our existing system of police administration. The fact that police officers aren't getting the penalties they deserve is another indication that they abuse their power. In many police agencies, the worst penalty an officer may get is being dismissed, as already noted in the preceding paragraph. Off-duty police officers have been involved in minor automobile accidents and gotten into arguments with the other motorist. The off-duty cop would tell the motorist they are a police officer and then draw and shoot. This group of police officers will only be dismissed, not put in jail as a result of their actions (Kane & White, 2009). In light of this scenario, it becomes clearer how the police use their position of power. If you murder someone because of a dispute, you'll be fired rather than sent to prison, according to this new policy. An off-duty police officer who was shot by a civilian in a fight would be prosecuted with murder and sent to prison if the positions were reversed. It's easy to see how drastically different these two scenarios are when looking at them side by side. In the preceding paragraph, it was said that police officers shoot a black suspect more quickly than a white suspect when they view their photo. This demonstrates the existence of discriminatory police personnel. The race of the suspect is often a deciding factor in whether or not bullets are fired. That has no place in the process of determining who should be shot. Race-baiting police officers might use their position of power to abuse the group of individuals they hold prejudice towards (Moore et al., 2012).

They lose sight of the primary goal of their authority, namely the protection of the public. Finally, in order to demonstrate that police officers, misuse their position, it should be recalled that in many cases, officers must make judgment decisions. Because of this, the degree of force they must use is up to the officer's discretion. Because of this, there are going to be times when the incorrect decision is made (Miller, 2015). Officers have the authority to use force in the face of any risk, but it is up to them to determine what constitutes a danger. Unarmed individuals were seen as a danger by the police officers who shot them. However, an unarmed person does not pose a danger, which indicates that the shooter had a different reason. One theory is that it was motivated by racism, while another is that it was motivated only by the desire to wield dominion over others. To sum it up, it should be obvious that police abuse their position of power.

In short, the police did more harm than good in the government's effort to create a system that would help individuals feel safe and secure. The cops began to abuse the freedom they had been granted to behave as they saw fit. For example, they are not put on trial in the same manner that citizens are put on trial. Due to racial or cultural superiority, they abuse their position of authority by harming unarmed individuals. Because of this, citizens must take action to stop the present police system from becoming dysfunctional. If we don't do anything about it, the cops will continue to misuse their authority, maybe even more so. A minority race, such as African-Americans, is particularly vulnerable to this kind of abuse. Police departments may be improved by taking action. One that gives people a sense of security. It is, nevertheless, possible that if a change is not made quickly, it will be too late (Moore, 2008).

We now go on to a review of the scientific and legal literature pertinent to the misconduct of off-duty police officers. Texas City police officers' off-duty wrongdoing is the subject of the first section of the investigation. There is an ongoing academic controversy concerning whether or not to include off-duty actions in studies of police misbehavior and crime. The civil liability problems that emerge from these situations are discussed in detail in the third section. Review of related literature a great deal of the information we have about off-duty police misbehavior comes from the CCPC's reports and other academic sources. There are three main issues in terms of the statistics that have been collected thus far: 1) the abuse of guns, 2) alcohol intoxication, and 3) domestic violence. A service weapon was improperly displayed or discharged in 25% of off-duty misbehavior incidents examined by the CCPC (2020), according to the study. Texas city police department shootings that were not connected to any law enforcement or order-maintaining purpose were identified by Nelis (2011). There were a number of "bizarre violence" incidents that were difficult to identify among these instances (p. 77). Texas city police department (Texas Police Department) off-duty officers have been involved in a number of incidents where they have used their guns to intimidate and/or shoot a wide range of victims, including subway passengers, taxi cab drivers, bar patrons, and domestic partners/spouses, according to Kane and White

(2009) (CCPC, 1998, 2001a, 2001b, 2010). Off-duty cops who were inebriated were involved in a significant proportion of the misconduct instances examined by the CCPC (CCPC, 2004). Charges of driving under the influence and being unfit for duty were the most often seen in these investigations. In an effort to combat the issue of off-duty alcohol misuse, the CCPC suggested a number of specific rules, such as expanding the definition of "unfit for duty" to include off-duty officers who are inebriated and prohibiting off-duty police from carrying weapons while intoxicated (CCPC, 1998). When it comes to "off-duty public order offenses," driving while inebriated falls within the category. However, Jones (2020) does not give any precise statistics.

That differentiates alcohol misuse as a kind of wrongdoing. Off-duty police officers have been involved in bar fights, drunk driving, and personal issues, according to Kourmentza (2022). Disturbing patterns of police domestic abuse were also uncovered by Mitchell's 2020 findings. Verbal threats, stalking, damage to property, and physical attacks that resulted in significant bodily harm were all examples of domestic violence perpetrated by off-duty police officers. Off-duty misbehavior, including domestic violence, was the most prevalent reason for terminating an officer. Muir (2017) carried out journalistic investigations that have exposed the issue of police domestic abuse in professional publications (Kourmentza, 2022). Violence in police marriages has long been acknowledged as a result of police work's negative influence on domestic relationships (Texas State Law Library). This line of research also includes studies on police domestic violence using officer surveys and interviews, but the issue of prevalence remains an unanswered empirical question because of problems related to measuring the phenomenon (Lobnikar & Mesko, 2015). To get accurate statistics on IPV, victims must be willing to come forward but this is especially difficult for those in police families because of the extra risk to their careers that comes with reporting abuses to authorities (Manzella & Papazoglou, 2014). Research on police off-duty misconduct and crime: academic debate studies on police misbehavior and criminality when an officer is off duty have been hampered by a disagreement over whether these terms cover such crimes. Scholars in the field of policing have emphasized the occupational roots of police crime and the crimes committed while an officer is on duty and in the course of his or her usual professional tasks (Mayer et al., 2002). According to Kappeler et al. (2021), many off-duty crimes are not police crimes since they do not include any part of an officer's vocational job. To what extent do law enforcement training, expertise, and knowledge help legitimize off-duty indiscretions, or are these standards themselves the cause of such behavior? In their research of career-ending police misconduct, Miller and Braswell (2011) make a strong case for including off-duty wrongdoing, and this argument also applies to police crimes. First and foremost, the profession offers police a variety of criminal chances, both while on duty and outside of it. Another reason why police officers are more prone to commit crimes, whether while on or off duty, is because they feel their position of authority exempts them from punishment. Third, most jurisdictions allow off-duty police officers to carry service firearms and offer them full enforcement powers. This complicates the distinction between on- and off-duty police activity since "the expertise, gun, and badge that comes with being a police officer" sometimes helps the off-duty crimes of police officers (see also Murphy, 2000). Litigation to assess organizational accountability for off-duty officer misconduct raises important concerns for police researchers seeking to evaluate police deviance and crime.

Off-Duty Assault

An off-duty officer with 19 years of experience was charged with assault after getting into an argument with a person. The off-duty officer hit the person several times and then pulled a gun and pointed it at the person. The off-duty officer fled the scene after the real cops were called. The off-duty was stopped a short time later and taken into custody. The sheriff allegedly stated that the officer would be removed from duty as his Texas peace officer's license was revoked, voluntarily to keep charges from being filed. What leads this officer to create such havoc? Again, we must believe that he thought that he was a large and in charge cop that could use is badge to push people around thinking that his actions would not be held accountable.

Questioned Murder

An officer committed suicide or so the report was written and the justice of the peace was reported. The officer was working for a corrupt police agency and had run for office during his career. The officer was confident in his actions and enjoyed his family. While working for this corrupt agency, he was accused of performing the illegal actions that the agency was condoning by other officers. I believe the officer was going to come forward on the agency and the officer was murdered to protect the agency. The moment

I heard of the officer committing suicide, I did not believe the officer could have done this to himself. The officer was found alone in his house with a gunshot to his head. The police agency was built by the chief to protect itself at all costs and a few officers were working at the agency at the time that would have done this for the chief without question. This is the same agency that had a female call a married officer and tells him she was pregnant with his child. The officer stated, "if you tell anyone about this, you and your baby will never be seen again." Would this officer have done such an action? I believe that he would have as he and the chief were in the same position in that they could do no wrong in the agency and would push their weight around in the community. Unfortunately, the city council of this town would not get involved in the police actions and would let the chief perform any action that he wanted. I witnessed the chief personally change city ordinances without being voted on by the city council. Makes a big difference when the chief of police is married to the mayor and they are in a relationship with the city manage.

Parking Lot Stupidity

This story is of an off-duty police officer working security at a major shopping chain store. A woman was suspected of shoplifting and the officer followed her to the parking lot. The woman got in her car and as she drove away from the off-duty officer he pulled his weapon and fired shots through the back window of the car as it was leaving the parking lot. The driver was injured in the shooting but there was a child in a car seat in the back seat of the vehicle. The officer is responsible for a bad shooting but now the shopping chain is now responsible because they employed the off-duty officer. The officer acted as if he was an on-duty officer and caused himself to be fired and the shopping chain sued. The arrogance of off-duty officers is unreal. They think they own the world and the world must answer to them at all costs. The officer was not insured while working off-duty and made a decision that changed his life. Does shoplifting require using a weapon to stop the individual? What the officer needed to know was that he did not have the authority to make an arrest. He could have only detained the person until an actual police officer arrived on the scene. A police officer is not a police officer when working an off-duty security job. This is actually how the phase "rent-a-cop" was coined. They are rented to work as a security officer, not a police officer. Actually, commissioned security officers would have been the better solution for the shopping chain. The security officers are required to be commissioned by a company that carries insurance to cover incidents that may occur during the security operations.

Conclusion

Even though the issue of police officers misusing their power is blown out of proportion by the media, it is still a significant problem in the United States and has to be addressed. Abuse of power by police officers has been a contentious topic of discussion in the United States since the Boston Police Department was established in the state of Massachusetts in the year 1838. All of the solutions that I propose in this article, such as more thorough recruiting procedures, more thorough training regimens, and revisions to legislation that is intended to protect citizens, all have the same overarching goal: to stop police officers from abusing their power in the first place. The majority of incidences of police violence are, in almost all cases, the result of poor cops acting on behalf of their own personal agendas. Conducting exhaustive background checks on prospective police officers is the most effective method for removing unfit individuals from the ranks of the police force. In order to get a deeper comprehension of our culture and society as a whole, the purpose of this research is to shed light on political prejudice and the tendency to form opinions based on racial bias, regardless of whether such opinions are positive or negative.

If we could find a way to recruit individuals without bringing in people who would make poor policeman, we may be able to significantly cut down on the amount of violence that police officers use. According to David J. Skorton, the spirit of this nation has been characterized by racism for far too much of this country's history (2020). The United States of America has long been recognized as the land of the free, and this reputation should continue indefinitely.... When it comes to instances of police brutality, what do you feel the rest of the world believes of the nation that prides itself on being the "land of the free"? If the United States could figure out a way to prevent the hiring of unfit individuals into law enforcement positions, the country's rate of police brutality would drop significantly.

The second most effective option for reducing the incidence of police brutality would be to provide officers with more extensive training. Officers of the law need to be able to communicate clearly with the members of the community that they have taken an oath to serve and protect in order to be able to perform their duty to "serve and protect." They should practice community engagement as part of their training processes before they are promoted to the position of regular traffic officer. According to Brendan McQuade, "There is something about policing itself that makes it exceedingly difficult and resistant to change," and this is one of the reasons why things like "unconscious bias training" and "de-escalation training" sometimes seem like they're going in circles.

The process of overhauling the legal system is very challenging, as was said before. However, if we were able to get sufficient support and concrete suggestions for ways to enhance law enforcement, we may be able to lessen instances of police brutality. Because of the fast rise of law enforcement groups in the 1800s, the system is in desperate need of a major redesign. In addition to more in-depth training, prospective law enforcement officers need to have pre-duty community engagement experience. If more stringent training methods are used, then incompetent police personnel will be quickly eliminated before they are recruited.

The third and last strategy for minimizing police brutality is to enact laws that guarantee the safety and rights of all persons, regardless of the features that distinguish them from one another. I think that we can all agree that members of the police force are exploiting loopholes in the rules and regulations that are already in place. One of these shortcomings was shown, for instance, when law enforcement officials broke into the home of a lady in 2014. She gave the law enforcement authorities her house key so that they could conduct a search inside her home. Instead, they shattered the glass and blasted the surrounding area with tear gas with the expectation of locating a member of the other gang who had taken cover inside. When West sought to sue the organization to collect damages, the police officers were able to avoid liability because to a legal loophole. Because of a legal loophole referred to as "qualified immunity," the police officers were not required to make up for the money that was lost. This is a clear example of unethical behavior, and it should serve as a cautionary tale about the potential damage that may be caused by legal loopholes in general.

As shown by the situation I've described, the law cannot have any loopholes that put public officials or law enforcement officers in a position where they are above the law.

As the last point, we need to build more extensive and complete recruitment and training methods for law enforcement professionals and public authorities, as well as improve the laws and freedoms that should be protecting the people who live in the United States of America. If we set comprehensive recruitment criteria, "bad apples" may be identified early on and eliminated from consideration for employment before they are ever considered. This will prevent the problem from occurring in the future. It is essential that law enforcement officials get more in-depth training if they are to be properly prepared to perform their duties in the field. A more stringent application of the laws and regulations that are already in place would not only help to keep the general public safe, but it would also protect law enforcement professionals from the illegal conduct of members of the general public. In the United States, police brutality is a significant problem, and there are a number of steps that may be taken to reduce the incidence of this problem in the first place.

Chapter Nine

Lack of Education in Texas Law Enforcement

Introduction

The world is evolving each day, and the law enforcement methodologies are also upgrading day by day. The developments of new styles in the law enforcement agencies have intrigued the police to use diverse methods for the safety of the nation. Texas police are somewhat trying to anticipate the role of the policemen to enhance the safety measurements on the land, and they use specific methods of choosing the eligible and powerful officers to perform tough duties with ease. Physical strength and mental stability are the main components that can help them to become valuable workers who are always there to help the citizens. The law enforcement agencies are formed to serve the citizens, and they have to remain alert, always alert, to provide them with safety. All the countries have their parameters and standard to test the credibility of the members, and the most important step is to encounter that these members are eligible to serve the law enforcement agencies. The trained members check the power and skills of all the participants who intend to join the force. The law enforcement agencies in Texas represent or expose that some brutal and untrained agents fail to execute their services. They'd rather tease the public and create chaos for them rather than bring comfort in their lives. Many of them take advantage of their position. The legislators are so invested in passing bills against the agencies hiring the notorious officers. The troublesome officers and their notorious acts are famous in the State of Texas and the law enforcement agencies working in the State of Texas. The main concerns of the department before hiring a police officer are his generation, responsibilities, and what people anticipate from the police officers. The department has to work very efficiently to choose to most vigilant officers to out-perform themselves when needed and protect people from any danger. This is the:

Lack of Education in the Texas Sheriff and Police Chief Positions

The parameter established by the State of Texas is to have the appropriate qualification to apply for a particular post, and the duties of the police have been upgraded with time; police are not only there to prevent crime, they are also supposed to interact with the community on several events. The police officers tend to arrange community programs where they communicate with children and people to spread awareness among them about self-defense, and they should also teach people how to react in a state of emergency. The police department of Texas has to elect sheriffs and hire police chiefs and other senior and junior officers who are eligible, physically fit, and qualified to deal with the most drastic situations. Many recognition programs have let the department gain recognition and anticipate the young girls and boys to join the institution. The department needs to have people who are mentally stable and fit and who know how to deal with or tackle the most difficult and heart-wrenching situations. A drastic accident or a cruel robbery, or a brutal murder can be something that will shake your nerves and upset you mentally (Wu, Stephen, 407-419). The stamina and power of the person will be tested as they have to go through very horrendous and sensitive occasions, and the ultimate way to deal with the problem is to remain determined and composed. The person has to control their calm and deal with the situation, but the troublesome officers who have no calm to control their nerves would cause more problems. They have no power to help the victims or capture the people who are committing crimes. The State of Texas has been the victim of mass shooting incidents where thousands of people have died dreadfully shrieking in pain, and they didn't even know what was their fault for being treated so badly. The shrieking voices of the children pleading for relief are hopefully looking at the police officers and officials to rescue them, and if they are not eligible enough to tackle the situation, the nation would not be able to trust the public service officers.

The legislators have encountered this particular issue in Texas, and they are figuring out ways that how the people could be safe from the notorious officer as some of the people have lost their lives because of the cruelty of the troublesome officers. Systematic failures are very commonly observed throughout the state, and the shooting incident became way more horrendous regarding such failure. The mentally challenged, bullied people who are at their lowest choose to attack the ones who are harmless and innocent. The systematic failure is indicated by the management, and they highlighted the interventions to implement. Many complaints were registered by the people, and that is why the legal agencies are alert to take action. They are about to pass a bill against these officers who are untrained and unprofessional. The ultimate reason for the failure of the department is that many officers lack training and they don't have formal education. Systematic errors exist because the officers are not educated enough to provide the rights to the people and protect them from evil. If the officers are not well trained and educated, they will surely fail to serve the people. The national law accreditation program for law enforcement is supposed to be introduced by the Texas Police Department. The department is on the verge of saving the lives of the people and giving the officers a chance to get proper training so they will be able to serve the nation. The most extensive shooting has been encountered in Texas, and still, the authorities fail to control such incidents. The legislative council of the state is supposed to introduce the programs that would allow them to hire efficient officers to maintain the security and safety of the people. There are many safety issues in the state, and the law agency needs to be supremely vigilant to save people from a dreadful death. There are Rangers in Texas as well who are trained to deal with the situations where the schools and colleges are under attack, or they are able to control massive terror activity that can happen instantly and cause serious damage (Axtell, Kayleigh, p. 2).

The police training in the State of Texas should be reformed as per the new consequence and upgrading of using weapons. The range of destructive material is so high, and many police officers are unaware of the interventions to deal with the toxic weapons. They will not be able to combat the challenges on the field. When the schools or colleges are under attack and the people are on the verge of dying, the supremely eligible shooters or the officers are supposed to take charge who can work selflessly and save the lives of the children and protect them. The assurance that the police officers will save them help the citizens then they will feel safe and protected. Many officers have been involved in the killing of innocent citizens. The ultimate process of education and professional training should be given to the officers to take charge in a state of emergency. African-Americans are also a community who suffer great hatred and bullying by the people, and some of the police officers also practice bullying and racism, as we have encountered in the most famous case of George Floyd, who was killed by a police officer (Li, Yudu; and Ben Brown, pp. 391-415). Better-equipped departments should step forwards to instill security and safety in the region. The moral integrity of officers will teach them to get away with all the elements of hatred and racism. This training will build empathy in them to deal very sportingly with the people and help them rather than considering their social and economic status and treating them with kindness. Training methods should be reformed, and the department should make sure that all the notorious officers who should not remain in the department of defense need to have officers who are supremely honest and optimistic. They should have racial discrimination towards others as we have encountered cases where African-American students were killed by the policemen of Texas. The brutality should stop, and the element of humanity should persist in the law enforcement community.

Lack of Education

The one thing the State of Texas has been deficient in is the educational requirements to become a Texas Peace Officer. Currently, the State of Texas only requires 12 hours of college to attend a police academy. Also, a physical and psychological exam is required with a clean criminal background. Firstly, the physical is a joke as any clinic will sign off on a physical and the psychological exam can be passed with the simplest of intelligence. The college hours can be in underwater basket weaving and you still attend an academy. The academies have been watered down so much that they are just wanting people to attend and pass according to their standards. The academy couldn't care less if you pass the state exam to become a Texas Peace Officer, no sweat off their back. I have witnessed people that could not spell cat if you gave them the c and t. Unfortunately, these standards will keep the uneducated, immature, and arrogant officers on the street and the cycle continues. On a brighter note, several police agencies do have more strict educational requirements to be eligible to apply. Unfortunately, this does not correct a plague that continues across law enforcement.

The one item that I feel needs to be covered is the requirements to be a sheriff in the State of Texas. This is an elected official, probably with the most authority in the county and all you must meet is the minimum qualifications. The State of Texas allows a sheriff to be elected without being a Texas Peace Officer with two years to obtain the certification. The sheriff oversees the county police force and jail operations. This includes numerous people working in the county sheriff's office and many more working in the jail. The budgets that must be managed can reach millions of dollars, yet we allow an uneducated and unskilled person to head this position. In my research, there are over 150 sheriff positions in the State of Texas and less than 1% have a college degree. This means that a person with no management skills, operational skills, public relations skills, staff development skills, or no budgetary management skills to oversee millions of dollars and operations plans. No major corporate organization would hire a person that does not have the skillset to perform the job at a high level. The integrity of the position should be higher and the general public should have the skillset to hire individuals that can adequately run the operation versus a person that has just been in law enforcement for a long period.

Law enforcement alone does not give the person the knowledge of skills to perform the job and be a keeper of the citizen's tax dollars. Since the citizens have proven that they will continue to elect unqualified people to hold this position, the State of Texas needs to make some changes and make the requirements to become a sheriff in Texas stricter. The sheriff should have at least a bachelor's degree and at least 10 years of management and budgetary experience. This would put the sheriff in a higher position as there have been numerous times the deputies under the sheriff have more experience and education than the sheriff. I feel that communities are losing the law enforcement game by allowing someone to hold the highest position in the county with a high school diploma. This is a joke and the State of Texas needs to stand up and realize the system is broken. I have heard from the uneducated officer that the certifications in law enforcement take the place of formal education. Unfortunately, just being in law enforcement and meeting the continuing educational requirement as required by the State of Texas does not give you the formal education to manage at a high level. I have proven that the continuing educational classes that officers attend are often falsified, watered down, or cut short leaving the officer with a false sense of education.

The same goes for the other elected officials for a city or county. City council members and commissioner court officials should have higher educational requirements as well. These people oversee the operations of a city or county and do not have any formal education or skills to be in these positions. Most of these people are elected on the good-ole-boy system and time and time again they have proven to fail. Recently, one county has had the county judge and several commissioners arrested and indicted on charges. We see the all-mighty powerful attitudes in this elected position just as we see them in the law enforcement environment.

When will it stop? When will the communities determine whether elected officials should have the pieces of knowledge, education, and skills to hold the position? When will the State of Texas decide the law enforcement requirements should be raised to meet the demands of today's society? When will law enforcement officers quite turning to the dark side of the badge? The simple answer to all of these questions is NEVER. Why, because this is the way it has always been, why fix what we know is broken? Law enforcement officers and elected officials will continue to do illegal activities and the communities and cities will continue to turn their back on the obvious breakdown in our society.

The purpose of writing this book is to years of witnessing the good, bad, and ugly of law enforcement and local governments. We decided that it was time for someone to speak up and share the dark side of the badge. Will this change things? No, the bad will continue to be bad even though there are good people in law enforcement that truly wish to SERVE AND PROTECT.

Reforming of Police Stations

The officers still indulge in old practices, and they fail to grasp the new interventions instantly to solve the problem of safety and security in the state. Sometimes individual instances of excessive use of force trivialize their job, and the police stations around America are reforming. The police department of Texas also has to reduce the excessive use of force against innocent citizens and remember the oaths they took while starting their services (Aguirre, Daniel). The school shooting issues have been a highlight to enhance the legal forum in Texas as several cases have been encountered. The police department across the nation are currently reforming to reduce the excessive use of force by police officers, and they use their authority to charge people and tease them for their interests. These activities take place to attain self-satisfaction as some of the officers might have encountered some severe kind of violence in their lives. There are consequences when a person faces some humiliation in childhood, and they exert it in the form of violence. The training programs are introduced to focus more on de-escalation tactics. The whole process is conducted to change the perspective of the police officers and to build trust in the officer that they are the ultimate saviors. These saviors are meant to save the people who are the victim of any violent incident or who have encountered any problem, and they need to take the assistance of the police officers. Police officers' training should be mandatory, and they have to get away with the lethal weapon treatment, which would be beneficial for them to use the firearm in time of emergency. They need to be efficiently trained to participate in combat without being fearful of the weapons.

Lack of Professional Training Leads to Complacency in Law Enforcement

The training of police is very tough as the Texas Police Department demands that the officer have to do recruit training for 18 weeks and counting filed differently as they spend 60 hours on firearm training and almost 44 hours on self-defense training. Tasers and guns are provided to practice. The appropriate training is given to operate the weapon, but when the person has not trained appropriately, they will not be able to save people in their hour of need. These methods are introduced to strengthen the department and let people be supremely trained and help the people who are in dire need of help. The elements of professional training are mandatory for complacency in law enforcement. Law enforcement complacency is marked by self-satisfaction when it is accompanied by unawareness of the danger.

The training and professional guidance would help the officers to remain content in avoiding complacency. It is avoided during the training that the officers should and must avoid complacency. It has to be avoided at any cost, and to avoid complacency in a high-risk profession like law enforcement is very difficult. If we examine the sportsmen, they are very well trained and will do it convincingly, and they will be considered the most efficient officers who avoid complacency. The officers have to sustain mental and physical stability. The problem we have encountered is that the negligence of police officers encourages criminals to get indulge in the activities without any fear.

The officers lack proper training to deal with the complication of the situations and react instantly, and the dreadful results are observed in the state (Dukes, Warren V., pp. 1-21). There are research and study which disclose that the excessive use of force trivializes the work of an officer. A study exposed by the Bureau of Justice Statistics that indicate only 0.5 percent of the 44 million Americans who have an encounter with a police officer suffered threats or experienced force. The people of color have faced the leash back and poor relationships with the police officers and faced brutality. Tempers control training is also something that causes bad law enforcement in the country. The law enforcement agency needs to hire people who are supremely eligible to train these officers to follow the rules properly in enforcing the law.

Relations between Police Officers and People of Color

To enforcement of the law is mandatory as the security of people and the officers is also ensured by the implementation when the security laws have to be implemented. The people of color have a strained relationship, and brutality has been encountered, and this is also an important hurdle in imposing the laws perfectly. The element of rage has been encountered, and the hatred among the people of color has this affirmation and lack of confidence in the police officers, and they believe that these officers would tease them and they would not be able to get any facilities from them. The distrust of police is shown by the African-Americans, and the demographics are not only with the African-American people; the people from different ethnicities are also being harassed by white supremacy. The element of white supremacy is flashed in all the sectors, and there are officers who have shown aggression and hatred towards people who are not from America. Sometimes the stress of a high-risk job also accompanies the police officers, and they exert aggression when they dare to deal with such stressful situations; they have to remain content and keep their calm; they should not be so aggressive, and they should always call for backup. The flaws in training contribute to spreading violence by police as they are trained to use the firearm, and the psychological training of being calm and patient lacks training majorly, so the training reformers have to be established properly.

Warriors to Guardians

In this study, we have encountered various issues that the people of Texas and America face while the police officers are dealing in the country. The obligations and reservations of polices officers are also very complicated, and they have to contemplate so many things which cause them serious issues.

The police officers have to deal with the risk factors when they have to deal with traffic challenges. Sometimes a natural disaster happens, and the ultimate person who will rush to help the people despite all the factors and risks would be a policeman. The policemen have to be there in every situation risking their lives for the prosperity of the country. They need to get the training that will show their physical strength, but their mental and psychological strength is supremely important. Even a normal human being can get frustrated in a particular situation and react aggressively. These officers should also be trained like the armed force officers (Reiter, Kathryn). The element of training and assistance is the only thing that will modify the mindset of these officers. The misconduct of the officers can be observed in many departments because of the restrictions and problems that trainers have to face. These are the major complication that doesn't let the officer behave properly and give their profound services in their field, but there are challenges that these officials have to face while serving at their best because of the natural challenges these officials are unable to over the challenges. The challenges should be eradicated. The ultimate way of changing the methods is to modify the policies.

The police department exposes that they appreciate that every human life is important, and they have to value all lives beyond color or religion. The cultural shift that has to take place to change the warriors into guardians can only be done when the policies can be changed and modified and replaced by new and improved interventions where the officers should get appropriate training to deal with the situations. The conditions are so drastic. The police department around the country is being modified, and the Las Vegas Metropolitan Police Department has used the new interventions or the policy that states that the department respects the value of every human life, and the application of deadly force is a measure to be employed in the most extreme circumstances. The authorities in Texas have to implement these methods to solve the issues of security and safety in the state. The intervention of dealing with the risk factor has been changed, and the police of Texas need to have particular training. The video showing the heavy machinery used for destruction and fighting has also been criticized that this evokes the emotion of harshness among the human beings or the officers who tend to provide their profound services for the country. They should get training to use the machines, but they should not see the videos that how the machines are spreading mass destruction. These videos spread the hatred and elements of destruction and aggression encountered in their minds. These psychologically affect the minds of these officers. The zero policies should be eliminated, and the officers should not be punished for committing a mistake. We never know the intent of a person and how and why he or she has committed the mistake, so these practices must be avoided. These officers should also feel like part of the community, and they should not feel bad about their existence. The methods can transform the bunch of warriors into guardians, and people can change their narrative toward these officers.

Security Challenges in Texas

There was an incident where the team of 367 officers was unable to control the situation when the school went under attack. *Texas Tribune* released the report of 77 pages in which the problem of the killer was mentioned that signs were ignored by the family, but the police failed to manage the situation systematically, and it was all chaotic. The ultimate security challenges being faced by the people of Texas are robbers and theft, killings, and other crimes. The drastic crime which has been encountered in Texas is shooting in schools; this is something supremely uncertain, and it causes a severe amount of trauma and fear among people, and they need to be treated with contentment, and if the police officers were not trained properly, they would not be able to maintain peace in the affected areas, and the nation or people will remain uncertain about the situation. The situation can only be handled when the police officers are very well aware of all the factors to deal with the risk element and spread positivity among people and assure them peace and sanity. Shooting incidents in schools are encountered widely in America. Texas has also been a victim of the shooting and the uncertain killing of young children or college students. The most important thing to keep the schools safe is to first hire officers who are able to do quick actions. The terrifying and horrid incident is when someone enters the school and opens fire on innocent children and teachers who are not harming anyone. The people lose their loved ones. We need to appreciate the efforts of the policemen who reach the spot-on time and deal with the situation and encounter the problem. They have to capture the terrorist and maintain peace in the affected area. They have to rescue the children, which is a great challenge. The educators and students are the victims of the guns in the school. The process of keeping the schools safe is mandatory. American children have been the victim of this gun violence in the name of religion, race, and social status.

Preventions from the School Shooting in Texas by Enforcement of Law

The basic consent of the legal agencies is to save the lives of innocent people who are victims of such violence. The most dreadful thing is that the schools have a great security system, and they have a very profound amount of security cameras and security guards. Still, some students manage to bring a gun into school, and they attack their classmates. The outsiders enter the schools and attack the people so violently and kill people who are there to study; the only objective of being at school is to study, but they get killed because of one spark of emotion (Jagodzinski, C. Lawrence, pp. 185-197). Gun prevention agencies are generated to solve this drastic problem. The police failed to prevent the situation and save the lives of people as the parents were scared to send their children to school because they were scared that their child would be the next victim. The fear is natural, but only law enforcement agencies can ensure the security of people who are visiting the schools. Police and the gun prevention organization have thought about the interventions about implementing the methods that would help to save the lives of people. Law enforcement and serious punishments should be granted to all the terrorists who tend to change the lives of people through these drastic incidents and their hatred. This is not the result of the hatred that should not be shown by taking the lives of other people.

These problems can be easily eradicated as this is one of the major issues which is encountered in Texas. The law enforcement agencies have established the department, such as the Everytown for Gun Safety Support Fund (Everytown), the American Federation of Teachers (AFT), and the National Education Association (NEA). These institutions are constructed on certain laws and the implementation of strict security interventions and methods that would have to be implemented. The schools also have to enhance their security services, and the record of the students should be maintained, and their mental and psychological health should be evaluated. All the details about their family backgrounds should be checked. These attacks on schools are something that cannot be controlled because of a weak security outlook and records. The profound intervention through law enforcement can be the only way to develop plans, and these methods can help to save the lives of children and the teachers who are modifying lives. The research-informed intervention plan after evaluating why the gun attacks is anticipated by people and these interventions would be supremely helpful in changing the system of the country and change the whole thing. The education professionals should be saved as they are changing the lives of people who should be saved from these horrendous attacks. The evidence should be collected, and expert-endorsed actions school should be taken and save lives. Law enforcement by police need can be the only way to change the narrative of prevention, and the lives of people could be saved, and the children could go to school with great ease and move into school without any fear. The ultimate method is that the officer should be trained according to the given time period under proper trainers to serve the state with valor and power. Law enforcement should be so strong that people should feel scared of accountability.

Retirement and Rehire of Law Enforcement Officers Leads to Lazy Job Performance and Complacency

The ultimate barrier to the progress of the department is retirement and rehiring. This should be strictly prohibited; only then will the department move back on track. This practice needs to discourage in the law enforcement agencies in Texas. The police officers get permanent jobs that are offered by the government, and they will get many incentives. The law enforcement officers have the liability of attaining the incentives and living their lives with great security (Alexander, Bob. Old Riot, New Ranger). The security of a job sometimes makes them supremely lazy, and they are not able to contemplate the requirement of their job. The assurance of getting the money every month and after retirement would make them less responsible, and they are not able to fulfill their duties. This practice has been encountered by law enforcement officers, and they become way lazy. They retire around the age of 57, so they know that even if they are performing at a moderate pace, they will not be questioned why they are not performing their duties very profoundly. The whole issue of not implementing the laws and lazy job performance is that they are not able to give their best performance; the people in that particular area would be affected by this practice. When the person has to go through any accountability or is accused of any charge, they will not lose their jobs, and they will get their jobs back after they excuse for their mistakes. The rules are not strict, and the employees are aware that they can take advantage of which are offered by the department. They will surely get their jobs back, and they will not be fired by the department. There should be strict accountability for the people who are being lazy to perform their job properly. These are the basic problems that are being encountered in the police department, and the feasible number of bonuses is the reason that the police officers fail to contribute to making the department way more effective.

The legislative members should be supremely alert to uncertain people who are doing some mysterious activities. The data of criminal records should expose the details of all such people. The ultimate and basic problems that departments face in law enforcement agencies is the retirement and retirement. The police department is highly affected by these practices and the police executive research forum that there is an 18% increase in resignations and a 45% increase in retirement. The pandemic fatigue enhanced the methods, and the negativity and strict job hours are intriguing the police officers to go for these actions, and sometimes they are supposed to opt for the jobs which are outside the law enforcement department. This department is supremely challenging, and the officers have to remain supremely active and respond to risk situations very actively. These are also the reason that people choose to retire. The jobs in law enforcement agencies now have become a bit challenging. The people now have to go through these challenges sometimes; they feel agitated. The element of agitation would also intrigue people to get away with the job. The people who initially opt for government jobs and believe that they will get the security of a job fail to realize that they have to give away their profound services without fearing their own lives, and they have to fulfill their jobs by sacrificing their lives and their family times. The enforcement of the law becomes weak when people fail to put in their effort, or sometimes they leave the job because they fail to give their hundred percent in their desired job. The laws have been modified in America, and the interventions which are implemented very broadly are topics such as body cameras, use of force, no-knock warrants, disciplinary systems, and civilian oversight. These methods are used, and the policemen are supposed to get the training to use the new and improved methodologies and interventions to help them save the lives of people and provide them a gleeful life. These new methods have made the job way more challenging, so the police officers fail to contribute with great conviction and give their efforts properly. These practices make the foundation of the institution very weak. They fail to move ahead with the technology enhancements such as biometrics, gunshot detectors, and police drones, but the jobs are not highly paid, which can also be a reason that the people opt for new jobs and they don't put in their efforts to strengthen the department. Law enforcement has weakened because of such behavior of the officers.

Long Working Hours Lead to Making Poor Decisions

The law enforcement departments have various obligations to follow up, and they need to move ahead with great methods and interventions to implement the supremely effective methods. The job has countless requirements to be fulfilled, and these requirements are based on the situation and which situation they have to tackle. The long working hours drain out the energy of the workers, and they fail to give their appropriate contribution to their job (Pollock, Wendi; Natalia D. Tapia; and Deborah Sibila, pp. 42-52). The behavior of the person depends on the comfort and ease they have to face at their workplace. This job is already very tough and energy draining as the employees have to remain supremely active all the time, so they should get short hours at work so they can perform with their full energy. These energies will also boost their morale. The high the energy is, the better the performance would be, and this is the reason that they fail to make very complicated decisions instantly as they remain indulged in the exhausting long hours.

Measurements to Improve the Performance of the Officers

The measurement which should be taken seriously by the department is the provision of the proper training and refusal of all such practices which demolish the reputation of the department. These officers can perform diligently when they would be able to have sound minds and sound bodies. When the person is not getting appropriate sleep and rest, the level of mobility elevates, and the problem will also enhance the psychological problems and most common problem which is encountered during the most hectic schedule, and they fail to make appropriate decisions which can boost their careers, and they end up making poor decisions, and sometimes they make some impulsive moves which can put an impact on their career and they can be rude and unkind to the citizen. The reciprocation of the long working hours impact the body language and mood of the person, and they can have heated encounter with the citizen and they can get indulge in some problems like fights and arguments. The long working hours cause social and economic issues as well.

The other important thing that could be used to prevent the particular situation is the provision of a higher number of workers to split the burden. The department of police in Texas should hire more officers in the force, so the workers have flexible working hours. The ultimate purpose of having easy and flexible working hours for the policemen is because efficient services are supremely important for providing excellent services for the citizens. The policemen have to stay on their toes and perform their duties vigilantly, and they have to deal with the most drastic and emergency situations, so if the police officers will remain fit and healthy and they would have sufficient sleep, they will be able to contribute very prominently in capturing the culprits and deal with the hideous incidents. These problems can only be solved when we have brave and vigilant heroes who are there to save people on the streets and save their lives. The safety can only be felt when the nation knows that the law enforcement department is there to provide them with the most profound and active services when come one gets indulged in any problem, and they can rely on the police department for rescue (Bishopp, Stephen A., pp. 1-20). The ultimate saviors have to remain active and alert to solve the issue. The situation of overfatigued is aggravated by understaffing associated with demographic shifts and the threats to homeland security. When the culprits are aware of the power of the police department, they would be aware that they will be supremely proactive, and the culprits can get caught easily. These problems will be solved instantly, and new interventions will help to provide ultimate grace to the department people are aware that these officers are reliable and helpful in making the homeland supremely safe, and they can move around without any fear.

False Certification to Complete the Required Timespan to Gain Certification

The measurement which is mandatory to be taken officially is to identify the people who false certificates through different tests and identify them. There are many flaws in all the departments, and this is the reason that the officers serving public service offices show negligence in their duties. They fail to fulfill their duties and disappoint the citizens. The citizens are completely dependent on the law enforcement agencies, and they have faith that these law enforcement officers are supposed to help them in their time of dire need. The flaws of the departments let us face the repercussion of the poor decisions of the officers. The police department in Texas and other states of America has various flaws and which is strengthening the process of appointing ineligible police officers who are not vigilant, and they are a threat to society. The ultimate study and research we have done have exposed that there are various social issues that are prevailing in the State of Texas and the people failed to get the security they wanted. The citizens are not hopeful because various untrained officers have no appropriate knowledge of their duties, and they cause severe harm to the citizens (Miller-Fox, Geri, pp. 57-379). The problem of undereducated and untrained officers has been encountered in the state; there is another flaw that has been encountered while unveiling the details about the department; many officers get false certification for completing the training hours. They fail to perform their duties because they have not got the proper training, and they don't know all the details about the problem and the ways to solve the ultimate security problems. The falsified certifications are the reason that we have many ineligible officers who are causing serious problems in the provisions of the security services. The police department plays a major role in contemplating the requirement of security in the state and saving the lives of people.

The ultimate problem of school killings or school attacks is largely encountered in the State of Texas, and the law enforcement agencies have to play a very proactive and vigilant role in saving the people of the country. The State of Texas is on the verge of serious security issues, and the children at the school need very active and expert security officers to protect the innocent lives which are brutally taken by the obnoxious terrorists. The police officers who get the leverage to complete the training hours with false certifications are also responsible for such problems. The whole study exposes the most horrifying thing people in Texas face are the shooting in school's incident, and the chaotic behavior of the police department is something that has anticipated more people to release their anguish and anger in such a way. The ultimate result is that the Texas department should train the officers so vigilantly and efficiently that they can take charge of such situations instantly and be supremely vigilant in getting hold of these criminals and cracking down the criminal activity. The officers should and must be very loyal and honest with their job, and they should not lie about their certification and get proper training. This is how the horrendous act of shooting can slow down, and innocent people will be saved by the rage of these mentally challenged people who leash out on others for their own insecurities and harm them.

Falsified Records

Continuing education in the law enforcement world is a constant as Texas Peace Officers are required to obtain 40 hours of continuing education during each two-year cycle to keep their license. Unfortunately, the types of training are limited with having to repeat the same classes over each cycle. Also, due to time constraints and limited manpower, many departments are unable to allow their officers to leave work status to obtain an education that will enhance their job performance. As a result, many officers falsify records that will allow officers to meet the 40 hours of continuing education requirement and keep them on the streets performing their duties. Personally, I watched one office allow officers to sign training rosters for ten classes at one time allowing the officers to obtain over 200 hours of continuing education hours and never attend a single class. The officers went down the table signing rosters for multiple classes and the rosters were filed with the state without question. I have seen this happen with multiple agencies allowing officers to obtain falsified continuing education hours and never attended classes.

On the other hand, I have witnessed departments send officers out of town to attend classes with taxpayers' dollars paying for travel, meals, hotels, and classes when the officers could have attended the same class in their hometown with a certified instructor. Personally, I teach knife/counter-knife training and offered to teach the whole department at no cost. Instead, the department elected to send three officers to an out-of-town training to obtain the same training that I offered at no cost. The officers spent three days at this training at a great cost to the taxpayers. The department felt no remorse for sending them out of town as the department was known for wasting money. When the officers returned from the training, they were excited about the information that they had learned and stated it was the best training they had ever seen. Upon questioning them about what they had learned, they had not learned the very basics of knife fighting or knife defense. The problem is that they could have received a higher quality of instruction at no cost to the taxpayers by staying at home and learning from an instructor that was certified to teach the valued techniques.

The whole research and analysis let us adhere to the facts that how different issues in the law enforcement department in Texas cause serious security issues for the citizen. The police department is the most prominent department which is supposed to hold people together and maintain discipline in the state. The supervisors and chiefs of the department are the real trouble makers who failed the nation by hiring the most incompetent workers who fail to complete their duties vigilantly and fail to protect the lives of the people. The children who are the drastic victim of the terror attacks on schools lose their precious lives, so the security agencies have to protect them from the evil and hideous people who are the reason for destruction and disruption in the state. The lack of education is the first thing which we have encountered that doesn't allow the people to work in peace because they don't feel secure. The ultimate freedom that a person is supposed to feel is missing because the law enforcement agencies are unable to provide the services which they are supposed to provide. With the complacency of law and getting appropriate positions in the department, one has to complete the training, but the officers who are behaving notoriously have false certification. The failure to complete their training hours and do proper training to solve the issues of security. They haven't learned the methods which they are supposed to try to save the problem and provide the most auspicious and profound security services to the people. The long working hours also cause a problem for the citizen as the long working hours of the workers let them fail to work prominently and provide efficient services. The misconduct of the officers is also something that is causing these issues. The department of police should have the most vigilant and active members who don't fear losing any conflict as they are meant to provide the best protection to the members of society and solve their problems. The outsiders and criminals should know that after harming the citizens or breaking the law, they have to face strict repercussions. These repercussions should be in the state of money or any physical punishment to teach them a lesson that they should never get the courage to perform the crime. The people should feel safe and protected because the law enforcement agencies should take charge of the security issues and make the atmosphere the most suitable for all the citizens in the state. May peace prevail in the state, and the children can go to school without any fear and hesitation.

Chapter Ten

Why Bad Policing Continues in Texas

Introduction

The Texas Police system needs a complete overhaul to get away from uneducated and untrained officers being hired and allowed to keep their jobs and how top law enforcement officials and the communities keep turning their back on bad policing. No day is the same—the work of a police officer is demanding but varied. And it requires emotional stability, physical strength, flexibility, and quickness of mind. Thanks to a flexible intervention concept, patrols made up of two officers are able to quickly go to the scene of the incident and collaborate closely with train staff and other police forces. A police officer cannot prepare to deal with certain interventions such as accidents, death cases, limitation of dangers, and criminal acts. Uneducated and untrained officers can ruin the reputation of the department (Albrecht, Heyer & Stanislas, 2019).

Police work is recognized in the literature as highly stressful. Suffice it to say that, since the early 1980s, Spielberger had devised a tool aimed precisely at measuring stress in the police forces called the Police Stress Survey. Numerous researches have been carried out in Europe, the United States, and Australia in order to investigate the multiple aspects of policemen's wellbeing, quality of working life, and mental health. When one wants to understand the effects of working life on the psychological wellbeing and psychological adaptation of a police officer, as well as for other professional fields, it is appropriate to take into account the multiplicity of dimensions in the positive and negative aspects (Andrews, 2018).

Image of the Police Officer

The stereotypical image of the policeman as an individual who carries out a dangerous and stressful job must be reviewed taking into account how satisfying and fulfilling this can be. Scholars investigated the positive and negative aspects of police work in the perception of policemen themselves. The most cited positive aspects are contact with citizens and the fact of working among people, the perception of help and usefulness for society, cooperation with colleagues, and freedom/responsibility.

In very similar previous research, the most mentioned positive aspects are primarily the excitement and challenges associated with being a policeman, followed by statements relating to helping people and job security. But when we combine factors such as job security with wages, benefits, and retirement arrangements, this package of compensatory factors turns out to be the most attractive. The negative aspects mentioned are in order: inadequate working hours, public blame (public condemnation of the police, negative stereotypes, distrust, and disapproval of citizens towards them), inadequate pay, and difficult relationships with administrators, politicians, or lawyers (Andrews, 2018).

In general, a more complex picture emerges from these researches: The same characteristics can be perceived as satisfactory or unsatisfactory depending on the case, and even the dramatic events typical of the policeman's work, when they occur, can be experienced as eustress by those agents who they love the excitement associated with their work. It is difficult to find in the literature a certain answer to the question of whether or not police officers constitute a category at risk for both physical and mental health. The second refers to the selection effect: Policemen are selected on the basis of their resistance to stress. Cops are therefore no longer at risk of stress discomfort than others, as they are chosen from among those who are most likely to manage difficult situations effectively. The third concerns the culture of the police often described through rules that value compliance with the male gender role, and therefore encourages the concealment of emotional problems. In this case, this lack of difference between policemen and other job categories would be due to the false answers to the questionnaires given by the policemen who do not want to admit their emotional problems. In the same work, the researchers also find a relationship between burnout and the use of violence. Violent conduct is more likely among police officers who have developed cynical and detached attitudes toward citizens. Contrary to expectations, the dimension of emotional exhaustion is negatively correlated with the use of violence: emotional exhaustion translates into a lower level of activity, greater avoidance of people, and, therefore, a lower likelihood of violent behavior (Andrews, 2018).

The numbers show that U.S. police killings of civilians occur more frequently in communities of color. Although certainly significant, the data is not sufficient to understand the extent of the protests following the death of Floyd, nor the nature of the discontent towards the police forces they express. The unrest is particularly intense in those urban areas that the sociologist Loïc Wacquant has defined as the "hyper-ghettos," in which racial segregation and economic marginalization intersect and overlap, reinforcing each other.

In the American "hyper-ghettos," the state is perceived by many as overly repressive and, at the same time, as unable to defend their rights. A recent study gives an idea of how widespread the sentiment is in communities of color. The authors—Vesla Weaver, Tracey Meares, and Gwen Prowse—conducted interviews and focus groups with a sample of over 1,500 individuals, selected from residents of twelve predominantly black neighborhoods in five American urban centers. The words of these citizens evoke the image of a two-sided state: always present when it comes to monitoring and punishing small infractions (think of Floyd's counterfeit banknote), but slow and ineffective when called upon to act to protect citizens. To understand the protests and violence following Floyd's death, it is necessary to take into consideration this context of radical distrust of the police, and, more generally of public authorities (Summers & Rossmo, 2018).

K-9 Catastrophes

When we talk about K-9 officers we are opening up a new world of confusion and lack of education and training. I have had the opportunity to be a K-9 officer for many years and have developed a dislike for many K-9 officers. Many of the K-9 officers that I have worked with or around only wanted to be a K-9 officers for the prestige of finding drugs and being in the spotlight. They knew nothing about animals, how to train them, and most of all how to care for them. I have never understood why most K-9s seem to act like they are on drugs all of the time and want to eat someone's face off. The trainers and officers will tell you that they want them to be aggressive, but this is misusing the dog and not allowing the dog to work at the top of their game. Many K-9 officers only look at their dogs as a tool to make them look better and give them something to brag about and mistreat the dog or give them no attention when at their home. Even though the K-9s are trained, they need to be socialized and crave attention and love. This is why you hear about officers leaving their dogs in the patrol unit and forgetting about them and they die of heat exhaustion. Lack of education and knowledge of canines result in bad experiences with the dogs. While many officers want the prestige of being a K-9, they need to understand the responsibilities that go along with the job. Unfortunately, I have witnessed officers that abuse and mistreat their dogs which causes them to be unable to be around the general public. I have yet to understand why officers will not let the general public pet the K-9s. My canines love attention and I do not worry about my canines even attempting to bite someone. On the other hand, when I tell them it is time to go to work, they snap to attention and do their jobs. Another misconception is that K-9s have to be trained in a different language. This is ridiculous in that a K-9 will listen to the trainer or officer before listening to any other person.

Police Officers Should Be Held Accountable

In our national reality, occasionally there are cases of police violence that fall on an individual; this is due to a lack of training in the police force or even to an irrational reaction of the intervened. In this regard, the best way to know what to do in the face of a police intervention other than vehicular, specifically, on public roads: It is knowing our rights and knowing the duties of police officers, in other words, we must know the law. In this article, we will briefly develop each assumption of police intervention using simple terminology oriented to the citizen; however, if the reader wishes to analyze them in a technical and detailed manner, they can enter the inserted links (Summers & Rossmo, 2018).

The National Police, based on of Political Constitution, has the purpose of guaranteeing security and restoring internal order so that the functional duty of the police force is to prevent, investigate and combat crime. While the arrest, for its part, is a consequence after the intervention, it is about the effective conduction of the intervened person to the corresponding police unit; detention is a measure of personal coercion (a limitation to the right to freedom protected by law) regulated in the Criminal Procedure Code (CPP).

Likewise, if we are taken to the police station as a result of the identity control process, an arrest is not made, since the correct term to use is retention. The police force, without the need for a fiscal or judicial order, can request their national identity document from any person and can carry out the pertinent checks in the place where they are, when they consider that it is necessary to prevent a crime or obtain useful information for the investigation of a punishable act. If the person is required to accredit his identification, the police officer will return the document or documents and authorize his departure from the place, proceeding in accordance with his internal regulations. If in case the requested party does not show any documentation or the document presented generates doubts about its authenticity or correspondence of identity, depending on the seriousness of the fact investigated or the scope of the police operation carried out, it must take it to the nearest police station for exclusive identification purposes (Summers & Rossmo, 2018).

The detainee may not be admitted to a cell or dungeon, nor kept in contact with other detained persons. The retention in the police station will not exceed four hours, after which they will be allowed to leave. The police force, within the dependency, must grant the detainee again the facilities to prove his identity or to notify his family or person indicated about his retention.

If the detainee is identified at the police station before the expiration of the four hours, he must be allowed to withdraw. For identification purposes, the police may take the general law, photographs, fingerprints, weight, measurements, or similar measures, even against his will, in which case an order from the prosecutor will be required. If in case the four hours elapse, and the proceedings are exhausted without achieving the identification of the detainee, the police officer must allow his withdrawal from the police station.

In the case of drug trafficking, for example, it has been realized that the police, as they are commonly understood, can only be one of the law enforcement bodies with powers to control drug trafficking and use. Thus, in America, in addition to the local and state police and the FBI, other important government agencies are involved in drug activities such as the DEA (Drug Enforcement Agency), the customs police, the coastguard, and even the military. An important role is also played by the Internal Revenue Service, given the internationally recognized importance of tracing and confiscating the assets, especially financial ones, of criminal organizations. Police activities are of particular interest to the social sciences (Skillicorn, 2021).

The attention to the characteristics of policemen as a professional category, as well as the recognition of the fact that they have a wide discretion in the use of the plethora of legal powers at their disposal, led the researchers to study what J. Skolnick (v., 1966) defined working personality. The "police culture" was then analyzed, that is the processes of social integration of the profession that can influence relations between the police forces and citizens. One issue that is given particular attention concerns the way in which the police deal with problems—including crime—related to particular ethnic groups, to homosexuals, or to social categories with atypical lifestyles, such as gypsies and homosexuals.

Despite the differences between the systems and practices of the police in different countries, in the contemporary debate on the roles of law enforcement agencies, there is a surprising agreement on what should be their primary functions. It has been observed with regard to the most visible symbol of police activity—the officer on patrol duty—that he rarely has anything to do with serious crimes. For example, Thomas Feltes (v., 1994), in a study on Germany, has highlighted how the tasks related to traffic control constitute 25-60% of the activity of agents on duty in the streets of German cities. A significant share of police work is also absorbed by the handling of administrative paperwork defines a core of "key objectives for police reform" (Skillicorn, 2021).

This debate—and in some cases, the practical feedback it has had at the level of the police organization—has focused in part on a re-examination of the notion of "community" in its social and political values and on the need to establish a closer link between the police and the community. In Britain, there is a recognized dilemma in this regard, as a "community" may want more neighborhood and street surveillance agents, while certain criminal activities, such as drug trafficking, require specialized police. The interesting thing about this debate is that it changes clichés about the types of police organizations. In France, for example, a country where the model of state police organized on a national basis is believed to dominate, a closer link is being experienced between the police forces and local communities, which respond to a project defined in non-essential terms, both of decentralization and rather of "territorialization," or even of "association" and "local" security policies. Certain powers of the prefectures have been devolved to mayors and departmental councils, and a number of municipal police forces have been created, however, with limited powers. The most important fact is that "a profound transformation is underway in the order of priority and in the definition of police roles ... the republican model of the police was centered on the priority given to public order." This is what the former Minister of the Interior has acknowledged, Easter, who affirmed that "it is necessary to move from a police system at the service of the State but not attentive to public expectations to community-oriented police, guardian of the law but committed to responding to the needs of citizenship."

Attempts to develop community service police are linked, in some advanced countries, to the problem of providing "security" in postmodern societies. For example, wealthier citizens may be in a position to purchase additional police services from the state or private companies as a status good. In Britain, citizens are encouraged to take greater responsibility for the safety of their properties and living quarters through "neighborhood surveillance" systems (Skillicorn, 2021).

First of all, in fact, the federal courts have long since clarified how it is the content of the message conveyed by the manifestation of thought, and not the way, the times, and the places of the event itself, to receive full constitutional protection. So those who protest publicly cannot be punished for the ideas he expresses through the protest, but he can be punished for not respecting the rules that regulate the ways in which any protest must be put in place. Whoever sets the flag on fire cannot be punished for disagreeing with government policies, but he can be punished if he violates the rules that establish when, where and how a fire can generally be started. And so on. It is therefore evident how the two categories of norms (content-based and content-neutral) are not always impermeable and distinguishable from each other and how limiting the way in which a thought manifests itself can, in some cases, mean limiting made the very expression of thought.

Unlike what happens in other systems, the American one allows, in fact, arrest even where a bagatelle offense is integrated (which we would often define as administrative, but which in that system is a crime), with the result that the true or presumed violation of any rule, relating for example to the use of city streets during the demonstration, can result in mass arrests and easy sabotage of the demonstration if the police so decide.

This is a change that, the article emphasizes, reflects a more general trend of the entire American justice system. On the one hand, in fact, incarcerated people are decreasing within urban areas, while on the other hand, they have increased at a similar rate in rural areas. The same goes for arrests, which again fall in the first areas to grow in the second. And when fewer arrests occur, the likelihood of a violent outcome of the action also drops drastically, as shown by some research conducted on the subject (Skillicorn, 2021).

Some analyzes have attributed the improvements to less severity in dealing with offenses such as marijuana possession or prostitution, but other reforms on the side of law enforcement themselves seem to have also played their part. Police killings in cities like Philadelphia, San Francisco, and Baltimore dropped after those departments began following a series of Department of Justice recommendations, while in Chicago, a reduction in violence followed more restrictive policies on the use of force and a new system to make agents more accountable for their actions.

The issue, controversial for years, of further incentivizing the initiative already underway in Texas, relating to arming school teachers of all levels and levels, is also returning to the fore so that they can respond effectively and, above all, promptly in the event of a mass shooting. Attorney General Ken Paxton spoke about it explicitly, declaring, "We cannot prevent the bad guys from doing bad things… but we can arm and prepare teachers and other public administrators so that they can react quickly. This, in my opinion, is the best answer."

This approach to the problem of mass shootings had been, we recall, especially supported by former President Donald Trump and strongly criticized for the risks inherent in the possibility that the weapons supplied to teachers could be found and accidentally used by the students themselves. Yet, in another recent massacre, namely that of Parkland, the commission set up to study the tragic event explicitly recognized that having armed teachers in the institute would have made a difference on the tragic balance sheet.

Once again, on the issue of mass shootings, it seems that both politicians and representatives of the U.S. public opinion are more engaged in a run-up in terms of visibility, demagogy, and ideological opposition, rather than trying to tackle the problem altogether. Every day, hundreds of school children are filed in Texas courts for a variety of offenses, such as swearing, misbehaving on the school bus, or fighting in the yard. Children are sometimes arrested for smoking cigarettes, dressing "inappropriately" or arriving late for school. In 2010, the Texas police handed out some 300,000 tickets to children as young as 6 years old for minor offenses committed at school. The penalties imposed range from a simple fine to community service and imprisonment. What used to be settled with a lecture from the teacher or a phone call to the parents sometimes ends up in arrests and a criminal record that could prevent a young person, years later, from going to university or getting a job (Huber, 2020).

In 2011, the Texas legislature changed the law so that 10- and 11-year-olds were no longer fined for their behavior in class. (In this state, you are criminally responsible from the age of 10.) However, a more ambitious bill, which was intended to end this policy—an initiative of Texas Senator John Whitmire, who called the system of "ridicule"—has not been adopted and therefore cannot be reconsidered for two years. Even the federal government got involved. Justice Minister Eric Holder said there was a "clear need to end" police repression to bring discipline to schools.

The particular emphasis on policing classrooms reflects the expansion, over the past two decades in Texas, of police surveillance in all its forms in response to fears, often unwarranted, that have spread in the United States in the 1980s and 1990s following an alarming rise in crime. Fears are fueled by the crack epidemic, alarmist academic studies, and the media. As the noose of policing has tightened across Texas, schools have suffered the consequences. Over the past two decades, the number of school districts with a police department has increased twenty-fold. "Zero tolerance" was originally a term used in the context of combating drug trafficking. Today, this expression is very often used to describe very repressive disciplinary measures in the school context (Sherman, 2020).

Stupid Is as Stupid Does

This story is a short one in that the officer was stupid and caused the death of his K-9. The officer and his K-9 were on top of the Astrodome in Texas. Why they were on top of the Astrodome would be the first stupid action that would need to be answered. During their stint on top of the Astrodome, the officer threw a ball for the K-9 to retrieve. However, the ball went off the top of the Astrodome and the dog went after the ball, falling its death. The officer was stupid in his actions but was not reprimanded for his actions. Fast-forward to the present, the officer is again a K-9 officer with an ISD. This officer should never be able to be a K-9 officer due to his lack of knowledge, experience, and past history dealing with K-9s. Unfortunately, we see this in the police world, that an officer can knowingly mess up and the situation will get overlooked. This needs to change and officers need to be held more accountable for their actions.

K-9 Abuse

I was called and asked if I wanted to watch a K-9 train finding drugs. Being a K-9 officer, I jumped at the chance to watch a K-9 work. During the training, I noticed that the K-9 was trained to have an aggressive response to finding drugs. The aggressive action was to scratch when detecting drugs. I asked the officer why he would want an aggressive response and he stated that he did not care of the K-9 scratched the paint off the side of the car. I told him when his dog scratched the side of an expensive car on a false response, his department would be paying the bill. The officer blew me off as he thought he was the best K-9 officer around and that his K-9 was the best. During the training, I watch his K-9 do some good work but lost all respect for the K-9 officer with the next action. The officer told the K-9 to sit and the dog hesitated for a moment before responding. The officer lifted the K-9 in the air by its leash and windmilled the K-9 about six feet off the ground and then slammed the K-9 on the ground beside him and scolded the K-9 for not following directions. I immediately stopped the officer and told him that he did not deserve to be a K-9 officer and if I ever saw him do any action like that again that I would personally handle the situation.

Love of the K-9

On the other side of the spectrum, many K-9 officers do love their K-9s and treat them well. In this incident, the officer had a beautiful K-9 and took excellent care of K-9. He loved his K-9 so well that he treated him like gold. However, the K-9 officer would keep his own kids locked in their bedrooms and feed them food under the door. The officer is still a K-9 officer but should have been arrested for child abuse.

Why Policing Continues to Fail

In the capital of Texas, police failures are nothing new. In five years, at least 35 people have died during police interventions. In Austin, as in the rest of the United States, black residents are too often targeted by men in uniform. A deputy police chief was suspended in the fall of 2019, accused of racist remarks made for a decade. A discussion then began on how to reinvent our public security. The police violence of 2020 will give impetus to this reform. In the Texas town, Michael Ramos, a black and Hispanic man, died under the gunfire of an officer in April. A month later, in Minneapolis, an African-American, George Floyd, was killed by a white policeman, Derek Chauvin. This murder triggers massive street pressure for budget cuts. Since then, Austin, a progressive island in a Republican state, has become the most advanced metropolis in the United States in terms of the defunding of law enforcement (Huber, 2020).

Until last year, funding for law enforcement in the Texas capital accounted for 40% of the municipal budget envelope. The new budget, voted in August 2020, puts on hold a 50% increase in these expenses over seven years, reports the *Texas Monthly*. Appropriations for police officers are reduced from $434.4 million to $292.9 million per year. This reduction entails the elimination of 180 police positions—150 of which are vacant—out of a total of around 1,800 officers. The training of four new promotions of police officers is delayed, and the budget dedicated to overtime is reduced. Other law enforcement funds will finance assistance to victims of domestic violence. "It means a second shelter for these people," says Kelly White, president of The Safe Alliance, which already runs a shelter in Austin for these victims (Wiest, 2021).

The defunding of the police also benefits the emergency medical services of the Texas capital. Between the funds from law enforcement and those dedicated to the fight against the Covid-19 epidemic, they earned 10 million dollars. This represents "72 more positions," "a hell of an investment," according to Andy Hofmeister, deputy head of these services. Thanks to police resources, two new ambulances are now running 24 hours a day. The municipality intends to bring the police back to their first mission: maintaining order. The second part of the reform initiates this reorganization: 76.6 million dollars have been immobilized in a so-called "separation" fund. A sum was taken from the budgets of services hitherto attached to the police, and which the city could make independent. These 76.6 million would then always be used to finance these missions, even if they come out of the police fold. The scientific police office thus became a separate entity in February, following serious problems revealed in 2016 (Huber, 2020).

After the Texas shooting, Democrats immediately called for a ban on military-style rifles and high-capacity magazines, tempered by pessimism that few or no Republicans would support anything beyond enhanced background checks and red-flag laws. Most Democrats agree on that. That's not what the

White House says. Centrist Democrats, led by Biden, have pushed since taking power to give more resources to police departments—and have distanced themselves sharply from calls after the killing of George Floyd to defund police departments. The president's pandemic relief plan, the U.S. Bailout, directed $10 billion in federal spending toward public safety. During his State of the Union address in March, the president pounded on the lectern, saying, "We should all agree that the answer is not to defund the police. It's to fund the police. Fund them. Fund them." The federal government has also invested millions in strengthening school defenses. In April, the Department of Justice announced $53 million in new funding to improve school safety across the country, in addition to nearly $64.7 million for proposals to prevent and respond to violent episodes (Huber, 2020).

If in doubt, the president's remarks at the executive order signing ceremony made it clear which side he is on. He criticized "those who seek to drive a wedge between law enforcement and the people they serve." And he praised the "brave local officers and Border Patrol agents," who he said had "stepped in to save as many children as possible" in Texas. Days later, as details emerged of local police mishandling of the Uvalde massacre, the Justice Department announced a review of law enforcement actions (White & McKenna, 2020).

The electoral card is the document that allows voting and certifies the regular registration of the citizen in the electoral lists of the municipality of residence. It must be presented at the polling station together with a valid identity document. It contains the personal data of the voter, the indication of the electoral section to which they belong, the voting center to go to, and the indication of the constituencies to which they belong. It is a permanent document that must be kept with care until the spaces are exhausted. At each election, a stamp will be placed on the card to certify that the vote has been taken. It is also essential to obtain discounts on the cost of travel tickets when voting. Each member of the polling station, if he were an employee, also has the right to compensatory rest, or to one day of rest for each day in which he was engaged in the polling stations, if that day for his activity does not appear to be working (Goff & Rau, 2020).

At least 85,000 law enforcement officers across the U.S.A. have been investigated or disciplined for misconduct over the past decade, an investigation by USA TODAY Network found. George Floyd has renewed the call for transparency in policing and the actions of police officers.

Most misconduct involves routine infractions, but the records reveal tens of thousands of cases of serious misconduct and abuse. They include 22,924 investigations of officers using excessive force, 3,145 allegations of rape, child molestation, and other sexual misconduct, and 2,307 cases of domestic violence by officers.

Dishonesty is a frequent problem. The records document at least 2,227 instances of perjury, tampering with evidence or witnesses, or falsifying reports. There were 418 reports of officers obstructing investigations, most often when they or someone they knew were targets.

Less than 10% of officers in most police forces get investigated for misconduct. Yet some officers are consistently under investigation. Nearly 2,500 have been investigated on 10 or more charges. Twenty faced 100 or more allegations yet kept their badge for years.

Cops Covering Cops

The "good ol' boy" system is when a leader unabashedly chooses favorites among their subordinates. There are many fair and impartial leaders within the police. The choice, not dictated by chance, to carry out ethnographic research on the police stems from the desire, somewhat dormant over the years, to tell a world that is still unknown to most today. Carrying out research on the police, for someone like me who is in the sector, has advantages but inevitably disadvantages. After all, approaching a policeman and asking him how he carries out his investigation activity made up of stalking, wiretapping, news from informants, or what may be the features of an elusive robber, is certainly not easy. Either because telling yourself allows you to let others know your vices and virtues, or because the interviewer, in this case, is perfectly able to distinguish the true from the false. Hence the research, also affected by this factor, was carried out informally without resorting to canonical interviews, thus managing to capture police knowledge through the most disparate moments and situations (Skillicorn, 2021).

The literature on the police exclusively concerns the interrelations with deviant phenomena and the consequences they have on society, so as to indicate methods and resources that the State uses for solutions to the problems of marginalization. Statistics and prospective surveys then take into account data that on certain occasions do not have a real and effective "control." Ethnographic research in the field would need data that are inaccessible to most. Interrogations, searches, raids, and more or less violent actions are transmitted with the characters of officialdom so as to reveal data without any real human meaning. Respect for the general principles of law and the functions of the penalty, the execution of measures or their exercise inevitably leaves aside the human and personalistic side of the facts.

It is widely believed that police studies have the task of opening the doors to an apparently strong but obscure power so as to give a modern and democratic aspect to a cross-section of society repeatedly labeled as the servant of masters and executioners of the defenseless. It is evident that the information is channeled here in a certain and safe way so as to show the citizen user what he wants to see. He certainly does not want to witness the not-so-zealous methods of looking for evidence or the violent action aimed at capturing a dangerous fugitive. His tastes are different. However, an explanation is necessary. Research that tries to explain and understand the deviance of the police and the theory of their suspicion is certainly not an easy thing, so much so that some methodological premises are necessary. We must in fact try to understand which term we must assign to the concept deviance. The linguistic meaning of a certain term can change by coming into contact with real situations or data, and the meaning attributed to that term also depends on the use made of it. Hence, the objective of the research necessarily had to pass through some ideal stages ranging from a form of determined deviance, excess of zeal, to the opposite extreme, expression of an atypical form of crime, that of the police (Wiest, 2021).

Captain Chaos

An officer receives a call for a welfare check at a residence. The officer, thinking this is nothing but another run-of-the-mill welfare check, arrives at the residence and immediately exits his vehicle. Only today's welfare check turns violent as the resident in the home opens fire on the officer. The officer secured safety behind his patrol unit as the occupant of the house targets his vehicle and the officer. It was only a short time before backup arrived and the resident continues to fire on the officers. Other departments and other county officers arrived on the scene as the resident continued to fire on the officers. Unfortunately, the sheriff would not give permission to the sniper to take out the resident for the safety of all the officers on the scene. One thing that stood out during this incident was that a ranking officer had a mental breakdown and dropped to his knees and raised his hands to the heavens in the middle of the front yard while shots were being fired. Other officers had to drag the high-ranking officer out of the yard and to safety before he was shot. Though this high-ranking officer had a mental collapse, he is still a high-ranking officer with the department. In the end, a sheriff from another county had to give the approval for the sniper to take out the shooter. This is yet another example of people that get elected to positions that they do not have the knowledge, experience, or skill to do in a professional manner. Yes, the high-ranking officer that had a mental collapse was a retire/rehire to draw retirement and a paycheck leading to a dual retirement paycheck. This why we need to take a hard look at rehiring retired officers and get away from young, arrogant, uneducated, and simply immature officers. The State of Texas should look at changing the requirements to become a Texas Peace Officer and agencies really need to crack down on officers that are not willing to follow policy and live up to the Protect and Serve ideology of law enforcement. This was covered in more detail in an earlier chapter.

Lack of Prosecution

Research showed that from 2015 to 2020, the Texas Rangers completed more than 560 public corruption case investigations, but only 67 of those cases have been prosecuted. However, the Texas Department of Safety would not respond to the subject.

In an incident where several officers had used excessive force on an inmate while he was handcuffed proved to no big deal as the special prosecutor stated that charges would not be filed. Had charges been filed, three officers would have been charged with Class B misdemeanor false statement to a peace office. Noticed how the excessive force charges or allegations just went away.

The Real Problem

My research has shown that a problem exists not only in Texas but across the nation. Police officers are committing crimes, with at least half being felonies. The problem is that officers will relinquish their peace officer certification in place of receiving charges for the crimes. This problem lies with the prosecutors in the cities and counties in that they do not want to prosecute police officers for their crimes because it makes them look bad when it comes time for re-election. Across Texas, hundreds of law enforcement officers permanently surrendered their peace officers license in a four-year period. Of some 297-license surrendered by peace officer nearly all of the cases, the officer was accused or charged with a crime, most often felonies. The problem is that the surrender of the peace officer's license was a tradeoff to avoid jail or prison time. A 2015 nationwide study of state-by-state police license decertification's performed by the In-

ternational Association of Directors of Law Enforcement Standards and Training found Texas had the fourth-highest number of licenses decertification's in that same year. When we have elected prosecutors that will not perform their duty to the citizens of the cities or counties, what future do we have of forcing the law enforcement community to change their way of performing their duties? When police officers are not held accountable for their actions and can avoid legal troubles by surrendering their peace officers license, the communities lose and the law enforcement of Texas takes another blackeye. When law enforcement is allowed to operate at a dysfunctional level and the courts will not take action, the citizens are the ones that lose in this fight. Even after this book has been written, cops still are doing stupid things that cause the public not to trust them. It is a shame that cops are not seeing the writing on the wall that there are groups of people that want to destroy them, but they still bring the spotlight on them. Cops breaking the law has been part of our past and will continue to be part of our future because the people that are being hired as cops should never be cops. They could not be trusted before the badge and the badge gave them the false power to keep doing stupid things.

Cover-ups

Many lawsuits have been filed alleging that the Texas Department of Public Safety covered up a story of a Texas Ranger's role in a fatal car accident. The officer was returning from a special operations assignment when he crashed his DPS unit into another vehicle. The officer was proved to be driving 84 miles per hour in a 45-mile-per-hour posted limit. The officer crashed into the other vehicle, causing the driver of the other vehicle to die a few days later. DPS rules state that officers working special assignments must rest for six hours before driving home. The officer involved in this incident had violated this rule numerous times but the agency failed to enforce its own rule. The DPS officer was never charged with any violation when the average person would have been charged with manslaughter, or criminally negligent homicide, or at least reckless driving. The officer was not charged nor did he receive any discipline. This officer was covered up by DPS seniors and now this officer is now leading high-profile investigations of shootings.

The images of George Floyd's arrest, which have gone viral, have inevitably renewed and exacerbated the long-standing criticism of the operating methods of American law enforcement, accused, among other things, of abuse of power and racism. Critical issues, these, never definitively resolved in ineffective and not very credible reform attempts undertaken by the police department. The anger and desire for revenge caused by an increasing discontent with the work of law enforcement officers, however, raises important questions regarding internal security. More radical approaches such as those of the Defund the Police movement risk turning into serious threats to American national security (Wiest, 2021).

Born from the vibrant protest in the aftermath of the arrest and killing of Floyd, the radical movement "Defund the Police" makes the abolition of the police department its banner. Composed of more or less extreme fringes, this new organization proposes, in its most conciliatory and moderate part, a real-location of funds destined for the police bodies in favor of larger investments in the health and social system of the country. Strongly criticized by police unions who highlight its potential danger—the most extreme fringes yearn for the total abolition of any public order control mechanism—the movement has acquired a growing relevance so as to play an important role in the presidential elections of 2020. On that occasion, President Trump's mud machine had, in a completely misleading way, hypothesized that Joe Biden was supporting activists and against the police.

The request for a radical change in application also requires a reflection on the transformation of police authority, power, and responsibility. In the aftermath of Floyd's death, some IT giants, including Amazon and Microsoft, have communicated their intention to make their respective facial recognition technologies unavailable to the police, fearing the danger that this technology could favor racial profiling by the forces of the order. The risk, according to the CEOs of the IT giants, would be a distorted use of technologies such as, for example, the monitoring of social media, potentially vulnerable to the racial prejudices of law enforcement operators. Technology that, however, a few years earlier on the occasion of the wave of outrage caused by the killing of Michael Brown in Ferguson, Missouri, in 2014, had been introduced precisely to discourage misconduct and make the activities of law enforcement agencies through the installation of cameras on uniforms (Garcia & Polson, 2018).

Holder anticipated his message in a speech in the newspapers, addressed to all of Ferguson, its inhabitants, and its authorities and by extension to a country that still suffers from misunderstandings and racial discrimination at work as in the administration of justice in the era by Barack Obama, the first African-American president. The path of the investigations, which ultimately will have to provide the answers, with the arrival of Holder gave a sign to proceed. In the afternoon, in Missouri, a grand jury was called, the special secret jury that will have to evaluate the circumstances of the shooting and decide if there are grounds for indictment. He will first have to examine the account of witnesses who saw Brown, unarmed, killed by six gunshots in the head and chest fired by Officer Darren Wilson, a veteran with six years of service, on 9 August last while on his way to visit the grandmother with a friend. According to the *New York Times,* the versions currently collected by the prosecution would be contradictory and the case could take weeks or months to complete (Wiest, 2021).

However, the Department of Justice, under the impetus of Holder, is also considering the opening of a special investigation that will put the entire Ferguson police on the dock, accused of aggressive and racist behavior not only in the case of the killing. Tourists are often exposed to various threats to their own safety and heritage in relation to phenomena such as terrorism, crime, and the lack of precise information on the local context of reference; in the event that a tourist becomes the victim of psychophysical and/or property injuries as a result of the criminal activity of third parties (e.g., a robbery, an assault, a kidnapping, an attack, etc.), legal and reputational responsibilities may arise to jeopardize the operation of the entire supply chain and to eliminate the widespread perception of safety that should be the basis of an expanding tourism (Wiest, 2021).

Given the premises, the most significant impact of crime on a tourist destination is the negative image of the destination, resulting in a reduction in tourist demand. The analysis of the impact of criminal threats on tourism assumes the role of a key element in any business project on the subject with particular regard to the reputational impact to which tour operators are exposed.

The impact of a bad reputation linked to insecurity produces harmful effects in all economic sectors involved, although this damage is amplified in the tourism sector based in particular on a virtuous circuit of esteem, admiration, and trust on the part of the tourist. The analysis of the reputational impact of the social and criminal dangerousness of a country must be distinguished in its dual meaning of:

- impact at a macro level, which refers to the effects of the criminal phenomenon on society in general, on the social community, or on the tourist destination;
- impact at the micro level, with reference to the effects of the criminal phenomenon on individuals (Wiest, 2021).

Final Thoughts

While the thin blue line is described as a term that typically refers to the concept of the police as the line which keeps society from descending into violent chaos or holds the frontier between chaos and civilian life, between crime and the American dream, I believe the thin blue line is the very thin line in which a cop can decide to be admirable and honorable in the position or use the badge to turn to the dark side and forget the oath that was taken when they entered the position.

Please understand that this book was not written in an effort to cast a shadow on law enforcement but to open the minds of society to the fact that many things are hidden in the police community leaving society to believe that all cops are fighting against crime and injustice. I have had the opportunity to work with some great people in the law enforcement world. These people were honorable and would not stand for injustice, especially in protecting the public. Unfortunately, I have had the opportunity to work with those people in law enforcement that only had the idea and concept of what they could gain from the position. I have witnessed laws being violated and management turning a blind eye to the situation and thus casting a shadow on the police world as a whole. When management turns a blind eye and allows injustice and criminal activity within the police brotherhood, the brotherhood is broken and the public has the right to know about these violations and unjustifiable acts by the police themselves.

Law enforcement was once an honorable position to hold within any community, but with the rise of police corruption and brutality cases, society is getting wise to its actions and want change. Unfortunately, many of the police brutality cases that have been brought to light and portrayed worldwide have garnered attention, many of these cases were only brought to light over racial issues. The authors of this book believe in the rights for all, but by making the police community as a whole look like racial Mongols, they fail to look at the big picture and see that racial discrimination occurs from all sides of race and to portray only one form of racial injustice is unfair and discrimination within itself.

Society as a whole need to open their minds and understand that they have control in keeping law enforcement in check. Communities elect officers and allow officers to be hired that do not fit the profile of a true police officer. Society needs to move away from the "good ol' boy" way of putting police officers in the position that should be held with honor and respect. Law enforcement officers that have the attitude that the badge and gun give them the right to act a certain way should be remove from office or fired immediately. The authors are amazed at the number of times police officers, judges, and county officials are hired or elected when they have no right to be placed in a position of power. A sheriff of a county is the highest authority in that county but we keep electing these people that have no education and management experience to actually hold the position. Law enforcement experience alone does not qualify a person to hold such a prestigious position. Society has contributed to casting such a big shadow in law enforcement but this same society should look themselves in a mirror and realize that they are the true cause of these actions.

Unfair treatment of society and communities by law enforcement should never be tolerated, but societies should realize that there are good police officers that truly want to serve and protect these communities and should be respected for their efforts to battle against their brothers in law enforcement that turn to the dark side. This same brotherhood should be evaluated to realize that this should be a brotherhood in arms fighting for the same cause. Humans will continue to make mistakes and these mistakes can be forgiven unless they undermine the integrity of a position of honor. It is okay to judge someone if you are willing to be judged yourself. If you have a full understanding of the person and the position do not judge them, instead, look yourself in the mirror and do your due vigilance and educate yourself before judging.

It will continue to be a problem if society does not educate themselves on candidates for a position before electing them or hiring them to perform in a professional position. If you continue to elect or hire people that are not qualified to perform the position to its utmost quality, then keep your mouth shut and live with you decision. Being a cop is not an easy job and should have qualified people to fill these positions, but history has proven that un-educated, inexperienced, overweight, and lazy people keep getting hired to fill positions that reflect the law enforcement as a whole.

In the law enforcement world, I have worked with many officers that I would call my brother. On the other hand, I have worked with those that I would not trust in any situation. There is a handful of officers that I have worked with that I know they would have my back, but only two that I would trust with my life, and I would give up my life for them. When your life is on the line every day you report to duty, you learn really quickly who you can trust. So, unless you have actually been in the game, and learn the rules before throwing stones, your house might be made of glass.

References

(2020, June 16). *What the federal government can do to help fix policing in America*. Brennan center for justice. *Https://www.brennancenter.org/our-work/research-reports/what-federal-government-can-do-help-fix-policing-america*.

Aguirre, Daniel. "Improving Police Supervision with Tuition Reimbursement Programs." (2019).

Albrecht, J. F.; Heyer, G. D.; & Stanislas, P. (2019). Policing and Minority Communities. Springer.

Ammerman, N. T. (1993). Report to the Justice and Treasury Departments regarding law enforcement interaction with the Branch Davidians in Waco, Texas.

Andrews, A. L. (2018). Moralizing regulation: The implications of policing "good" versus "bad" immigrants. Ethnic and racial studies, 41(14), 2485-2503.

Anozie, V.; Shinn, J.; Skarlatos, K.; Urzua, J. (2004). Reducing incentives for corruption in the Mexico City Police Force, La Follette School of Public Affairs University of Wisconsin, Madison.

Appier, J. (1998). *Policing women: The sexual politics of law enforcement and the LAPD* (Vol. 79). Temple University Press.

Applewhite, D. A. (2021). A year since George Floyd. *Molecular biology of the cell, 32*(19), 1797-1799.

Armacost, B. E. (2003). Organizational culture and police misconduct. *Geo. Wash. L. Rev., 72*, 453.

Axtell, Kayleigh, et al. "The Anatomy of a Crisis: Law Enforcement Leaders' Perspective on Police Enforcement." The Scholarship Without Borders Journal 1.1 (2022): 2.

Baenziger, A. P. (1969). The Texas state police during reconstruction: a reexamination. *The Southwestern Historical Quarterly, 72*(4), 470-491.

Barak, G. (Ed.). (2015). *The Routledge international handbook of the crimes of the powerful* (pp. 515-525). London: Routledge.

Bayley, D. H.; & Perito, R. (2011). Police Corruption:. U.S. Institute of Peace.

Bayley, D. H.; & Perito, R. (2011). *Police Corruption:* U.S. Institute of Peace.

Bishopp, Stephen A., et al. "Negative affective responses to stress among urban police officers: A general strain theory approach." Deviant Behavior (2018): 1-20.

Bjelopera, J. P. (2012). *Organized crime: An evolving challenge for us law enforcement*. DIANE Publishing.

Bracewell, T. E. (2018). Multidisciplinary team involvement and prosecutorial decisions in child sexual abuse cases. Child and adolescent social work journal, 35(6), 567-576.

Brice, D. (2012). Finding a Solution to Reconstruction Violence: The Texas State Police. *Still the Arena of Civil War: Violence and Turmoil in Reconstruction Texas, 1865-1874*, 187-212.

Bruce, D. (2003). Democratic Reform of Police—Any Lessons for Kenya from South Africa? Centre for the Study of Violence and Reconciliation, April, Johannesburg, South Africa, *http://webcache.googleusercontent.com/search?q=cache:ZWI_tXmF9eQJ:www.humanrightsinitiative.org/publications/police/papers/democratic_reform_and_oversight_of_police.doc*.

Brunson, R. K.; & Weitzer, R. (2009). Police relations with black and white youths in different urban neighborhoods. *Urban Affairs Review, 44*(6), 858-885.

Bryant, N. (2021). Police Brutality: Macroeconomic Effects in the United States.

C. (2021, August 12). *Public perceptions of the police*. Council on criminal justice. *Https://counciloncj.org/public-perceptions-of-the-police/*.

Caldero, M. A.; Dailey, J. D.; & Withrow, B. L. (2018). *Police ethics: The corruption of noble cause*. Routledge.

Campbell, M. C. (2011). Politics, prisons, and law enforcement: An examination of the emergence of "law and order" politics in Texas. *Law & Society Review, 45*(3), 631-665.

Campney, B. M. (2021). Police Brutality and Mexican American Families in Texas, 1945–1980. *The ANNALS of the American Academy of Political and Social Science, 694*(1), 108-121.

Chaney, C.; & Robertson, R. V. (2013). Racism and police brutality in America. *Journal of African American Studies, 17*(4), 480-505.

Chatillon, A.; & Schneider, B. E. (2018). "We Must Summon the

Courage": Black Activist Mothering Against Police Brutality. In *Marginalized Mothers, Mothering from the Margins*. Emerald Publishing Limited.

Chen, E. Y.; Robichaux, K.; Gordon, M. R.; Coverdale, J. H.; Shah, A. A.; Davis, M. P.; & Nguyen, P. T. (2021). A pilot program's healthcare response to human trafficking in Houston, Texas. Journal of Human Trafficking, 1-11.

Chêne, M. (2009). Low salaries and the culture of per diems and corruption, Transparency International/U4, (U4 Helpdesk query 220), Chr Michelsen Institute, Bergen, Norway, *http://www.u4.no/helpdesk/helpdesk/query.cfm?id=220*.

Chopko, B. A.; Palmieri, P. A.; & Facemire, V. C. (2014). Prevalence and predictors of suicidal ideation among U.S. law enforcement officers. *Journal of Police and Criminal Psychology, 29*(1), 1-9.

Crenshaw, K. W.; Ritchie, A. J.; Anspach, R.; Gilmer, R.; & Harris, L. (2015). Say her name: Resisting police brutality against black women.

Cross, T. P.; & Schmitt, T. (2019). Forensic medical results and law enforcement actions following sexual assault: a comparison of child, adolescent and adult cases. Child Abuse & Neglect, 93, 103-110.

Davis, R. C.; Auchter, B.; Wells, W.; Camp, T.; & Howley, S. (2020). The effects of legislation mandating DNA testing in sexual assault cases: Results in Texas. Violence against women, 26(5), 417-437.

Davis, R. C.; Jurek, A.; Wells, W.; & Shadwick, J. (2021). Investigative outcomes of CODIS matches in previously untested sexual assault kits. Criminal Justice Policy Review, 32(8), 841-864.

Davis, T. A. (2005). *Gender inequality in law enforcement and males' attitudes and perceptions toward women working in law enforcement*. The University of Texas at Arlington.

Dukes, Warren V. "Measuring double consciousness among black law enforcement officers to understand the significant role of race in law enforcement occupational cultures." Journal of Ethnicity in Criminal Justice 16.1 (2018): 1-21.

Embrick, D. G. (2015). Two nations, revisited: the lynching of black and brown bodies, police brutality, and racial control in 'post-racial' Amerikkka. *Critical Sociology, 41*(6), 835-843.

Fagan, J.; & Piquero, A. R. (2007). Rational choice and developmental influences on recidivism among adolescent felony offenders. *Journal of*

Empirical Legal Studies, 4(4), 715-748.

Franklin, C. A.; Garza, A. D.; Goodson, A.; & Bouffard, L. A. (2020). Does training affect rape and domestic violence myth endorsement among police personnel? A trend analysis.

Freelon, D.; McIlwain, C. D.; & Clark, M. (2016). Beyond the hashtags: # Ferguson, #Blacklivesmatter, and the online struggle for offline justice. *Center for Media & Social Impact, American University, Forthcoming.*

Fyfe, J. J. (1980). Geographic correlates of police shooting: A microanalysis. *Journal of Research in Crime and Delinquency, 17*(1), 101-113.

Fyfe, J. J.; & Kane, R. (2006). *Bad cops: A study of career-ending misconduct among New York City police officers.* John Jay College of Criminal Justice.

Garcia, N. M.; & Polson, E. C. (2018). Community policing relations: Texas law enforcement practices in one community. Journal of Ideology, 39(1), 3.

Garza, A. (2014). A herstory of the #BlackLivesMatter movement.

GBD 2019 Police Violence U.S. Subnational Collaborators. (2021). Fatal police violence by race and state in the USA, 1980–2019: a network meta-regression. *The Lancet, 398*(10307), 1239-1255.

Goff, P. A.; & Rau, H. (2020). Predicting bad policing: Theorizing burdensome and racially disparate policing through the lenses of social psychology and routine activities. The ANNALS of the American Academy of Political and Social Science, 687(1), 67-88.

Goodson, A.; Garza, A. D.; Franklin, C. A.; Updegrove, A. H.; & Bouffard, L. A. (2020). Perceptions of victim advocates and predictors of service referral among law enforcement personnel. Feminist Criminology, 15(5), 611-633.

Green, M. W. (1999). *The appropriate and effective use of security technologies in U.S. schools: A guide for schools and law enforcement agencies.* U.S. Department of Justice, Office of Justice Programs, National Institute of Justice.

Hamilton, A. R.; & Foote, K. (2018). Police torture in Chicago: Theorizing violence and social justice in a racialized city. *Annals of the American Association of Geographers, 108*(2), 399-410.

Harrington, P.; & Lonsway, K. A. (2006). *Investigating sexual harassment in law enforcement and nontraditional fields for women.* Upper Saddle River, NJ: Prentice Hall.

Harrison, J. (2012). Women in law enforcement: Subverting sexual harassment with social bonds. *Women & Criminal Justice, 22*(3), 226-238.

Holmes, L. (2020). Police Corruption. In *Oxford Research Encyclopedia of Criminology and Criminal Justice*.

Holmes, M. D. (2000). Minority threat and police brutality: Determinants of civil rights criminal complaints in US municipalities. *Criminology, 38*(2), 343-368.

Huber, N. (2020). Intelligence-led policing for law enforcement managers. Available on *https://leb.fbi.gov/articles/featured-articles/intelligence-led-policing-for-law-enforcementmanagers*. Last accessed, 15.

Interpol (n.d.). Global standards to combat corruption in police forces/services, *http://www.interpol.int/Public/corruption/standard/Default.asp*

Jackson, J.; Asif, M.; Bradford, B.; & Zakria Zakar, M. (2014). Corruption and police legitimacy in Lahore, Pakistan. *British journal of criminology, 54*(6), 1067-1088.

Jagodzinski, C. Lawrence. "School safety upgrades and perceptions of safety protocols in prevention of school shootings." School violence in international contexts. Springer, Cham, 2019. 185-197.

Jones, J. S. (2020, September 21). *Though often mythologized, the Texas rangers have an ugly history of brutality*. Washington Post. *Https://www.washingtonpost.com/outlook/2020/09/21/though-often-mythologized-texas-rangers-have-an-ugly-history-brutality/*.

Jurik, N. C.; & Halemba, G. J. (1984). Gender, working conditions and the job satisfaction of women in a non-traditional occupation: Female correctional officers in men's prisons. *Sociological Quarterly, 25*(4), 551-566.

Jussila, J. (2001). Future police operations and non-lethal weapons. *Medicine, Conflict and Survival, 17*(3), 248-259.

Kane, R. J.; & White, M. D. (2009). Bad cops: A study of career-ending misconduct among New York City police officers. *Criminology & Public Policy, 8*(4), 737-769.

Kourmentza, e. (2022, April 1). *Police officer job description*. Recruiting resources: how to recruit and hire better. *Https://resources.workable.com/police-officer-job-description*.

Kraska, P. B. (2007). Militarization and policing—Its relevance to 21st century police. *Policing: a journal of policy and practice, 1*(4), 501-513.

Law enforcement code of ethics (n.d.). University of Texas system. *Https://www.utsystem.edu/offices/police/law-enforcement-code-ethics*.

Lawson Jr., E. (2019). Trends: Police militarization and the use of lethal force. *Political Research Quarterly, 72*(1), 177-189.

Levenson, L. L. (2001). Police corruption and new models for reform. *Suffolk UL Rev., 35*, 1.

Li, Yudu; and Ben Brown. "Police chief turnover in Texas: An exploratory analysis of peer-evaluation survey data pertinent to police performance and turnover." Police Quarterly 22.4 (2019): 391-415.

Lobnikar, B.; & Mesko, G. (2015). Perception of police corruption and the level of integrity among Slovenian police officers. Police Pract Res, 16(4): 341-353. Loyens, K. (2014). Rule bending by morally disengaged detectives: An ethnographic study. Police Pract Res, 15(1): 62-74.

Lowande, K. (2021). Police demilitarization and violent crime. *Nature human behaviour, 5*(2), 205-211.

Lowenfeld, A. F. (1990). U.S. law enforcement abroad: The constitution and international law, continued. *American Journal of International Law, 84*(2), 444-493.

Lysiak, M. (2013). *Newtown: An American Tragedy*. Simon and Schuster.

Manzella, C.; & Papazoglou, K. (2014). Training police trainees about ways to manage trauma and loss. Int J Ment Health Promotion, 16(2): 103-116.

Martin, R. (2011). Police corruption: An analytical look into police ethics. *FBI L. Enforcement Bull., 80*, 11.

Matusiak, R. E.; & Matusiak, M. C. (2018). Structure and function: Impact on employment of women in law enforcement. *Women & Criminal Justice, 28*(4), 313-335.

Mayer, J. D.; Salovey, P.; & Caruso, D. (2002). The Mayer– Salovey– Caruso Emotional Intelligence Test (MSCEIT), Version 2.0. Toronto, Ontario, Canada: Multi-Health Systems.

McCormack, M. (1986). Corruption in the subculture of policing: An empirical study of police officer perceptions. (Doctoral Dissertation, Fordham, University, 1986) United Microfilms International, Ann Arbor, Michigan.

McCormack, L.; & Riley, L. (2016). Medical discharge from the "family," moral injury, and a diagnosis of PTSD: Is psychological growth possible in the aftermath of policing trauma? Traumatol, 22(1): 19-28.

Meier, K. J.; & Nicholson-Crotty, J. (2006). Gender, representative bureaucracy, and law enforcement: The case of sexual assault. *Public Administration*

Review, 66(6), 850-860.

Merritt, A.C.; Effron, D.A.; & Monin, B. (2010). Moral self-licensing: When being good frees us to be bad. Soc Personal Psychol Compass, 4(5): 344-357.

Merritt, A. C.; Effron, D. A.; Fein, S.; Savitsky, K. K.; Tuller, D. M.; & Monin, B. (2012). The strategic pursuit of moral credentials. J Experiment Soc Psychol, 48(3): 774-777.

Mesloh, C.; Henych, M.; & Wolf, R. (2008). *Less lethal weapon effectiveness, use of force, and suspect & officer injuries: A five-year analysis.* National Criminal Justice Reference Service.

Miller, L. (2000). Law enforcement traumatic stress: Clinical syndromes and intervention strategies. Trauma Response, 6(1): 15-20.

Miller, L. S.; & Braswell, M. C. (1992). Police perceptions of ethical decision-making: The ideal versus the real. Am J Police, XI (4): 27-45.

Miller, M. L.; & Schlenker, B. R. (2011). Integrity and identity: Moral identity differences and preferred interpersonal reactions. Eur J Pers, 25: 2-15.

Miller-Fox, Geri A. "Emotional Labor Training Typology for Basic Peace Officer Training Curricula." Administrative Theory & Praxis 40.4 (2018): 357-379.

Mitchell, T. (2020, August 17). *6. Police views, public views.* Pew research center's social & demographic trends project. *Https://www.pewresearch.org/socialtrends/2017/01/11/police-views-public-views/.*

Monin, B.; & Miller, D. T. (2001). Moral credentials and the expression of prejudice. J Pers Soc Psychol, 81(1): 33-43.

Moore, C. (2008). Moral disengagement in processes of organizational corruption. J Bus Ethics, 80(1): 129-139.

Moore, C.; Detert, J. R.; Trevino, L. K.; Baker, V. L.; & Mayer, D. M. (2012). Why employees do bad things: Moral disengagement and unethical organizational behavior. Pers Psychol, 65(1): 1-48.

Morris, S. B.; & Deshon, R. P. (2002). Combining effect size estimates in meta-analysis with repeated measures and independent-groups designs. Psychol Methods, 7(1): 105-125.

Muir, R. (2017, August 31). *Great expectations: what do the public want from the police?* The police foundation. *Https://www.police-foundation.org.uk/2016/09/great-expectations-what-do-the-public-want-from-the-police/.*

Mullen, E.; & Monin, B. (2016). Consistency versus licensing effects of past moral behavior. Annual Rev Psychol, 67: 363-385.

Murphy, K. R. (2000). What constructs underlie measures of honesty or integrity? In R. D. Goffin, E. Helmes, R. D. Goffin, E. Helmes (Eds.). Problems and solutions in human assessment: Honoring Douglas N. Jackson at seventy (pp. 265-283). New York, NY, US: Kluwer Academic/Plenum Publishers.

Murphy, K. R.; & Dzieweczynski, J. L. (2005). Why don't measures of broad personality dimensions of personality perform better as predictors of job performance? Hum Perform, 18(4): 343-357.

Nelis, D.; Kotsou, I.; Quoidbach, J.; Hansenne, M.; Weytens, F.; Dupuis, P., et al. (2011). Increasing emotional competence improves psychological and physical well-being, social relationships, and employability. Emotion, 11(2): 354-366.

Nelson, J. (Ed.). (2001). *Police brutality: An anthology*. WW Norton & Company.

New York Times (2015). America's dirtiest cops: Cash, cocaine and corruption on the Texas border (written by Josh Eells).

Newbold, G. (2005). Women officers working in men's prisons.

Newham, G. (2002). Tackling police corruption in South Africa, Centre for the Study of Violence and Reconciliation, June, Johannesburg, South Africa, *http://www.csvr.org.za/wits/papers/papoli14.htm.*

Nix, J.; Campbell, B. A.; Byers, E. H.; & Alpert, G. P. (2017). A bird's eye view of civilians killed by police in 2015: Further evidence of implicit bias. *Criminology & Public Policy, 16*(1), 309-340.

Nuriddin, A.; Mooney, G.; & White, A. I. (2020). Reckoning with histories of medical racism and violence in the USA. *The Lancet, 396*(10256), 949-951.

Officer expectations and duties. (2021, January 11). Police. *Https://police.unc.edu/recruitment/officer-expectations-duties/.*

Olzak, S. (2021). Does protest against police violence matter? Evidence from US Cities, 1990 through 2019. *American sociological review, 86*(6), 1066-1099.

Parker, B. J. M. (2016). Women in Law Enforcement: A Relief, Not a Burden.

Peeples, L. (2020). What the data say about police brutality and racial bias—and which reforms might work.

Police power | American law. (n.d.). Encyclopedia Britannica. *Https://www.britannica.com/topic/police-power.*

Police powers. (n.d.). Lii / legal information institute. *Https://www.law.cornell.edu/wex/police_powers.*

Polk, O. E.; & Armstrong, D. A. (2001). Higher education and law enforcement career paths: Is the road to success paved by degree?. *Journal of Criminal Justice Education, 12*(1), 77-99.

Pollock, Wendi; Natalia D. Tapia; and Deborah Sibila. "Cultivation theory: The impact of crime media's portrayal of race on the desire to become a US police officer." International Journal of Police Science & Management 24.1 (2022): 42-52.

Punch, M. (2000). Police corruption and its prevention. European journal on criminal policy and research, 8(3), 301-324.

Reiter, Kathryn. "Time Limits on Assignments in Law Enforcement." (2019).

Richardson, C.; & Pisani, M. J. (2012). *The informal and underground economy of the South Texas border.* University of Texas Press.

Rios, J. (2016). Flesh in the Street. *Kalfou, 3*(1), 63-78.

Ristroph, A. (2017). The constitution of police violence. *UCLA L. Rev., 64,* 1182.

Ritchie, A. J.; & Mogul, J. L. (2007). In the shadows of the war on terror: Persistent police brutality and abuse of people of color in the United States. *DePaul J. Soc. Just., 1,* 175.

Russo, C. W. (2019). Hiring and Retention of Female Police Officers. The Encyclopedia of Women and Crime, 1-3.

Sechrest, D.; & Burns, P. (1992). Police corruption: The Miami case. Criminal Justice and Behavior, 19(3), 294-313.

Sherman, L. W. (2020). Evidence-based policing and fatal police shootings: Promise, problems, and prospects. The ANNALS of the American Academy of Political and Social Science, 687(1), 8-26.

Skillicorn, D. B. (2021). Cyberspace, Data Analytics, and Policing. Chapman and Hall/CRC.

Springer, N.; Engelmann, I.; & Pfaffinger, C. (2015). User comments: Motives and inhibitors to write and read. *Information, Communication & Society, 18*(7), 798-815.

Staudt, K. (2009). *Violence and activism at the border: Gender, fear, and everyday life in Ciudad Juárez*. University of Texas Press.

Stewart, D. M. (2011). Collaboration between federal and local law enforcement: An examination of Texas police chiefs' perceptions. *Police Quarterly, 14*(4), 407-430.

Stinson, P. M.; Liederbach, J.; Brewer, S. L.; Schmalzried, H. D.; Mathna, B. E.; & Long, K. L. (2013). A study of drug-related police corruption arrests. *Policing: An International Journal of Police Strategies & Management*.

Stratton, B. T. (1986). Integrating women into law enforcement. In *Police selection and training* (pp. 307-324). Springer, Dordrecht.

Sturges, P.; and Cooke, L. (n.d.). Finding the grey in the blue: transparency and disclosure in policing, Loughborough University, U.K.. *http://www.greynet.org/images/GL9,_page_119.pdf.*

Summers, L.; & Rossmo, D. K. (2018). Offender interviews: Implications for intelligence-led policing. Policing: An International Journal.

Tankebe, J. (2010). Public confidence in the Police: Testing the effects of public experiences of police corruption in Ghana. *The British Journal of Criminology, 50*(2), 296-319.

Tate Santana, M. (2018). Trafficked in Texas: Combatting the sex-trafficking epidemic through prostitution law and sentencing reform in the lone star state. Vand. L. Rev., 71, 1739.

Teague, H. A. (2018). Black and blue in North Texas: The long neglected history of anti-Black police violence in North Texas, 1880-1930. Journal of Black Studies, 49(8), 756-781.

Texas state law library. (n.d.). *Guides: protest rights in Texas: interactions with police*. Guides sll texas gov. *Https://guides.sll.texas.gov/protest-rights/police.*

Texeira, M. T. (2002). "Who protects and serves me?" A case study of sexual harassment of African American women in one U.S. law enforcement agency. *Gender & Society, 16*(4), 524-545.

Vaughn, M. S.; Cooper, T. W.; & del Carmen, R. V. (2001). Assessing legal liabilities in law enforcement: Police chiefs' views. *Crime & Delinquency, 47*(1), 3-27.

Weisburd, D.; & Greenspan, R. (2000). Police studies toward the abuse of Authority: Findings from a National Study, National Institute of Justice: Washington, D.C.

White, S. R.; & McKenna, J. M. (2020). Improving school policing programmes through strategic collaboration. Policing: A Journal of Policy and Practice, 14(2), 512-525.

Wiest, J. B. (Ed.). (2021). Theorizing Criminality and Policing in the Digital Media Age. Emerald Group Publishing.

Williams, J.; & Kleiner, B. H. (2001). Sexual harassment and discrimination in law enforcement. *Equal Opportunities International*.

Wilson, D. G.; Walsh, W. F.; & Kleuber, S. (2006). Trafficking in human beings: Training and services among U.S. law enforcement agencies. *Police Practice and Research*, 7(02), 149-160.

Wood, L.; Schrag, R. V.; Baumler, E.; Hairston, D.; Guillot-Wright, S.; Torres, E.; & Temple, J. R. (2020). On the front lines of the COVID-19 pandemic: Occupational experiences of the intimate partner violence and sexual assault workforce. Journal of interpersonal violence, 0886260520983304.

Wu, Stephen. "Leadership Matters: Police Chief Race and Fatal Shootings by Police Officers." Social Science Quarterly 102.1 (2021): 407-419.

Zappia, D. J. (1996). Police chief Adam Elmer Jansen: an honest man 1947-1960. University of San Diego.

Zhijie, S. (2015). Dynamic Research on Police English Corpus.